The Landon Lectures

The Landon Lectures

Perspectives from the First Twenty Years

EDITED BY

William L. Richter

AND

Charles E. Reagan

ISBN No. 0-9616658-1-5
Friends of the Libraries of Kansas State University

Library of Congress Catalog Number: 87-81227

Contents

Editors' Preface

The Landon Lecture Series was inaugurated in 1966 by Kansas State University President James A. McCain to honor Kansas' most distinguished elder statesman, Alfred M. Landon.

Governor Landon was sworn in as governor of Kansas on January 9, 1933, and was the Republican Party nominee for president of the United States in 1936. Governor Landon delivered the first lecture in the series, "New Challenges in International Relations," on December 13, 1966.

Speakers who come to Kansas State University to honor Governor Landon with their appearance are drawn from the public arena of world-renowned politicians, journalists, cabinet members, and other prominent figures involved in current public issues. The Landon Lectures of Presidents Nixon, Ford, and Reagan are among those reprinted in this volume.

Twenty-two of the 73 Landon Lectures given during the past twenty years have been selected for this collection. All of the major political issues of this period, including the civil rights movement, the war in Vietnam, the energy crisis, the Middle-East conflicts, Watergate, the Women's movement, and the relations between Congress and the President, are treated by the speakers whose lectures are in this volume. We have also included the reminiscences about the Landon Lectures of the five persons who have chaired the lecture series.

Both of us would like to thank the many people who have contributed their time and talents to making this book possible: Eugene Kremer, President of the Friends of the Libraries of Kansas State University, who proposed the collection and whose organization is the publisher; Virginia Quiring, Associate Dean of the Libraries and business agent for the volume; Patricia Weisenburger, Librarian of the Weigel Architecture and Design Library and our production manager; Tony Crawford, University Archivist, responsible for selecting the photographs from university archives; Julie Widman, Landon Lecture Secretary; and Larry Hirst, the designer of the book.

We would particularly like to thank the Patrons of the Landon Lecture Series, under the leadership of the late J. Robert Wilson and Edward Seaton, whose faithful support of the Series has made it the prestigious series it is.

William L. Richter
Charles E. Reagan

Manhattan, Kansas

The Landon Lectures

Alfred M. Landon (1887–) was governor of Kansas from 1933–1937, and in 1936 was the unsuccessful Republican candidate for President. He then directed his interests to his businesses but remained an influential voice in American politics. He is regularly visited by political figures of both parties and is widely considered as the "elder statesman" of the Republican party. Throughout his long career he has remained an outspoken and independent thinker whose ideas have had significant influence on the course of American politics.

New Challenges in International Relations

Alfred M. Landon

Governor Landon delivered the inaugural lecture of the Landon Lecture Series on December 13, 1966, at the K-State Union. It ranged widely over international issues which would be important for several years to come. He addressed themes to which later speakers in the series would return again and again: Vietnam, Third World Nationalism, international trade, east-west relations, nuclear arms, and other enduring world issues. Most notably, he advocated the normalization of relations with the People's Republic of China.

The positions which he articulated in this lecture and in other public statements in the mid-1960's ultimately became national policy following the Nixon-Kissinger "opening" to China in the early 1970s.

DECEMBER 13, 1966

We must face the challenges of new realities of international life today.

The world is an armed camp. An uneasy peace is maintained, while a power struggle continues to build up between the Soviet Union and China, with the United States neutral between them. On the other hand, we support South Vietnam's opposition to Communist aggression.

India, the second largest nation, wrecked by Socialistic leadership, is racked by internal dissension and menaced by external threats.

The potential colossus of China—the world's most populous nation—is experiencing a severe internal revolution.

The end of the Vietnam war is not in sight. And the vital questions of barring the use and spread of nuclear weapons and the military use of space remain unanswered.

Everywhere, a new nationalism—having recently vanquished European empires—is now transcending ideologies and old alliances, and is paradoxically supporting world peace, based on fear—not trust. World Communism, the United Nations, NATO, and the Atlantic Alliance are fragmenting on the rocks of this new nationalism.

The New Nationalism

This new nationalism is one of independence and self-determination. It is not the old dynasty nationalism with its ancestral roots in medieval feudalism. Nor is it the aggressive nationalism of modern dictators built on the doctrine of force.

World War One wiped out the last of the monarchs representing the centuries-old dynasty nationalism. And World War Two eliminated two megalomaniac dictators—Hitler and Mussolini—and their Japanese brethren. The policies of two more aggressors—Stalin and Sukarno—have been thrown by their people on the scrap heap of history. Only one of the five megalomaniacs of our time is left—China's troubled Mao. The ruthless Red Guards turned loose by him on his unhappy countrymen are a sad recreation of Hitler's Jackboots and Mussolini's Blackshirts.

Meanwhile, China's world influence has suffered severe reversals—in Latin America, Africa, India, and Indonesia—and also in the United Nations which, by the greatest majority vote in some years, recently refused to seat Communist China.

This new nationalism is transcending Communism. Both outside—as well as inside China—the theories of Marx and Lenin for the establishment and maintenance of worldwide Communism are being revised. The turmoil in China is essentially concerned with a struggle between the fundamentalists and revisionists.

The Soviet Union is departing so far from the original concepts of Marx and Lenin as to render them almost unrecognizable. Soviet Communism is moving slowly and subtly, but surely, toward incorporation of certain capitalistic principles of reward for individual talent and incentive.

Behind the thinning and now porous Iron Curtain, Communism has failed to meet the hopes and aspirations of its people. Its hierarchy is changed. Developing public opinion has eroded and loosened its monolithic structure.

The heretofore captive East European satellites are no longer captive nor satellites. They are pushing away from economics and political control and domination by Moscow. And it must be admitted that—by the same token—Western Europe is also pushing away from economic and political domination by the United States of America.

This new nationalism has wrought momentous changes. It is changing the post-war alliances within both the Communist and non-Communist world. It presents great difficulties for the United Nations and the ideas of world federation, or Atlantic union.

By fostering national barriers, the new nationalism in one sense obstructs international cooperation. Paradoxically, by reducing ideological barriers, this new nationalism in another sense permits greater international cooperation based on the principle of equality of nations.

International Trade

In October, 1961, when the White House was divided on whether to support the fledgling European Economic Community, or whether to request a year's extension of the Reciprocal Trade Agreements Act, I urged support of the E.E.C. as the most realistic step toward economic and political stability, and hence world peace. Why? Because the E.E.C. was founded on the simple principle of removing nationalist barriers to international trade.

The principle of a high protective tariff is basic to a government-protected, or owned, or managed economy. High tariffs inhibit cross-cultural relations. Freer trade, on the other hand, enables the peoples of different nations to become better acquainted with the customs, beliefs, ways of life, and government policies of one another. With the greater expansion and ease of communication today, freer trade induces mutual international understanding.

When international understanding is thus achieved, political tensions are reduced and voices of reason are easier heard and understood. The way is then prepared to move toward world stability, increased prosperity, higher standards of living and education, and peaceful competitive existence in international markets. These conditions, in turn, form the foundation for cooperative political policies among nations.

Two and one-half years of bargaining within the European Economic Community are coming to a close with expectation of the most substantial tariff reductions in history. The effects of this action will spread all over the world—from Europe to Latin America, Africa and Asia. I quote from a recent statement by the Japanese Ambassador:

> We Japanese believe that contacts through trade tend to facilitate mutual understanding among nations of differing ideologies and social structures.

This development is not as dramatic and grandiose as a League of Nations, a United Nations, or world law based on a world court. However, international trade is the only proven method for initiating a workable peace with international security and understanding—security and understanding that might save the United Nations organization which is now bankrupt financially, politically, and structurally. The world needs the United Nations as a forum to discuss and expose international grievances and concerns.

Early this year, our President requested Congress to repeal legislation obstructing United States trade with Communist countries. Congress adjourned without acting on the President's trade recommendations. Meanwhile, the English, French, West Germans, and Japanese are filling the orders of China, the Soviet Union and Eastern Europe. Our allies are trading with Communist countries. We are not.

The defensive "white elephant" military structures of SEATO and CENTO existed only on paper. Despite our rebuilding efforts, NATO's days are numbered. These alliances were not designed to provide the common ground for better acquaintance with, and understanding of, the Communist world. Nevertheless, our own nationalism persists to inhibit the expansion of America's world trade. The American Congress has not learned a prime lesson of history—that economic isolationism leads to political isolationism as well as the converse, and that either is counterproductive in this day and age, as even the Soviet Union is reluctantly learning.

Sino-Soviet-American Relations

The world is truly in an era of great change. World peace and stability depend on harmonious relations between China, the Soviet Union, and the United States. The time has come for each to completely reappraise its foreign policies. Each major power must ask itself whether it correctly perceives new realities, whether momentous world changes have evoked commensurate policy responses. Specifically, each must introspectively assess whether continuing confrontation with its military strength is the most effective means to assure world peace and stability and hence its own security.

What are these new realities? They include: the Soviet modernizing of Communist dogma, the Sino-Soviet split, European self-determination and independence from Soviet and American domination, the advent of Chinese nuclear power, the growing non-alignment of developing nations, the recession of the Communist tide, and worldwide acceptance of the concept of the welfare state. In a nut shell, these are the new challenges wrought by the new nationalism.

The potential colossus of China, weakened internally and externally by Mao's unrealistic fanatic militancy, bitterly attacks both the Soviet Union and the United States. The irony is that these attacks help to induce better relations between these super powers—exactly what China fears.

The Soviet Union faces hostility from China on her Eastern front—the closest and most obvious mark for its new nuclear bomb—with the longest border line in the world, and territorial disputes and memories of bloody invasions centuries old. The passage of time has not eliminated from the folklore of Russian memories the ravages of Genghis Khan's hordes, or Napoleon's French, or German armies twice in the last fifty years. It was Mao's leadership that chased Russia out of Manchuria.

On her Western front, the Soviet Union fears a united Germany as the devil fears holy water. In all of Russian history, there has been one basic foreign policy and that is to avoid facing a war at the same time on two fronts.

By the same token, China—without a navy—faces the United States of America on her Pacific front and the Soviet Union on her land front.

Both the Soviet Union and China face the United States of America uncertain as to the international policies of the greatest economic power, welfare state, and military power in the world. The Soviet Union lately links together both China and the United States of America in formal public attacks. The corollary of such attacks is what the Soviet Union fears.

We have this definite situation that the Soviet Union needs the pressure of America on China in the Pacific, despite Premier Kosygin's continued assertions that "... if the war [in Vietnam] were ended, relations [with America] would certainly improve." China, in turn, needs the pressure of America in Europe on the Soviet Union, despite Mao's attacks on both. The peace of the world is in suspense while this jockeying goes on.

Hence, America is presented with an unusual opportunity to initiate a "live-and-let-live" policy of competitive economic existence with the Soviet Union, or China, or preferably both. Such American initiatives are necessary to reduce tensions, violence, war, and threats of war, in other words—to normalize international relations. Encouragingly, these policies seem to be developing.

In recent months, President Johnson has made three highly significant foreign policy moves that have generally escaped the public attention and discussion they deserve, and have yet to be explained to the American people. Foremost among the foreign policies of the Truman, Eisenhower, Kennedy, and Johnson administrations were the reunification of Germany and the political and economic isolation of Communist China. These two policies, together with the implications of the President's commitments at the Manila Conference, signify possibly momentous changes in our foreign policy.

Reappraising Our China Policy

The first of these three significant moves by President Johnson occurred in July, 1966, when he proposed at least a tentative reappraisal of our China policy with his offer of reconciliation with China. I quote President Johnson:

> Lasting peace can never come to Asia as long as the 700 million people of mainland China are isolated by their rulers from the outside world.
>
> We persist [in efforts to improve relations] because we believe that cooperation, not hostility, is the way of the future. That day is not here yet. It may be long in coming, but it is clearly on the way, and come it must.

In September, 1966, Vice President Humphrey followed President Johnson's incipient design by speaking of "building bridges to China." I have been urging such a policy for a long time, but without success. Recently, spokesmen for the United States Chamber of Commerce are on record as stating that increased communication with the Peking government is in order. And, according to a recent report of the American Friends Service Committee, our present policy of non-intercourse with China is leading to disaster. Said the Committee, and I quote:

> Two of the largest and most powerful nations of the world have since 1950 lived largely in isolated ignorance of one another and in an atmosphere of mutual fear and hate. . . . Some attempt to break the present deadlock is long and dangerously overdue.

The point to be emphasized here is not that our China policy is soon to be reversed. China has replied to the President with more lies and abuse. Rather, the question of great interest to both the United States and the Soviet Union is—After Mao, what? It is in anticipation of answering this important question that the pending reappraisal of our China policy acquires added significance.

Abandoning German Reunification

The second of the three meaningful moves was inherent in Mr. Johnson's assertion of last August that better relations with the Soviet Union "must be our first concern." By implication, the President thereby signaled our intention to abandon the priority of the reunification of Germany. I quote from Joseph C. Harsch in the *Christian Science Monitor:*

> ... the President has formally stated that reunification of Germany can come about only within the reunification of Europe. Germany's cause is no longer Step One in healing the split in Europe caused by the cold war. The unity of Germany is a hoped-for result of closer East-West ties. It is no longer the precondition.

Two recent developments in Germany might possibly be related. They are: (1) the downfall of the Erhard government replaced by an uncertain coalition of the Christian Democrats and the Social Democrats; and (2) a resurgence of German nationalism as evidenced in two state legislative elections.

A *quid pro quo* for this momentous change in our European policy could be for the Soviet Union to use its good offices in bringing about a settlement in Vietnam that would be worthy of our sacrifice of blood and money. An end to the Vietnam war, according to Premier Kosygin, would pave the way to improved relations. Recently he said, "We want a relaxation of tension; we want an understanding with the United States."

The Soviet Union would have much to gain. She would be free of a threat on her Western front which would allow her to concentrate on the growing Chinese military threat on her long Eastern front.

The Manila Conference

The third and last move fraught with momentous consequences for all the world concerns President Johnson's pre-election Manila Conference. I quote from a recent report by the Research Institute:

> First the Conference left untouched the one crucial issue: Where does the Vietcong figure in the war's final settlement? South Viet Premier Ky made clear where he figures the Vietcong: destroyed as an organization, its members "abiding by the law"—the South Vietnam law as enforced by the government headed by Ky.
> It is inconceivable that Hanoi or the Vietcong will negotiate on

any such terms, unless Ky should retract his words publicly. It is equally inconceivable that he will yield on any of them.

The stage is set, hence, for a long drawn-out tug-of-war among the Manila conferees—with no end to the fighting itself. The allied stalemate may be harder to break than the field impasse.

And concluding from this report:

If Ky were alone, he might be brought to heel fairly soon. But he has real support from the South Koreans, Thais and Australians. They do not want to see the Vietcong in a peacetime Saigon government either; they are in this to stop Red expansion, no matter what it takes.

This is different from what the Filipinos, New Zealand—and the United States—are ready to accept: Let the Vietcong into the government. Philippine President Marcos is ambitious to become Asia's peacemaker even at the cost of including the VC.

This is the United States position, as well, although President Johnson did not press it openly at Manila.

The Manila Conference was a complete failure as far as agreement on any Vietnam peace settlement is concerned. Before the ink was dry, Premier Ky of South Vietnam emphatically dissented from President Johnson's interpretation of the Manila Conference proceedings, just as he did with President Johnson's interpretation of the so-called Honolulu Pact. Again I quote from the Research Institute report:

After Manila . . . Ky has only one clear course left: Keep the U.S. fighting until the Vietcong has been totally smashed. This means more men and arms, more escalation, a much wider war.

It should also be noted that the much heralded free election law in that unhappy country gives Premier Ky and his military junta a veto over any measure the civilian assembly adopts.

One result of the Manila Conference was the dramatic pronouncement by our President that the United States is a major Asian power and is assuming guardianship in its name over all of Asia. This appears to be an assertion of national responsibility of appalling proportions. Should Congress implement Johnson's Asian manifesto, it would seem that America would become permanently and deeply involved—politically, militarily, economically—in all Asia.

Nearly two months have passed without any explanation by our President of his sweeping pronouncement. Why is the President silent? Americans are kept in the dark as to just what was said at Manila by our President—and what his intentions are.

Of equal present and future importance is how other governments interpret President Johnson's Manila manifesto. Do they consider it as a definite projection of U.S. foreign policy? Or do they consider his expansive statement as merely a gesture of good intentions designed to obscure the utter failure of the Conference to agree on peace in Vietnam? Have they learned that American presidents' words do not "always weigh a ton"—as Mr. Coolidge said?

Perhaps, when interpreting our President's Manila statement, other governments might recall previous American international commitments which we did not honor—as, for example, the Open Door for China which we ignored when Japan invaded Manchuria in 1931. Or they might recall the Buffalo speech of John Foster Dulles during the 1952 presidential election campaign pledging the new administration—if elected—to liberation of the captive nations of Eastern Europe—a pledge that was to contribute to the Hungarian revolt of 1956 in expectation of American support that was never forthcoming.

Or, our President's Manila pronouncement might be explained as "speaking softly but carrying a big stick." If this is the correct interpretation, then the question must be asked—just how big a stick does America intend to carry in Asia in the light of spreading nuclear power. Do we really need such paramountcy in Asia?

In October, 1964, China formally proposed a conference of the five nuclear powers preliminary to a conference of all nations to abolish nuclear weapons. I immediately urged American acceptance at least for the purpose of discussion. Secretary General U Thant somewhat unprecedentedly publicly endorsed my statement the next morning. But the Johnson administration dismissed offhand China's overture, on the ground that it was mere propaganda, that China's nuclear bomb was obsolete, and that it would be twenty or more years before China would perfect the means of delivering it. But, in less than two years, China has demonstrated that it has already achieved the capacity to develop an on-target missile delivery system and a bomb with thermonuclear characteristics.

Finally, there is the question—if President Johnson meant what he seemed to say at Manila—where is he going to get the money to bring his Great Society to all of Asia? And this in addition to the pressing question of where is he going to get the money to finance both a big war and yet continue his Great Society for the home folks?

If our President's new Asian policy is undertaken, the greater question must be asked: What responsibility—moral or otherwise—do we Americans actually have to bankrupt ourselves for President Johnson's unrealistic policy for world salvation?

If this policy is described as a part of the program to contain Communism, let us observe how Communism is containing itself by its unworkable theories, as can be seen in Communist dominated countries everywhere. Indonesia is the latest example, plus a number of African states that have kicked out both Chinese and Russian attempts at Communist domination.

It will be the responsibility of our Congress to implement President Johnson's Manila manifesto, or to refuse to assume its frightful consequences, when and if the President requests the necessary appropriations to implement it. Even a token Congressional appropriation would be tantamount to the assumption of responsibility that would lead to various future complications.

While the President's astounding Manila manifesto does not require treaty ratification by the United States Senate, it is so vital to American interests that I believe that the Senate Foreign Relations Committee ought to probe all its facets and to expose all its implications, and our obligations under it, for the attention of the American people as well as peoples elsewhere.

There must be a clear and complete understanding not only between the American people and their government, but also among the governments that participated at Manila as to what exactly are we Americans expected to do for our Asian wards, what specific commitments and limitations were made by President Johnson, and how lasting will they be. For some unknown reason,

President Johnson has chosen not to discuss these great concerns with the American people. Meanwhile, other governments should clearly understand that President Johnson's exuberant Asian commitments require Congressional action under our system to become operative.

The simplest way to clear this all up is to get the complete transcript of the Manila Conference before the Senate Foreign Relations Committee for introduction in the *Congressional Record.*

African Embargoes

There remains one other critical development that threatens to enlarge even further the stretching world commitments of the United States. I speak of the growing pressures to impose economic embargoes through the United Nations on Rhodesia and the Republic of South Africa. To enforce its decision to end the South African mandate over Southwest Africa, the United Nations may soon impose economic sanctions on South Africa, as well as Rhodesia.

When Britain attempted to bring Rhodesia to heel by imposing sanctions, President Johnson promptly concurred. But these sanctions have failed. Now Prime Minister Wilson is apparently caught bluffing again. When his bold words in his report to the British Parliament of his conference with the Prime Minister of Rhodesia are boiled down, they are nothing but the same old appeal for "special sanctions" by the United Nations on purchases of key Rhodesian products.

From the beginning, it has been evident that Prime Minister Wilson is trying to bluff Rhodesia back into line by threats.

If the United Nations adopts a more forcible policy, who is going to enforce it?

I quote from John Knight's "Editor's Scrapbook":

Mr. Wilson would like nothing more than to have the United States pull his chestnuts out of the fire. As the *Economist* of London has said: "To pretend that Britain alone can resolve this problem is just as stupid as to think it can be handed over to the U.N. That duty (sanctions) does not rest with the British government alone. The cloud in Mr. Ian Smith's sky may seem no bigger than a man's hand; but the real question is whether the hand is President Johnson's."

And the *London Sunday Observer* comments that it must be up to the United States to make effective the sanctions on Rhodesia, the Republic of South Africa and Southwest Africa.

The only effective means of enforcing economic embargoes is by naval blockade, not to mention air cover. To effectively blockade the coast of South and Southwest Africa would be a prodigious and very expensive undertaking. Our navy is already fully committed. Our First Fleet is patrolling the California coast, and the Second Fleet the Atlantic coast. Our Sixth Fleet operates in the Mediterranean area, and our Seventh Fleet in the straits between Taiwan and China and the rest of the Pacific area, including South Vietnam.

Any effective embargo of Rhodesia would require a blockade of South Africa. The volume of South African trade alone with Great Britain might well involve the solvency of the British pound.

How can we support the solvency of the British pound and yet enforce such economic embargoes on Rhodesia or South Africa, or both, and yet fight a major war in South Vietnam, not to mention all the other American commitments at home and abroad?

This African affair will not be settled in one week or one month. It can be as long as the engagement in Vietnam.

Conclusion

From every side, then, there is a pressing need for the Senate Foreign Relations Committee to review and assess the position America occupies as the result of its exuberant evangelical world leadership in Europe, in Asia, in Africa and in this hemisphere.

While I staunchly believe in and support President Johnson's policies of new contacts with both the Soviet Union and China as the basis for better international understanding, I believe Senator Fulbright's announced plan for a full and comprehensive review by the Senate Foreign Relations Committee in both public and closed hearings is both timely and essential.

Long ago, I said the United Nations could not succeed in its objectives if it left out Communist China.

President Johnson has taken the first steps with both China and the Soviet Union. There has been no commensurate response from either.

Our President is leading from strength, both economically and militarily. There is as much need—perhaps more—for our national administration's intelligent concentration on strengthening our economic foundations and backlogs as its concentration on strengthening our military.

It is now up to the Soviet Union to demonstrate the change of front—that Premier Kosygin desires—by performance rather than by words. After all, credibility is as essential in political relations as it is in trade.

Let me conclude by saying simply this: We should respond to the new nationalism and other new challenges in international relations in our continuing search for world peace. I believe we are on the threshold of abandoning our foolish and unrealistic China policy. At the same time, we are hopefully making progress toward improving relations with East European nations.

Now, at last, a realistic basis exists for discussions between the Soviet Union and the United States of a new policy for both countries.

Should China recover from her present insanity and join in responsible interaction with the Soviet Union and the United States—a new era in international relations would commence that would shape the destiny of this world by creating stability on which peace with security is ultimately based. This must be our hope. This must be our aim.

Ralph McGill (1898–1969) was the editor and later publisher of the *Atlanta Constitution*. In addition to many honorary doctorates, he won the Pulitzer Prize in 1958 for his editorials and the Presidential Medal of Freedom in 1964. He was the author of *The South and the Southerner* as well as an advocate of racial equality and a leader in developing what has come to be known as the "New South." He was a longtime friend of Alf Landon.

The Emerging South:
Politics and Issues

Ralph McGill

Ralph McGill was the second speaker in the Landon Lecture Series and the first of a long list of leading American journalists who have appeared on the Landon platform. McGill's address, delivered May 17, 1967, provides interesting insights into a transitional period in the politics of the American South. The flavor of the "Old South" is conveyed by McGill's use of the term "Negro," which has since fallen into disuse. More importantly, McGill identifies at least some of the features of the "New South," including the growth of a two-party system and the political integration of the region into the larger American system. It is remarkable that the trends McGill identified in 1967 could develop so rapidly that within a decade McGill's own city of Atlanta would have a Black Mayor and a former Georgia Governor would be elected President of the United States.

MAY 17, 1967

I am greatly complimented to be one of those invited to participate in the lecture series that bears the name of and honors the man Alfred Landon. He has lived—and continues to live—a life of usefulness and of excellence. He has made—and still makes—a contribution to our life and times that has been critically constructive. His participation in the national dialogue has been—and is—one that properly commands respect and appreciation.

My pleasure at being here and attempting to discuss something of the political development of the Southeastern United States— that controversial region known generally as "the South"—is increased because this same Alfred Landon was responsible for inspiring me to try to do something about it.

Some months after the Presidential campaign of 1936, I was on a visit to Washington for my paper. Mr. Landon happened also to be there. He was gracious enough to see a newspaperman unknown to him. We talked about the lamentable condition of party politics in the South. I raised in particular the low estate of what was then known as the Republican Party in the states of the old Confederacy. It was, in a sense, a non-existent party. Its members were contemptuously known as the "Post Office" Republicans. They were a few men who handled the Post Office and other patronage appointments when a Republican was elected President. These men also controlled the selection of delegates to the national conventions. In between, most of them made common cause with state Democratic factions and, at the county level, functioned as Democrats.

Mark Hanna of Ohio, maker of the Republican Party, is credited with establishing this skeleton-like organization. Some months before the national convention that nominated William McKinley, Mr. Hanna appeared in the then small town of Thomasville, Georgia, just north of the Florida line. A house had been rented for him. Mr. Hanna announced, to the great satisfaction of local pride, that he had come to Thomasville for his health. It was noted, however, that a surprising number of persons became interested in Mr. Hanna's health. Callers came every day. They came by train and carriage. Most of them stayed at the local hotels, except an occasional one or two who were guests at the Hanna home.

Mr. Hanna was practicing one of the arts of king-making. He had earlier determined to nominate Mr. McKinley on the first ballot. It occurred to him that while there was no Republican Party in Dixie, there were delegates. Before he reached Thomasville and took a house, letters and a few telephone calls had alerted persons in all the states of the Deep South to be ready to go to Thomasville and ask about Mr. Hanna's health. Mr. Hanna's health improved with each visiting delegation. When he returned home to Ohio he was interviewed about his health and that of the Republican Party. He said both were good. Indeed, he predicted that Mr. McKinley would be nominated on the first ballot. He was. He had a significant majority and a substantial portion of it was a solid block of votes by delegations from the Southern states. It was merely coincidental that chairmen who answered the roll call of these Southern states were all men who had been to Thomasville to inquire about Mr. Hanna's health. From that time until 1952 Southern delegations traditionally were tied by influence to leadership from Ohio. They were counted in the Taft corner for President William Howard Taft and they were later supporters of the presidential ambitions of Senator Robert Taft.

Indeed, it was a part of the political irony of our times that the nomination of General Dwight Eisenhower at the 1952 convention turned on a pivot of a southern state—Georgia—and a contest of the seating of the delegation. The old line Post Office Republicans had controlled the state convention and had ruled out delegates committed to General Eisenhower's candidacy. Two delegations showed up at the Republican convention of that year. The convention's credentials committee seated the Taft delegation. A contest from the floor followed. In a rare and historic decision the delegates reversed the convention's credentials committee and seated the delegation committed to General Eisenhower. This precedent was followed by a similar decision regarding contesting delegations from Texas, and within minutes, the stampede to General Eisenhower was on. I recall sitting in the press section during that decision and having Mrs. Oveta Culp Hobby say to me, "Who would ever have expected a Republican convention to turn on the state of Georgia and on a moral issue at that?"

Southern Republicans

Governor Landon and I had talked in 1937. At that time he discussed, among other things, the quality of Republican delegations from the South. His conclusion was that they were, on the whole, a rather second rate lot. There were individual exceptions, but in the main, these delegations were made up largely of men who, the governor said, would not be admitted to state Republican delegations from other sections of the country. In this he was entirely correct. They were a second rate lot and some of them were third and fourth rate. This was well known locally, but the Republican Party also was known locally not to be a party in fact, but merely a skeleton-type organization which made no effort to build a party organization at either the local or state level. Governor Landon further concluded that not until the Republican National Committee was willing to give assistance and consideration to responsible Southerners would there be a development of the two-party system in the South.

I printed this interview and it created a mild and temporary tempest. Two or three of the local Republican leaders issued indignant denials, but they soon subsided in the face of the undeniable facts of what Governor Landon had said.

There is today the beginnings of a two-party system in the South. The Republican Party as it exists is neither a united nor a happy one. Its leadership is all too often those who have deserted the Democratic Party because of opposition to civil rights legislation. Too much of the Republican effort in the South has been, and is, an attempt to win votes by adopting programs more racist than those of the Southern Democrats. It cannot be said that a single state Republican organization in the South has endorsed the Republican national platform planks on civil rights. In 1964, for example, Governor George Wallace of Alabama gave aid and comfort to a number of Republican candidates for Congress and for other local offices. Republican election gains were significant insofar as the labels meant anything. Republicans won victories. But in 1966 Governor Wallace turned against these same men when he determined to support a slate of state nominees who would be favorable to his wife's candidacy for the governor and to his later third party "Southern Democratic" movement. The Republicans in Alabama, therefore, bit the dust.

In 1966 there was a general falling-off of Southern Republican successes as compared with those in 1964. Senator Goldwater's political managers had determined on what they called the "Southern strategy." This was, in reality, a poorly concealed racist strategy. It was based on the belief that Senator Goldwater could not win the Northern Negro vote. They felt that he might conceivably carry some of the Northern states, but they believed he would, by satisfying Southern racists, gather in the whole bloc of Southern electoral votes and perhaps win in the electoral college.

In Georgia, in 1964, the present Governor, Mr. Lester Maddox, then engaged in an open running fight against public accommodation laws, cynically declared that Senator Goldwater's racial position suited him (Mr. Maddox). In Alabama, George Wallace abandoned his own third party racist program so that he would not get in Senator Goldwater's way.

This racist dilemma will continue to plague the Southern Republican development, but as I see it, it is, while sad and regretable, perhaps a necessary part of the trauma of developing a second party. Nor should the melodrama of race by the so-called Southern Republicans hide the fact that there are many reputable first rate men who are at work trying to create a Southern Republican Party of responsibility and prestige. Some of these men had managed to make considerable progress until the take-over by Goldwater forces in 1964. They were not, and are not, racists. They are men committed to what they believe to be the principles of a progressive conservation. Most of them were replaced as state chairmen and national committeemen by the Goldwater organizational take-over in 1964, but they are coming back. They are by no means lost to the struggle to create a responsible competing party.

The Southern Democrats are not without trauma and dilemma. The divisive effects of racism and the determination of rural leaders to maintain segregated school systems at no matter what the cost to educational standards in general have contributed to a substantial split in what used to be called the solid Democratic South. We now know that in fact we had no Democratic Party such as existed in states outside the South. In the Southern one-party states the Democratic Party was what the governor made it. There were factions, each calling itself Democrats, that contended for the governorship.

When in 1964 and 1966 it became necessary for Southern Democrats to function as a party, they found themselves without any efficient, effective state organizations. They had never needed such organizations, because there had been an absence of opposition. They found their own ranks split by racist divisions. There is increasing disposition on the part of young voters not necessarily to follow the party of their fathers, but to split their votes and act more and more as independent voters, rather than those with party affiliation. It cannot now be said that the Democratic Party in the South is well organized or that it will be so in time for the 1968 campaign.

Certainly racist influences will plague and embarrass both parties in the next Presidential campaign.

Social History

I believe it necessary that there be a greater national comprehension of the political and social history of the South, because the effects of that history are now, in truth, a national problem, political, economic and social. Let me say, further, that it is not my purpose to berate the South. It is my region. I was born in it. I have lived and worked in it. But the romanticized myth of the South has been, and is, a curse to those who live there. The myth still obscures the reality.

The creation of a system of segregation was an evil, the effects of which were deep and widespread beyond the easy assumption that it merely separated the races in travel, in education, and in housing. It subjected the Negro to a separation that made it impossible for him to know anything of participation in citizenship, much less the responsibilities of it. Segregation gave to the white Southerner a false sense of position and values. In trying to pay for two school systems with a per capita income that was inadequate to finance one good school system, he subjected all children to an education inferior to that provided children of other regions. He slowed the industrial development of his region. He delayed the appearance of managerial skills and the accumulation of capital. There was also the profound moral dilemma of always justifying and supporting an immoral system.

Political maturity was impossible under that system. It was, for example, not really possible for a second party to develop in the South until 1958 when the U.S. Supreme Court ruled the white primary unconstitutional. The white primary device was one that restricted the voters to white persons. There was no opposition party. The primary was the election. The white primary and the poll tax created political apathy among white persons. Today, in 1967, the percentage of Southerners who vote is well below the national average.

The white power structure that created the device restricting the ballot wanted to attain that result—a general lack of voter participation.

In Mississippi, in 1900, it openly was argued that "the poll tax gets rid of most of the Negroes and also gets rid of a great many undesirable whites at the same time."

In 1901 Henry Fontaine Reese, of Selma and Dallas County (Alabama), stood before the state legislative convention and appealed for a constitutional poll tax provision.

"When you pay $1.50 for a poll tax in Dallas County, I believe you disfranchise 10 Negroes," he said. "Give us this $1.50 for educational purposes and for disfranchisement of a vicious and useless class."

"There has been talk," said delegate Reese, "from the hills of north Alabama as to what the poor white boys want. I do not propose to put my people under the hand of Negro rule because it might disfranchise one or two bastards in the white counties of Alabama."

Participation in the fraud, admitted cheating, and dishonesty of the disfranchisement proceedings had an effect on what the late W. J. Cash called "The Mind of the South." A large majority of poor white persons were delivered, along with almost all Negroes, into the political control of a minority of white voters.

All this chicanery had to be justified. Out of it came the doctrines of white supremacy, of Negro inferiority, and a system of segregation whose moral, political, social and economic injustices, follies, and evils are just now being comprehended.

What is not fully comprehended is that the product of the South's evil of segregation with all its ramifications deprived not merely a top-heavy majority of the nation's Negroes, but also hundreds of thousands of white children of education and citizenship. This product has now been exported to all the nation. It is a part of the complexity of life and government in Kansas City, in Topeka, in Seattle, in Miami—in all the cities of the nation.

An immense migration out of the rural South and the Southwest began in the decade of the boll weevil in 1920–30. It slowed during the depression, but it became accelerated as the nation moved into the Second World War, and it has not stopped. The peak era of migration was in the decades of 1940–1950 and 1950–1960. Not all of this has been Negro. A substantial percentage has been poor white farmers, tenants, or croppers who are no longer needed on the land. But most of them have been Negro.

San Francisco will do as an example. This beautiful and historic city has always had a cosmopolitan population. In 1940 the Negro population in San Francisco was a little over 5,000. But in 1951 Japan practically wiped out our Pacific fleet. It became necessary to re-take the Pacific. To do this, we had to build some 60,000 aircraft, ships, landing craft, and weapons of all sizes. War plants from Seattle to San Diego filled up with workers, most of them off the farms of Southern states—Oklahoma, Texas, and other agricultural states. In 1945 San Francisco's Negro population was 50,000.

Slum Violence

Americans could better understand the discontent and the spontaneity of slum violence in the larger cities if they knew the background. In the span of time between 1940–1963, almost 3½ million Negroes left the South. The war-time shipyards, aviation, and other war plants were the magnets that accelerated this out-migration. Out-migration continued after this peak period as farm machines replaced human beings and mules. An official estimate reveals that 114,000 Negroes left 11 counties in Mississippi in the recent decade of 1950–1960. Two and a half million Negroes have left the South since 1960. The out movement has slowed for obvious reasons, but it continues. The condition of the farm population in the old cotton states will worsen in the years ahead.

Early this month a U.S. Senate sub-committee, composed of respected Republicans and Democrats, made public the results of personal investigation and the taking of evidence in Mississippi. It was a shocking report on the poverty of rural persons, mostly in the South, who are no longer needed on the land.

An estimated 15 million of over 38 million poor are rural Americans. Half the nation's farm-operator families have incomes less than $3,000. At least 500,000 rural families whose chief income is farm wages live well below the poverty level.

Conditions are even worse for the five million rural Negroes. More than half have incomes of less than $2,000. In fact, perhaps a third have cash returns below $500 or less per year.

Urban poverty may, after all, be seen if one persists and goes out of the way to look for it. But rural misery is, on the whole, rather scattered and more hidden. It is, therefore, even more neglected, demonstrating the truth of the axiom, "out of sight, out of mind."

The Senate sub-committee found shameful exploitation of the food stamp program. It recommended a careful, studied reform of the welfare program. We will, I think, ignore this report to our peril.

There is, of course, a chorus of grumbling about poverty programs and loud denunciation of recipients as "not working." The comparison is not exact, to be sure, but we do not become exasperated because the many years of experimenting with cancer research has not produced a cure. Generations passed before the scourge of tuberculosis was brought under control. Poverty is more costly and dangerous than cancer or any other disease. It produces, of course, its own by-product of disease and crime.

There is a long hot summer ahead. It is, indeed, almost at hand. The tensions resulting from the exporting from farms to cities of millions of poor, unskilled, illiterate and semi-literate persons across the last four decades; the huge increase in population, half of which is 25 years old or younger—plus the burdens of war—have increased and added complexity to our lives.

It is a part of the problem that our heavy increase in population corresponded roughly with the out-migration from the South and the rural areas generally. The Census Bureau tells us that this fall about 100 million of our 200 million population will be 25 years old and younger. Everything is crowded—campuses, cities, suburbs.

The New Left

We will be further tested, regionally and nationally, by riots, draft-card burners, imitators of Cassius Clay, and activities of the extremists of what is collectively called the New Left.

The New Left in America is not numerically strong. It is itself somewhat fragmented. It has, within the context of its far-out position, its own extremists advocating violence and also elements not yet fully committed to programs of anarchy. There are some who are training "urban guerrillas" to fight police and other law enforcement representatives from cellars, alley ways and hidden positions. There are others that plan protests, riots, and related tactics.

They can succeed only if Americans lose a sense of balance and act out of anger and emotional impulses. It is difficult to put down reactions to those who burn or degrade the nation's flag, who do lead Hanoi to think it can win the war in America, or who lend themselves to the more irrational forms of protest. But it is precisely this weakness in human nature that is relied upon by the extreme of the New Left. They know they, few in number, can succeed only if they arouse a massive social and political swing to the "right." Hence, we may expect to be subjected to continued irritations and provocations—all aimed at upsetting the national balance and purpose. The provocateurs want to demoralize the society they have come to hate. They will keep trying to prod us to abandon the basic strengths of our society to retaliate against them.

Congressman Hebert's outburst of a few days ago against one of the deliberately staged provocations, an insult to the flag, was to suggest that we "forget about the first amendment and jail those who seek to destroy our society but seek protection of its laws."

This, of course, plays into the hands of the provocateurs. The Congressman spoke spontaneously in indignation. If we are provoked into selective "forgetting" of any of the foundations on which our form of government is established, then these foundations will in time disappear by becoming meaningless.

The New Left is estimated to include about 200,000 persons. Its more extreme members, willing to use repeated irrational violence to bring on chaos and, hopefully, a condition of anarchy, cannot succeed, either on the campuses or in the city slums, unless Americans succumb to emotional, angry retaliations as excessive as the provocations and, thereby, themselves contribute to a sense and a presence of anarchy.

The New Left, including, as it does, adults who join in the acts of wholly irrational protests and demonstrations, already has had a considerable success. They have helped create an impulsive, blind reaction that has enabled reactionary forces in and out of the Congress to slow, or halt, the necessary and hopeful progress of recent years.

The spectacle of some of the one-time personalities in social progress turning to "peace protests" because today "peace is where the money is" is a further aid to the forces of reaction and, therefore, indirectly to the worst of the New Left.

Poverty and Education

There are 38 million Americans whose critical conditions of poverty are undenied. There are massive, shocking gaps in the education provided the poor and the children of the middle and upper income groups. There are millions of Americans, exiles from agriculture, particularly Southern agriculture, who are crowded into slum areas of cities. There is, in this nation, almost no housing for the very poor. The very poor include hundreds of thousands of Spanish-speaking have-nots and hundreds of thousands of "poor whites" from Appalachia and the obsolete small farms.

The young Negro in the South is aware of the progress made. But he still finds himself in predominately or all-Negro state schools and colleges which he knows to be second and third rate. He is aware of the injustice of the past and the slow pace of the present. This is why some of them listen to the Stokely Carmichaels. One can easily imagine the frustration, despair and emotional tensions of a young Negro in states governed by a George Wallace, a Lester Maddox, or others like them whose commitments have been to rigid segregation and an inferior citizenship for the Negro.

It should be obvious that the immediate and long-time needs of 38 million Americans should not be abandoned because of the often stupid, reckless, irrational protests and deliberately provocative acts of such governors as are symbolized by Wallace and Maddox or by those of the New Left who are hostile to the existing society. The racists benefit by neglect of the needs of the deprived American. The New Left also is aided and encouraged, and the cure of our most dangerous and damaging ills is unnecessarily delayed.

Jefferson believed that if the people could be helped to know and comprehend the facts, they would, in the end, act with common sense. We are in a period, complex, emotional, and difficult, when common sense, understanding, and patience are required of us.

Robert F. Kennedy (1925–1968) was named Attorney General in 1960 by his brother President John Kennedy. He led a successful drive against organized crime and corruption in the Teamsters Union. He was committed to securing the civil rights of blacks, especially in Southern states. In November of 1964 he was elected senator from New York. By 1966, Robert Kennedy had become a critic of the Johnson administration's policy concerning Vietnam. On March 16, 1968, Kennedy announced his candidacy for president. His speech at Kansas State was the first major speech of his campaign. On June 4, 1968, after winning the California primary, he was shot; he died two days later.

Conflict in Vietnam and at Home

Robert F. Kennedy

Robert Kennedy's appearance in the Landon Lecture Series on March 18, 1968, was memorable not only for the timeliness and forcefulness of his speech. It also was an event in itself—the first major public address following the announcement of his presidential candidacy. Kennedy had been scheduled to speak on domestic policy issues. A KSU press release the previous Friday, just prior to his candidacy announcement, listed his lecture topic as "Change and Conflict in the Community." As a presidential candidate he chose to address the *burning topic of the day, the Vietnam War. American involvement in Vietnam had escalated sharply since Lyndon Johnson's election in 1964, and American public protest against the war had grown proportionally. Kennedy's Landon Lecture sought to tap that growing protest and to link America's ills at home with its problems abroad. The dramatic eloquence of his rhetoric, for instance in the concluding paragraph of his lecture, is reminiscent of that of President John Kennedy and is echoed in the style and words of his younger brother, Senator Edward Kennedy, whose 1984 Landon Lecture is reprinted in this volume.*

MARCH 18, 1968

The reason I'm here is that someone sent me a history of this city. And I found out that it was founded by people from Chicago who came to Kansas to found a town named Boston which they later changed to Manhattan. So I knew I'd be right at home.

I am proud to come here at the invitation of Alfred M. Landon. I met him at the White House when he visited there. I know how highly President Kennedy respected Governor Landon, and the continuing contribution he made—and still makes—to the public life of the country.

I am also glad to come to the home state of another Kansan who wrote,

If our colleges and universities do not breed men who riot, who rebel, who attack life with all the youthful vision and vigor, then there is something wrong with our colleges. The more riots that come on college campuses, the better world for tomorrow.

The man who wrote these words was that notorious seditionist, William Allen White—the late editor of the Emporia Gazette and one of the giants of American journalism. He is an honored man today; but when he lived and wrote, he was often reviled on your campus and across the nation as an extremist—or worse. For he spoke as he believed. He did not conceal his concern in comforting words; he did not delude his readers or himself with false hopes and illusions. It is in this spirit that I wish to speak today.

A Year of Choice

For this is a year of choice—a year when we choose not simply who will lead us, but where we wish to be led; the country we want for ourselves—and the kind we want for our children. If in this year of choice we fashion new politics out of old illusions, we insure for ourselves nothing but crisis for the future—and we bequeath to our children the bitter harvest of those crises.

For with all we have done, with all our immense power and richness, our problems seem to grow not less, but greater. We are in a time of unprecedented turbulence, of danger and questioning. It is at its root a question of the national soul. The President calls it "restlessness;" while cabinet officers and commentators tell us that America is deep in a malaise of the spirit—discouraging initiative, paralyzing will and action, dividing Americans from one another by their age, their views, and the color of their skins.

There are many causes. Some are in the failed promise of America itself: in the children I have seen, starving in Mississippi; idling their lives away in the ghetto; committing suicide in the despair of Indian reservations; or watching their proud fathers sit without work in the ravaged lands of Eastern Kentucky. Another cause is in our inaction in the face of danger. We seem equally unable to control the violent disorder within our cities—or the pollution and destruction of the country, of the water and land that we use and our children must inherit. And a third great cause of discontent is the course we are following in Vietnam: in a war which has divided Americans as they have not been divided since your state was called "bloody Kansas."

Crisis of Confidence

All this—questioning and uncertainty at home, divisive war abroad—has led us to a deep crisis of confidence: in our leadership, in each other, and in our very self as a nation.

Today I would speak to you of the third of those great crises: of the war in Vietnam. I come here, to this serious forum in the heart of the nation to discuss with you why I regard our policy there as bankrupt: not on the basis of emotion, but fact; not, I hope, in clichés—but with a clear and discriminating sense of where the national interest really lies.

I do not want—as I believe most Americans do not want—to sell out American interests, to simply withdraw, to raise the white flag of surrender. That would be unacceptable to us as a country and as a people. But I am concerned—as I believe most Americans are concerned—that the course we are following at the present time is deeply wrong. I am concerned—as I believe most Americans are concerned—that we are acting as if no other nations existed, against the judgment and desires of neutrals and our historic allies alike. I am concerned—as I believe most Americans are concerned—that our present course will not bring victory; will not bring peace; will not stop the bloodshed; and will not advance the interests of the United States or the cause of peace in the world.

I am concerned that, at the end of it all, there will only be more Americans killed; more of our treasure spilled out; and because of the bitterness and hatred on every side of this war, more hundreds of thousands of Vietnamese slaughtered; so that they may say, as Tacitus said of Rome: "They made a desert, and called it peace."

And I do not think that is what the American spirit is really all about.

Let me begin this discussion with a note both personal and public. I was involved in many of the early decisions on Vietnam, decisions which helped set us on our present path. It may be that the effort was doomed from the start; that it was never really possible to bring all the people of South Vietnam under the rule of the successive governments we supported—governments, one after another, riddled with corruption, inefficiency, and greed; governments which did not and could not successfully capture and energize the national feeling of their people. If that is the case, as it well may be, then I am willing to bear my share of the responsibility, before history and before my fellow-citizens. But past error is no excuse for its own perpetuation. Tragedy is a tool for the living to gain wisdom, not a guide by which to live. Now as ever, we do ourselves best justice when we measure ourselves against ancient tests, as in the Antigone of Sophocles: "All men make mistakes, but a good man yields when he knows his course is wrong, and repairs the evil. The only sin is pride."

Reversals and Escalations

The reversals of the last several months have led our military to ask for 206,000 more troops. Recently, it was announced that some of them—a "moderate" increase, it was said—would soon be sent. But isn't this exactly what we have always done in the past? If we examine the history of this conflict, we find the dismal story repeated time after time. Every time—at every crisis—we have denied that anything was wrong; sent more troops; and issued more confident communiques. Every time, we have been assured that this one last step would bring victory. And every time, the predictions and promises have failed and been forgotten, and the demand has been made again for just one more step up the ladder.

But all the escalations, all the last steps, have brought us no closer to success than we were before. Rather, as the scale of the fighting has increased, South Vietnamese society has become less and less capable of organizing or defending itself, and we have more and more assumed the whole burden of the war. In just three years, we have gone from 16,000 advisers to over 500,000 troops; from no American bombing North or South, to an air campaign against both, greater than that waged in all the European theater in World War II; from less than 300 American dead in all the years prior to 1965, to more than 500 dead in a single week of combat in 1968.

And once again the President tells us, as we have been told for twenty years, that "we are going to win;" "victory" is coming.

But what are the true facts? What is our present situation?

The Present Situation

First, our control over the rural population—so long described as the key to our efforts—has evaporated. The Vice President tells us that the pacification program has "stopped." In the language of other high officials, it is a "considerable setback," with "loss of momentum," "some withdrawal from the countryside," "a significant psychological setback both on the part of pacification people themselves and the local population." Reports from the field indicate that the South Vietnamese Army has greatly increased its tendency to "pull into its compounds in cities and towns, especially at night, reduce its patrolling, and leave the militia and revolutionary development cadres open to enemy incursion and attack." Undoubtedly, this is one reason why, over two recent weeks, our combat deaths—1049—were so much greater than those of the South Vietnamese—557. Like it or not, the government of South Vietnam is pursuing an enclave policy. Its writ runs where American arms protect it: that far and no farther. To extend the power of the Saigon government over its own country, we now can see, will be in essence equivalent to the reconquest and occupation of most of the entire nation.

Let us clearly understand the full implications of that fact. The point of our pacification operations was always described as "winning the hearts and minds" of the people. We recognized that giving the countryside military security against the Viet Cong would be futile—indeed that it would be impossible—unless the people of the countryside themselves came to identify their interests with ours, and to assist not the Viet Cong, but the Saigon government. For this we recognized that their minds would have to be changed— that their natural inclination would be to support the Viet Cong, or at best remain passive, rather than sacrifice for foreign white men, or the remote Saigon government.

It is this effort that has been most gravely set back in the last month. We cannot change the minds of people in villages controlled by the enemy. The fact is, as all recognize, that we cannot reassert control over those villages now in enemy hands without repeating the whole process of bloody destruction which has ravaged the countryside of South Vietnam throughout the last three years. Nor could we thus keep control without the presence of millions of American troops. If, in the years those villages and hamlets were controlled by Saigon, the government had brought honesty, social reform, land—if that had happened, if the many promises of a new and better life for the people had been fulfilled—then, in the process of reconquest, we might appear as liberators: just as we did in Europe, despite the devastation of war, in 1944–45. But the promises of reform were not kept. Corruption and abuse of administrative power have continued to this day. Land reform has never been more than an empty promise. Viewing the performance of the Saigon government over the last three years, there is no reason for the South Vietnamese peasant to fight for the extension of its authority or to view the further devastation that effort will bring as anything but a calamity. Yet already the destruction has defeated most of our own purposes. Arthur Gardiner is the former chief of the United States AID mission in South Vietnam, and currently Executive Director of the International Voluntary Services. He tells us that we are "creating more Viet Cong than we are destroying"—and "increasing numbers of Vietnamese are becoming benevolently neutral toward the Viet Cong." As a consequence, the political war—so long described as the only war that counts—has gone with the pacification program that was to win it. In a real sense, it may now be lost beyond recall.

Our Regressive Ally

The second evident fact of the last two months is that the Saigon government is no more or better an ally than it was before; that it may even be less; and that the war inexorably is growing more, not less, an American effort. American officials continue to talk about a government newly energized, moving with "great competence," taking hold "remarkably well," doing "a very, very good piece of work of recovery." I was in the Executive Branch of the government from 1961 to 1964. In all those years, we heard the same glowing promises about the South Vietnamese government: corruption would soon be eliminated, land reform would come, programs were being infused with new energy. But those were not the facts then, and they are not the facts today. The facts are that there is still no total mobilization: no price or wage controls, no rationing, no overtime work. The facts are, as a Committee of the House of Representatives has told us, that land reform is moving backward, with the government forces helping landlords to collect exorbitant back rents from the peasantry. The facts are that 18-year-old South Vietnamese are still not being drafted; though now, as many times in the past, we are assured that this will happen soon. The facts are that thousands of young South Vietnamese buy their deferments from military service while American Marines die at Khe Sanh.

The facts are that the government has arrested monks and labor leaders, former Presidential candidates and government officials—including prominent members of the Committee for the Preservation of the Nation, in which American officials placed such high hopes just a few weeks ago.

Meanwhile, the government's enormous corruption continues, debilitating South Vietnam and crippling our effort to help its people. Committees of the Senate and House of Representatives have officially documented the existence, extent, and results of this corruption: American AID money stolen, food diverted from refugees, government posts bought and sold while essential tasks remain undone. A subcommittee of the Senate Committee on Government Operations has reported that the Vietnamese Collector of Customs had engaged in smuggling gold and opium—and that he was protected by figures even higher in the government. President Johnson has responded to criticism of corruption in Vietnam by reminding us that there is stealing in Beaumont, Texas. I for one do not believe that Beaumont is so corrupt. I do not believe that any public official, in any American city, is engaged in smuggling gold and dope; selling draft deferments, or pocketing millions of dollars in U.S. government funds. But however corrupt any city in the United States may be, that corruption is not costing the lives of American soldiers; while the pervasive corruption of the Government of Vietnam, as an American official has told us, is a significant cause of the prolongation of the war and the continued American casualties. As this government continues on its present course, and our support for it continues, the effect can only be to leave us totally isolated from the people of Vietnam. Our fighting men deserve better than that.

The Cost of Destruction

Third, it is becoming more evident with every passing day that the victories we achieve will only come at the cost of destruction for the nation we once hoped to help. Even before this winter, Vietnam and its people were disintegrating under the blows of war. Now hardly a city in Vietnam has been spared from the new ravages of the past two months. Saigon officials say that nearly three quarters of a million new refugees have been created, to add to the existing refugee population of two million or more. No one really knows the number of civilian casualties. The city of Hue, with most of the country's cultural and artistic heritage, lies in ruins: Of its population of 115,000, fully 113,000 are said to be homeless. There is not enough food, not enough shelter, not enough medical care. There is only death and misery and destruction.

An American commander said of the town of Ben Tre, "it became necessary to destroy the town in order to save it." It is difficult to quarrel with the decision of American commanders to use air power and artillery to save the lives of their men; if American troops are to fight for Vietnamese cities, they deserve protection. What I cannot understand is why the responsibility for the recapture and attendant destruction of Hue, and Ben Tre and the others, should fall to American troops in the first place.

If Communist insurgents or invaders held New York or Washington or San Francisco, we would not leave it to foreigners to take them back, and destroy them and their people in the process. Rather I believe there is not one among us who would not tear the invaders out with his bare hands, whatever the cost. There is no question that some of the South Vietnamese Army fought with great bravery. The Vietnamese—as these units, and the Viet Cong have both shown us—are a courageous people. But it is also true that a thousand South Vietnamese soldiers, in Hue on leave for Tet, hid among the refugees for three weeks, making no attempt to rejoin their units or join the town's defense; among them was a full colonel. And it is also true that in the height of the battle for Hue, as trucks brought back American dead and wounded from the front lines, millions of Americans could see, on their television screens, South Vietnamese soldiers occupied in looting the city those Americans were fighting to recapture.

If the government's troops will not or cannot carry the fight for their cities, we cannot ourselves destroy them. That kind of salvation is not an act we can presume to perform for them. For we must ask our government—we must ask ourselves: where does such logic end? If it becomes "necessary" to destroy all of South Vietnam in order to "save" it, will we do that too? And if we care so little about South Vietnam that we are willing to see the land destroyed and its people dead, then why are we there in the first place?

Can we ordain to ourselves the awful majesty of God—to decide what cities and villages are to be destroyed, who will live and who will die, and who will join the refugees wandering in a desert of our own creation? If it is true that we have a commitment to the South Vietnamese people, we must ask, are they being consulted—in Hue, or Ben Tre, or in the villages from which the 3 million refugees have fled? If they believe all the death and destruction are a lesser evil than the Viet Cong, why did they not warn us when the Viet Cong came into Hue, and the dozens of other cities, before the Tet Offensive? Why did they not join the fight?

Will it be said of us, as Tacitus said of Rome: "They made a desert and called it peace?"

It is also said that we are protecting Thailand—or perhaps Hawaii—from the legions of the Communists. Are we really protecting the rest of Southeast Asia by this spreading conflict? And in any case, is the destruction of South Vietnam and its people a permissible means of defense?

Let us have no misunderstanding. The Viet Cong are a brutal enemy indeed. Time and time again, they have shown their willingness to sacrifice innocent civilians, to engage in torture and murder and despicable terror to achieve their ends. This is a war almost without rules or quarter. There can be no easy moral answer to this war, no one-sided condemnation of American actions. What we must ask ourselves is whether we have a right to bring so much destruction to another land, without clear and convincing evidence that this is what its people want. But that is precisely the evidence we do not have. What they want is peace, not dominated by any outside force. And that is what we are really committed to help bring them, not in some indefinite future, but while some scraps of life remain still to be saved from the holocaust.

Our Weakening World Position

The fourth fact that is now more clear than ever is that the war in Vietnam, far from being the last critical test for the United States is in fact weakening our position in Asia and around the world, and eroding the structure of international cooperation which has directly supported our security for the past three decades. In purely military terms, the war has already stripped us of the graduated-response capability that we have labored so hard to build for the last seven years. Surely the North Koreans were emboldened to seize the Pueblo because they knew that the United States simply cannot afford to fight another Asian war while we are so tied down in Vietnam. We set out to prove our willingness to keep our commitments everywhere in the world. What we are ensuring instead is that it is most unlikely that the American people would ever again be willing to again engage in this kind of struggle. Meanwhile our oldest and strongest allies pull back to their own shores, leaving us alone to police all of Asia; while Mao Tse-Tung and his Chinese comrades sit patiently by, fighting us to the last Vietnamese: watching us weaken a nation which might have provided a stout barrier against Chinese expansion southward; hoping that we will further tie ourselves down in protracted war in Cambodia, Laos, Thailand; confident, as it is reported from Hong Kong, that the war in Vietnam "will increasingly bog down the United States, sapping its resources, discrediting its power pretensions, alienating its allies, fraying its ties with the Soviet Union, and aggravating dissensions among Americans at home." As one American observer puts it, truly "We seem to be playing the script the way Mao wrote it."

All this bears directly and heavily on the question of whether more troops should now be sent to Vietnam—and, if more are sent, what their mission will be. We are entitled to ask—we are required to ask—how many more men, how many more lives, how much more destruction will be asked, to provide the military victory that is always just around the corner, to pour into this bottomless pit of our dreams?

But this question the Administration does not and cannot answer. It has no answer—none but the ever-expanding use of military force and the lives of our brave soldiers, in a conflict where military force has failed to solve anything in the past. The President has offered to negotiate—yet this weekend he told us again that he seeks not compromise but victory, "at the negotiating table if possible, on the battlefield if necessary." But at a real negotiating table, there can be no "victory" for either side; only a painful and difficult compromise. To seek victory at the conference table is to ensure that you will never reach it. Instead the war will go on, year after terrible year—until those who sit in the seats of high policy are men who seek another path. And that must be done this year.

For it is long past time to ask: what is this war doing to us? Of course it is costing us money—fully one-fourth of our federal budget—but that is the smallest price we pay. The cost is in our young men, the tens of thousands of their lives cut off forever. The cost is in our world position—in neutrals and allies alike, every day more baffled by and estranged from a policy they cannot understand.

The Price We Pay

Higher yet is the price we pay in our own innermost lives, and in the spirit of our country. For the first time in a century, we have open resistance to service in the cause of the nation. For the first time perhaps in our history, we have desertions from our army on political and moral grounds. The front pages of our newspapers show photographs of American soldiers torturing prisoners. Every night we watch horror on the evening news. Violence spreads inexorably across the nation, filling our streets and crippling our lives. And whatever the costs to us, let us think of the young men we have sent there: not just the killed, but those who have to kill; not just the maimed, but also those who must look upon the results of what they do.

It may be asked, is not such degradation the cost of all wars? Of course it is. That is why war is not an enterprise lightly to be undertaken, nor prolonged one moment past its absolute necessity. All this—the destruction of Vietnam, the cost to ourselves, the danger to the world—all this we would stand willingly, if it seemed to serve some worthwhile end. But the costs of the war's present course far outweigh anything we can reasonably hope to gain by it, for ourselves or for the people of Vietnam. It must be ended, and it can be ended, in a peace of brave men who have fought each other with a terrible fury, each believing he and he alone was in the right. We have prayed to different gods, and the prayers of neither have been answered fully. Now, while there is still time for some of them to be partly answered, now is the time to stop.

What We Can Do

And the fact is that much can be done. We can—as I have urged for two years, but as we have never done—negotiate with the National Liberation Front. We can—as we have never done—assure the Front a genuine place in the political life of South Vietnam. We can—as we are refusing to do today—begin to deescalate the war, concentrate on protecting populated areas, and thus save American lives and slow down the destruction of the countryside. We can— as we have never done—insist that the Government of South Vietnam broaden its base, institute real reforms, and seek an honorable settlement with their fellow countrymen.

This is no radical program of surrender. This is no sell-out of American interests. This is a modest and reasonable program, designed to advance the interests of this country and save something from the wreckage for the people of Vietnam.

This program would be far more effective than the present course of this Administration—whose only response to failure is to repeat it on a larger scale. This program, with its more limited costs, would indeed be far more likely to accomplish our true objectives.

And therefore even this modest and reasonable program is impossible while our present leadership, under the illusion that military victory is just ahead, plunges deeper into the swamp that is our present course.

So I come here today, to this great University, to ask your help: not for me, but for your country and for the people of Vietnam. You are the people, as President Kennedy said, who have "the least ties to the present and the greatest ties to the future." I urge you to learn the harsh facts that lurk behind the mask of official illusion with which we have concealed our true circumstances, even from ourselves. Our country is in danger: not just from foreign enemies; but above all, from our own misguided policies—and what they can do to the nation that Thomas Jefferson once told us was the last, best, hope of man. There is a contest on, not for the rule of America, but for the heart of America. In these next eight months, we are going to decide what this country will stand for—and what kind of men we are. So I ask for your help, in the cities and homes of this state, in the towns and farms: contributing your concern and action, warning of the danger of what we are doing—and the promise of what we can do. I ask you, as tens of thousands of young men and women are doing all over this land, to organize yourselves, and then to go forth and work for new policies—work to change our direction—and thus restore our place at the point of moral leadership, in our country, in our own hearts, and all around the world.

Arthur Schlesinger, Jr. (1917–) is now Albert Schweitzer Professor of Humanities at City College of New York. He was educated at Harvard and Oxford and returned to serve on the faculty at Harvard. He wrote prize-winning biographies of Andrew Jackson and Franklin Roosevelt. In 1959, he helped John Kennedy recruit a liberal "brain trust" for his administration, and he became a special assistant to the President in 1961. After John Kennedy's assassination, he resigned his post and wrote his Pulitzer Prize winning history of the Kennedy administration, *A Thousand Days: John F. Kennedy in the White House.* In late 1966, he published a critique of American involvement in Vietnam, *The Bitter Heritage: Vietnam and American Democracy.* He was an advisor to Robert Kennedy during his campaign for the presidency. During the Nixon administration, Schlesinger wrote *The Imperial Presidency,* an attack on the centralization of power in the office of the President.

The 1968 Election:
An Historical Perspective

Arthur Schlesinger, Jr.

Arthur Schlesinger, Jr., who spoke on November 14, 1968, was the first of the Landon Lecturers who was neither a journalist nor an active politician. As a leading political historian and chronicler of the Franklin Roosevelt and John F. Kennedy presidencies, Schlesinger analyzed the 1968 presidential election from a perspective which emphasized major long-term changes in American society. In doing so, he elevated the discussion of the election from a focus on mere personalities and state-by-state returns to a consideration of more lasting issues: the erosion of the social base of New Deal liberalism and the crisis of leadership and direction within the Democratic Party. Schlesinger's characterizations of President Richard Nixon, as "mechanical" and Vice-President Humphrey, as a spokesman for the "Old Politics," might be compared with the Landon Lectures which each gave at Kansas State in 1970, both of which are included in this volume.

NOVEMBER 14, 1968

I am greatly honored to have the privilege of delivering an Alfred M. Landon Lecture on Public Issues here at Kansas State University. I was particularly pleased to receive President McCain's invitation to take part in this series not only because Governor Landon is an old and valued friend but because the occasion enables me, as a liberal and a Democrat, to express my own deep appreciation for the role Governor Landon has played in our national life. Through the political vicissitudes of half a century he has preserved his own distinctive voice—a voice of character, decency and pungent common sense. It has been the authentic voice of the middle border— the voice, after all, of Kansas; and "the Kansas spirit," as Carl Becker wrote sixty years ago, "is the American spirit double distilled." Governor Landon has not been afraid to say what he thinks; he has displayed a consistent and admirable irreverence for established ideas and institutions; and he has been a fearless enemy of intolerance and bigotry. He may once have been a Republican candidate for President ; but I hope he will forgive me if I say he has also been a representative of American radicalism in the best sense of the word—in the sense of using reason to strike at the roots of the matter and letting the chips fall where they may. His nation and his century stand in his debt.

We have recently concluded one of the oddest presidential campaigns in American history. It was a campaign of paradox. Each major party nominated the man whom many observers considered the weakest of its available candidates. Neither candidate developed an effective theme, made a memorable speech or uttered a fresh idea. Many voters regarded the contest—at least till the last week or so—with vast and imperturbable indifference. The number of votes cast in 1968 barely exceeded the number cast in 1964. If the same proportions of votes had been cast as in 1960, 7 million more Americans would have had to go to the polls this year. Yet, in spite of all this, the election ended as the most exciting presidential race in twenty years.

The closeness of the contest may be attributed in the short run, I believe, to a conflict between two fundamental principles of American politics. One principle has long since been formulated: it is TURN THE RASCALS OUT. If a party has done badly in office, the sound reaction of the American voter is to give the opposition a chance. The Johnson administration had permitted the American involvement in Vietnam to deepen and harden beyond any rational justification. It hardly seemed that the men who plunged us deeper and deeper into the Vietnamese futility should be rewarded by reelection. Many voters felt—and understandably so—that the Democrats simply did not deserve four more years of power.

This was one instinct at work in the electorate. But it was countered by another instinct. This second principle has not been so clearly formulated as the first; but it can be expressed, I think, somewhat as follows: HUMAN BEINGS ARE BETTER THAN

MECHANICAL MEN. The fact that this principle has not been formulated should not lead anyone to underestimate its potency. In alliance with the first principle, it led to Franklin Roosevelt's decisive victory over Herbert Hoover in 1932—the victory which established the Democratic party as the majority party for more than a generation. And, when the two principles came in conflict in 1948, the second overcame the first; the electorate in the end, despite dissatisfactions with his administration, chose the vivid and fallible humanity of Harry S. Truman over the unctuous calculation of his opponent. The two principles were again in conflict in this election. As the campaign wore drearily on, more and more voters were obviously beginning to be depressed by the idea of a mechanical man in the White House. As each week went by, moreover, Hubert Humphrey was more himself, more a free man and a human being. Had there been another week—perhaps another seventy-two hours—he would probably have won the election.

In the short run, this conflict of political instinct helped shape the 1968 result. But behind this conflict lay, I think, deeper problems. For under the surface profound changes have been taking place in American politics—changes in issues, changes in techniques. To see the 1968 election in full historical perspective one must first grasp the significance of recent alterations in the nature of the American political problem.

The American political problem received its last fundamental definition from Franklin Roosevelt. He was the creative political genius of his age; and he established the framework of thought and action which has governed our subsequent politics. He set the issues, delineated the constituencies, and refined the techniques. He was, in short, the architect of the New Politics of the nineteen thirties. He enjoyed, of course, a considerable advantage in his work of political reconstruction. The Great Depression had made the obsolescence of the older political ideas and issues evident to a great mass of voters. There was a hunger for innovation and reform; no arguments were necessary. It is chastening to think that in 1928 the term "liberal" meant essentially someone opposed to the Eighteenth Amendment. By 1934 it had come to mean something very different.

If the Great Depression facilitated Roosevelt's task of political redefinition, it also left its distinctive imprint on the substance of that redefinition. The New Deal emerged essentially as a protest against the conservative doctrines of human impotence in face of economic crisis. Its concern was with the problems of a society in economic stagnation. It contended—and rightly, I believe—that the national government was the best instrument available to the people for reviving and reforming the stricken economy. And it rallied a coalition of trade unions, city machines, ethnic minorities, family farmers and intellectuals—a disparate and often diverging group, based on the poor and the uneducated and unified by FDR's political skill. It was this coalition which produced the vast social changes of the thirties. It was this coalition which, perhaps less from conviction about the policy than from confidence in the leader, supported the internationalist course in foreign affairs in the forties. And it was this coalition which made the Democratic party the majority party in the nation.

The New Deal coalition, its ideas, policies and methods, were thus born in depression. But the United States has changed in the years since the thirties—in great part, because of the New Deal. Most strikingly, it has become an affluent society. Because our affluence is very unevenly distributed, and because many New Deal ideas and policies were relevant not just to depression but to justice and civilization, the New Deal coalition had contributions to make even in an age of affluence. But the very success of New Deal policies began to undermine New Deal political power.

A sense of common desperation had created the original coalition; but, by using the affirmative state to protect jobs, homes, bank accounts, and farm prices, by assuring compensation for the unemployed and pensions for the old, the New Deal reduced that sense of desperation. The component elements began to lose their early feeling of solidarity and to pursue their divergent interests. By 1952 the Republicans came back to Washington. It is true that this was less because of the popularity of the Republican party than because of the popularity of the Republican candidate. Yet something was changing in American politics. As one Democratic politician put it after the 1952 election, "The trouble is that we ran out of poor people." This was not, of course, true; for plenty of poor people remained in our society. But, unlike the ambitious immigrants of the eighteen nineties or the politically aggressive unemployed of the nineteen thirties, the poor of the fifties were all too often a demoralized and inarticulate minority who in many cases had inherited their poverty and passively accepted it as a permanent condition. As for the despairing job-seekers of the thirties, many were prosperous suburbanites by the fifties and the sixties. The "forgotten men" of FDR, as James Reston has pointed out, have become the "forgotten Americans" of Richard Nixon. Affluence thus tended to subvert the old New Deal coalition.

At the same time, the rise of the affluent society has given new questions prominence in our politics. The issues of the New Deal were fundamentally those of what might be called quantitative liberalism. The New Deal program tackled the elemental needs of the American people—a job, a suit of clothing, three meals a day, a roof over one's head, and a measure of security for old age. Because the New Deal secured the basis of life for so many, post-New Deal liberalism began to move on to the issues implied by the phrase, first used by Adlai Stevenson in 1956, "the quality of life." Qualitative liberalism identified new areas for action—such areas as civil rights, civil liberties, education, the humanization of our cities, the relationship between life and environment, the state of our arts. Moreover, foreign policy, which until the end of the thirties was a subordinate and marginal consideration, became a central question in our politics and lives.

The emergence of these new issues cut athwart the New Deal coalition. For politics in the '30s divided essentially according to the level of income. The poor demanded, and the rich opposed, that series of measures which brought about so beneficial a redistribution of opportunity, income and power in American society. But the issues of the '60s did not square the battle lines of the '30s. To an increasing degree, politics in the '60s—and this will probably be even more true of the '70s—began to divide according to the level, not of income, but of education.

Consider such foreign policy issues as the Vietnam war, foreign aid, negotiated disarmament, East-West trade, admission of mainland China to the United Nations; consider such domestic issues as racial justice, open housing, civil liberties, students, law and order, federal aid to cities, federal aid to education, even air and water pollution, even cigarettes and billboards. On these issues, it is the poor and uneducated whites who tend to be the most emotional and primitive champions of conservatism—who fear the niggers, despise the long-haired college kids and can't understand why we don't drop a nuclear bomb on Hanoi. The affluent and better educated, on the other hand, tend to care more about rationality, reform and progress. Louis Harris summed up the testimony of public opinion polls when he said recently, "The privileged have become the progenitors of change, while the underprivileged whites have become the steadfast defenders of the status quo."

Thus the new issues appear to have eroded the base of the old coalition. At the same time, significant changes in the means of communication—above all, the rise of television and public opinion polls—have begun to alter the shape of American politics. Traditionally we have had a three-layered political order with a row of middlemen standing between the politician and the voter. The local party boss, the trade union leader, the farm leader, the head of the ethnic federation—such men passed back and forth between their constituencies and the politician, representing each to the other. But all this began to change. The mass media and the public opinion polls tended to eliminate the middleman and to create a two-layered system. The people have struck out on their own. They base their judgments each evening on Walter Cronkite and David Brinkley and register their views each week through Louis Harris and George Gallup. They regard the old political establishment with contempt and respond to any candidate who sets himself against the old faces. The anti-establishment candidates appeal above all to the students, who thus far have been the only ones to develop modes of organization which will work in the electronic age.

The result has been to sap the strength of the traditional political institutions. The city organizations have mostly fallen into disrepair. (Chicago is almost the last remaining example of the old-fashioned machine; perhaps the Daley organization should be preserved in the Museum of Natural History.) Trade union membership has declined both relatively and absolutely; today only about one-fifth of the labor force is organized, and, in any case, labor leaders can no longer deliver a labor vote. The ethnic minorities have been turned against each other by the Negro revolution. The farmers are a declining force. In short, the Old Politics of the middlemen is now giving way to the New Politics of mass involvement.

The combination of the new, non-economic issues with the new means of mass communication was subjecting the New Deal coalition to severe strains by the late 1950s. It would have required creative political genius equal to that of Franklin Roosevelt's to reconstruct and revitalize that coalition. I believe that President Kennedy had that genius and was well on his way to finding new terms for old alliances when tragedy terminated his gallant life.

It is an irony of history that his successor, Lyndon Johnson, a devoted son of the New Deal, should have administered the coup de grace to the New Deal coalition. In domestic affairs President Johnson's vision of the Great Society offered genuine promise of reconstituting the old alliances. But he nullified this wise and admirable effort by his policies in foreign affairs and by his attitudes toward the national Democratic party.

The traditional foreign policy of the Democratic party—the policy of Wilson, Roosevelt, Stevenson and Kennedy—has been a policy which united realism and idealism. These leaders acquired their great influence around the planet because they understood that a fundamental component of national power is the capacity to move the conscience and reason of the world—because, in the words of the Declaration of Independence, they paid "a decent respect to the opinions of mankind." The traditional foreign policy of the Republican party, on the other hand, has been to deprecate the relevance of world opinion and to base American policy rather exclusively on military power on the theory that force is the only thing the other side understands. In Vietnam, the Dominican Republic, and elsewhere, President Johnson, by casting the United States in the role of an international bully, rejected the traditional foreign policy of the Democratic party in favor of the traditional foreign policy of the Republicans.

In so doing, he badly confused his own party, leaving it torn between loyalty to the Democratic President and loyalty to historic Democratic principles. The Vietnam War was the essential cause of the Democratic defeat in 1968; and the men who persuaded President Johnson that he should embark on the course of military escalation are the men directly responsible for that defeat. In particular, the Vietnam blunder drove the intellectual community into opposition to the Democratic administration. For better or worse, intellectuals in our society wield a political influence out of all proportion to the votes they cast. No Democratic President this century has been elected without their active and enthusiastic support. The intellectuals in the '30s had been the lynch-pin of Franklin Roosevelt's coalition. In estranging them, Lyndon Johnson hastened the demoralization and intensified the crisis of the Democratic party.

I have concentrated thus far on the crisis of the Democratic party not just because I am a Democrat but because it is an axiom of American history that the great political debates tend to take place first within the majority parties. Only if the majority party shows itself incapable of dealing with urgent national issues does the minority party have a serious chance to create a new majority. So the debate over slavery tore the Whig party to pieces in the eighteen fifties and enabled the Republicans to establish a new political consensus; so too the expulsion from the Republican party in 1912 of its progressive wing prevented the Republicans from meeting the problems of social justice in an industrial society and gave Franklin Roosevelt his opportunity to devise new programs and make the Democrats a new majority party.

This does not mean, though, that minority parties do not experience their own inner debates between the stand-patters and the modernizers. As men like W. H. Seward had tried to make the old Whig party face up to the problems identified by Jackson, so in the last thirty years men like Governor Landon, Wendell Wilkie, Nelson Rockefeller, John Lindsay have tried to make their party face up to the issues identified by FDR. And they have been just enough more successful than Seward to keep their party in intermittent connection with the vital issues of the age.

Both parties, then, have had to wrestle with the implications of the recent revolution in political issues and techniques. Yet in each party the pull of the past has been very great. Like all human institutions, political parties tend to cling to accustomed ways of perceiving and doing things. Moreover, older men, which means men whose ideas were formed in another time, tend through the sheer attrition of seniority to occupy positions of authority in a political party. This is notably true, of course, of Congress, which is why (to adopt James MacGregor Burns' useful distinction) the congressional wings of each major party tend to be more standpat than the presidential wings. The Old Politics becomes a self-perpetuating myth, kept alive by the political professionals, who have a vested interest in its preservation, and by newspapermen, who spend most of their time interviewing political professionals.

The inherent conservatism of political parties thereby increased the gap between the Old Politics and the new times. President Kennedy, I believe, had the vision and will to bridge that gap; but his murder both terminated his effort and increased the sense of alienation among the young, the poor and the blacks. Then President Johnson, after holding out his splendid conception of the Great Society with its promise of justice to the poor and the blacks, proceeded to sacrifice the Great Society to a squalid and irrelevant war in Vietnam. The revolt among the young against Vietnam was compounded by the revolt among the blacks against continued denial of their rights; this was further compounded by the revolt among low-income whites against self-assertion by the blacks; and all was further exacerbated by the pervasive sense of powerlessness afflicting nearly every class in society—the sense of the impotence of the individual amidst the towering impersonal structures of modern life. The young became the particular carriers of this spreading disquietude—and for reasons perhaps best explained, oddly enough, by General de Gaulle after the Sorbonne riots last June. The "anguish of the young," the old general said, was "infinitely" natural

> in the mechanical society, the modern consumer society, because it does not offer them what they need, that is, an ideal, an impetus, a hope, and I think that ideal, that impetus, and that hope, they can and must find in participation.

The goal of the discontented young, poor and black was precisely this goal of participation. They began to demand a voice in the decisions which would determine their destinies. The vital question now was whether this goal could be pursued within the established political process. The Democratic party of Lyndon Johnson seemed impenetrable; the Republican party of Barry Goldwater and Everett Dirksen unimaginable. The young saw the institutions of American society as organized to shut them out; and the more radical among them began to conclude that exclusion was inevitable in a system controlled, as they believed, by a military-industrial complex. Thus Mark Rudd of the Columbia SDS viewed the war in Vietnam "as an inherent part of the political-economic system that dominates our country." As the estrangement grew more acute and embittered, the more romantic or irrational students began, with sublime unrealism, to speculate about destroying the system through violent revolution.

This was the situation at the start of this year. Then in March the New Hampshire primary took place. Today the New Hampshire primary seems eight years rather than eight months ago; but it was an important date, and the nation owes a good deal, I think, to Senator Eugene McCarthy for his demonstration that protest had means of expression within the democratic process. McCarthy's cause was rationality in Vietnam; and Robert Kennedy soon added the further challenge of ending, or at least, tempering the schisms within our national community—a prospect which Kennedy, because of his exceptional identification with the victims and casualties of American life, was uniquely equipped to fulfill. Then murder ended his brave and generous life; and this horror, along with the murder of Martin Luther King, intensified the desperate sense among the excluded groups that some basic ugliness would rise ineluctably out of American society to strike down every leader who tried to embrace them in the promise of American life.

Yet the protest continued to seek outlets within the democratic process—behind McCarthy and later George McGovern in the Democratic party; behind Nelson Rockefeller in the Republican party. In the end, alas, neither party rose to the challenge. Both conventions selected men of the past—men whose minds had been formed a generation ago and who tended to see the nineteen seventies in the image of the nineteen forties. Both candidates represented the Old Politics, and their designations accentuated the sense of mass frustration—a condition dramatized in the disorders of the last days of the Democratic convention.

Among the intellectuals the reaction, for a season, was disgust and withdrawal. Among the non-intellectuals the reaction, for a season, was a drift to the only remaining means of registering protest against the Old Politics—that is, by supporting George Wallace. Commentators expressed astonishment that men and women who had been supporting Kennedy or McCarthy in March were supporting Wallace in September; but no one should have been all that surprised. The Wallace effort for a moment moved beyond its racist base and became a repository for general resentment and rancor throughout the land.

In the meantime, the major party campaign was markedly vacuous. Mr. Nixon, by evident design, waged a campaign of mechanical banality and evasion. This was intended, of course, to minimize the risk of saying anything which might offend anybody; and in the end his anti-campaign worked, though only barely. Mr. Humphrey, carrying the burden of an unpopular President, an unpopular administration and an unpopular war, seemed for a while frantic and ineffectual. Only in the last weeks of the campaign did he begin to emerge from under this burden, to speak with his own voice and seem at last his own man. As he did this, he started to win back the intellectuals from apathy and the trade unionists from Wallace.

In retrospect, Mr. Nixon may now regret the intellectual emptiness of his campaign. For our quadrennial elections are about the only time when the American people as a whole will sit still and listen to a discussion of political issues. They therefore provide a rare opportunity for political education and mobilization. Mr. Nixon systematically squandered that opportunity. As a result, he denied himself both a definite mandate and a wide basis of informed and active support for specific policies—the two things he now most needs if he is to govern effectively as a mistrusted minority President confronted by a hostile Congress and a suspicious electorate.

It should perhaps be added that, in spite of the candidates, the 1968 election did not altogether fail as an educational experience. Though the parties did little positive to clarify issues, the voters themselves began to crystallize their judgments in the course of the year, and the candidates had at least the sense to acquiesce. There is no more astute observer of political tendencies than Samuel Lubell; and I am impressed by the conclusion which Mr. Lubell reached on the eve of the election. "On the two most emotional issues—Vietnam and our racial crisis," Mr. Lubell wrote, "—my interviewing does indicate that the campaign has gained general public acceptance for policies which in time could unify the country."

On Vietnam, the electorate impressed on the parties the growing demand that we bring this hopeless war to an end and withdraw our military forces from the mainland of Asia. In the past Mr. Humphrey had been a steadfast supporter of President Johnson's policy of military escalation, and Mr. Nixon's only disagreement had been that President Johnson did not escalate fast enough. Yet both candidates—Mr. Nixon by silence and Mr. Humphrey by declaration—seemed to agree with the growing conviction that we must deescalate the war and move as soon as possible toward a negotiated settlement.

As for racial justice, the Wallace movement may have had the useful effect of making many voters think about the consequences of their prejudices. Wallace tempted them for a while; but then in the end they drew back, and Wallace's appeal contracted rather swiftly to the lower Confederacy. Probably Mr. Lubell is also right in suggesting that "the strength of Wallace's backing ... shocked many liberals and Negroes into realizing that excesses on the Negro side have to be curbed." In any case, I would agree with his conclusion that "the preponderant part of the electorate, in most of the South as well as in the North, is prepared to support a 'middle course' policy that would curb racial violence while still continuing Negro progress."

This clarification of national opinion is an immense gain. But it expressed the process of democracy rather than the leadership of the candidates; and this implies a dangerous disconnection between politicians and reality—a disconnection which, if continued, will encourage further secession from the democratic system. The lasting answer to this disconnection can only lie in moving beyond the Old Politics and making our major parties responsive to the issues and the methods of the nineteen seventies.

In the perspective of history, the 1968 election may well go down as the last hurrah of the Old Politics of this period—as, say, the 1928 election in retrospect was the last hurrah of the Old Politics of the twenties. And, as the 1928 election foreshadowed the political developments of the next decade—as, for example, in the rising Democratic strength in the cities—so the 1968 election may, if we read it aright, tell us something about the shape of American politics to come.

Two questions will be decisive. The first is: will the major parties now start to do what they failed to do in 1968—will they understand and accept the political imperatives of the new age? If they fail to do this, then we can expect a serious growth among both the New Right and the New Left, nominally at each other's throats but each feeding on the existence of the other and both united in their desire to abolish the institutions of civility and accommodation in our society, both united in their determination to wreck the political system. But, if the major parties succeed in the task of modernizing their ideas and methods, then we can hope to continue to fight out our battles within the political system, as, except for the Civil War, we have done throughout our history.

The second question is less important but still not altogether devoid of interest. It is: which party will create the framework for the politics of the coming time, as Franklin Roosevelt's Democratic party crated the framework for the politics of his time? Each party, it should be noted, has its assets in the contest for the future.

The great Republican asset is the possession of the Presidency. For the Presidency is the most influential office in the land; there is no better vantage point from which to bring a new political consensus into existence. The problem is whether the new Republican President has the imagination or the desire to do this. The Republican party has at this moment a great opportunity to return to its early and best traditions—the traditions of Abraham Lincoln and

Theodore Roosevelt. This liberal generation has tended to write off the Republican party as constitutionally devoid of intelligence and initiative; and, indeed, the record of the last half-century would go far to sustain this judgment. Yet one must not forget that, when an alliance of Conscience Whigs and Jacksonian Democrats formed the Republican party more than a century ago and when Lincoln became the first Republican President, it was a broadly based party devoted to the cause of human freedom. Nor should one forget that sixty years ago, when Governor Landon was a young fellow and men like Theodore Roosevelt and Robert M. LaFollette were Republican leaders, the Republican party was in the forefront of the struggle for progressive reform.

Moreover, the shift from quantitative to qualitative issues—from the economic conflict of the thirties to the cultural conflict of our own day—is sociologically favorable to Republican prospects. The Republican party, after all, is the party of the more affluent and therefore of the better- (or at least the longer-) educated. The Bull Moose strain, as we have noted, has never completely died within the Republican party; and there are intimations today of a revival of the Lincoln-Roosevelt tradition of moral and intellectual purpose.

As a Democrat myself, I would be sorry to see the Republicans seize the leadership of innovation and reform. And I am constrained to add that, despite a number of gallant individuals, like the mayor of New York City and the governor of New York state, I do not think this is likely to happen. A Republican party on the Lincoln-Roosevelt model would be very different from the Republican party of Mr. Nixon. "The Republican party," as Nelson Rockefeller put it in the primaries, "must become again a national party, the voice of the poor and the oppressed." It would have to embrace the immigrant groups; it would have to welcome the Negro; it would have to fight for civil rights and civil liberties. It would have to believe in the national government, like Hamilton; it would have to contend for federal aid to education, like Lincoln, and for federal protection of natural resources, like Theodore Roosevelt. Will Mr. Nixon do these things? Will he avail himself of the opportunity to reconstruct his party and form a new majority coalition?

Perhaps he will; the chemistry of the Presidency does strange things to people. One must add that nothing in his career and nothing in his campaign suggest that his vision and sympathy extend beyond the possessing classes. I may well be wrong; but one feels that under Mr. Nixon's leadership the Republican party will remain, as Emerson once said of the Whigs, the "shop-and-till party"—

> timid, and merely defensive of property. It vindicates no right, it aspires to no real good, it brands no crime, it proposes no generous policy, it does not build, nor write, nor cherish the arts, nor foster religion, nor establish schools, nor encourage science, nor emancipate slaves, nor befriend the poor, or the Indian, or the immigrant.

It seems entirely possible, then, that the Republicans may forfeit the enormous advantage the Presidency could give them in the contest for the political leadership of the seventies. How about the Democrats? They lack, of course, the strategic advantage of the Presidency. On the other hand, they have a tradition of innovation and reform, and they will now enjoy the opportunity of opposition. Freedom from power offers them a rare chance to contemplate their situation, think their problems through, reformulate their issues and open their places of leadership to young and unconventional men.

It can be said, I think, that Democrats are offered three different approaches to the job of reconstruction. These can be called the Humphrey way, the McCarthy way and the Kennedy way.

The Humphrey way is self-evident: it is to insist that the Old Politics is alive and well—and in America. I do not mean that this is the way Hubert Humphrey would necessarily have chosen if he had had a free choice. He is a sensitive and intelligent political man who in other circumstances might conceivably have led the opposition within the party to the Johnson administration and the war. But he became the prisoner of the Vice Presidency; and he was also the prisoner of an old-fashioned personal style which seemed clamorous and archaic on the new media. In any case, by 1968 he had no choice but to string along with the traditional middlemen—that is, with the bureaucracies of political organizations, of labor organizations, of farm organizations, of ethnic organizations. The result was an apparent effort to preserve the facade of the Roosevelt coalition without, it would seem, worrying too much about the mind and the soul. The hard question, of course, is whether the old bureaucracies can rally their constituencies any longer. The 1968 election does not decisively settle this question, though I am myself inclined to attribute Humphrey's last minute surge less to the effectiveness of the old bureaucracies than to the liberation of Humphrey himself and his subsequent capacity to move into the politics of mass involvement—this and the aid he got from practitioners of the New Politics after the modification of his position on Vietnam began to enable them to enter his campaign.

No doubt I am wrong; but I cannot help feeling that the Old Politics has run its course. My guess is that the future lies between the McCarthy and Kennedy ways. It should have been evident from the frictions of the primaries that these ways are not identical. Now that we can look back at the primaries with a measure of detachment, let us understand that, while Eugene McCarthy and Robert Kennedy agreed on the supreme issue of Vietnam, they most emphatically disagreed on two other issues of more enduring importance. They disagreed on their conceptions of the Democratic coalition, and they disagreed on their conceptions of the Presidency. These issues may sound abstract. But I would suggest that they go to the heart of the question of the future of the Democratic party.

I have said that the nation owes a great deal to Senator McCarthy. His courage in entering the contest against President Johnson on the issue of Vietnam broke the ice-jam in the Democratic party and set free a flood of popular feeling which marvelously changed the politics of 1968. Senator McCarthy is a thoughtful and perceptive man. He understood why the Old Politics would no longer work. He perceived that the traditional coalition and the traditional political methods were alike growing obsolescent. He read his friend (and mine) J. K. Galbraith and heeded the increasing role in American society of the 'technostructure'—all those who bring specialized knowledge, talent or experience to group decision-making. The technostructure, indeed, became the basis of the McCarthy campaign. Senator McCarthy seemed to accept the conclusion that the level of education had superseded the level of income as the dividing line in our public affairs. Noting the steady decay of the alliance of the educated few and the uneducated many which Franklin Roosevelt had put together in the '30s, noting too the steady expansion of the technostructure, McCarthy would seem to have decided that the future required a new alliance which would now be founded on the educated many.

Some have said that the difference between the Old Politics and the New lies in the fact that Old Politicians, like Humphrey, see America as made up of interest groups while New Politicians, like McCarthy, see America as made up of individuals. I wonder whether this is really so. Surely James Madison was everlastingly right in the *Tenth Federalist* when he said that interest groups "grow up of necessity in civilized nations, and divide them into different classes, actuated by different sentiments and views."

The real difference seems to me to lie in the fact that Humphrey appeals to anachronistic interest groups while McCarthy had the wit to appeal to the emerging interest groups. When a politician tells an audience of students that he would fire General Hershey or an audience of professors that he would fire J. Edgar Hoover, he is appealing to interest groups as specifically and deliberately as any politician who, say, told a farm audience in 1960 that he would fire Ezra Taft Benson. The new interest groups—the suburban middle class, the college students, the church groups, the peace groups— may be less familiar than the wool industry or the steel workers, less familiar even than the Negroes, the Puerto Ricans, the Mexican Americans, the Indians and the poor in general. That hardly makes them any less interest groups.

It was McCarthy's achievement to understand that voters were beginning to defect from the old interest groups. It was his effort to put together a coalition of the new interest groups. The inner logic of his remarkable campaign was to unite the college-educated, whatever their race, religion or previous condition of servitude: teachers, students, church leaders, enlightened businessmen, civic-minded suburbanites, the rising professional, managerial and technical classes. This, of course, is why his campaign was so popular in the suburbs. This is why he was the Democratic aspirant with the greatest appeal to Republicans. This too accounts for the "we happy few" flavor of the McCarthy campaign. It explains why his embattled followers on the streets of Chicago were mostly sons and daughters of the white middle class—why they have received so little sympathy or support from the blacks, the working-men and the poor.

Because McCarthy rested so much confidence in the purpose and intelligence of the coalition of the college-educated—and obviously too because he shared the national revulsion against the activist administration of Lyndon Johnson—he said in his campaign that "the New Politics requires a different conception of the office of President." Actually he offered not so much a new conception as a revival of the old conservative theory of the passive Presidency— as Theodore Roosevelt used to call it, the Buchanan-Taft thesis of the Presidency—and its adaptation to progressive purposes. McCarthy simply did not feel that his "constituency of concerned individuals" required Presidential leadership on the Wilson-Roosevelt-Kennedy model. Rather than simply providing leadership, he said, the President's duty is to "liberate individuals so that they may determine their own lives." The next President "should understand that this country does not so much need leadership. . . . He must be prepared to be a kind of channel." The powers of the Presidency should be decentralized. The Presidency "must never be looked upon as a kind of personal office." He opposed "the sort of Presidential power which extends itself in a personal way into every institution of government."

Senator McCarthy deserves great credit for raising such questions in this trenchant manner. He has made an important contribution to the revived debate about the nature of the Presidency. But no one should be deceived as to what he was saying. He made it perfectly clear that he did not propose to be a President in the tradition of Wilson, Roosevelt, and Kennedy—that he did not consider this kind of President good for the country.

This then would seem the essence of the McCarthy way: a coalition of the college-educated emphasizing what he called "the limits of [Presidential] power and the limitations that must be placed upon the exercise of power." McCarthy himself pointed up the contrast between his conception and Robert Kennedy's conception of the Democratic coalition when he told a university audience in Corvallis during the Oregon primary that public opinion polls showed Kennedy running best "among the less intelligent and less educated people in America. And I don't mean to fault them for voting for him, but I think that you ought to bear that in mind as you go to the polls here on Tuesday.".

The Kennedy way, in my judgment, stands in sharp contrast to both the Humphrey and McCarthy ways. Robert Kennedy saw the Democratic party as a coalition neither of political middlemen nor of college graduates but as a link between the two Americas—between educated and uneducated America, between rich and poor America, between white and black America. Unlike Vice President Humphrey, he did not suppose that the traditional political institutions could control their constituencies in the new age of television and public opinion polls. Unlike Senator McCarthy, he did not regard the "less educated" as necessarily the "less intelligent," and he was not prepared to surrender the working masses—even the cops and the cab drivers—to George Wallace.

Like McCarthy and Humphrey, Kennedy began his analysis with the crisis of the Roosevelt coalition; but I think he read the Roosevelt experience with more precision and penetration. He dissented from the Humphrey way because he understood that Roosevelt did not create his coalition through the institutions to which Humphrey had committed himself; these institutions were the effect, not the cause of FDR's success. He dissented from the McCarthy way because he understood that Roosevelt held his coalition together through exactly the sort of Presidential leadership which McCarthy condemns.

Charisma has its role in Democratic politics. Roosevelt persuaded the working class of the thirties to go along with him on issues like foreign policy, equal rights and civil liberties not because the "less educated" then had more enlightened opinions than their counterparts today but because his Presidential leadership had demonstrated his commitment to them and because, for these and other reasons, they trusted and loved him. I think that Kennedy supposed that today's white low-income groups could be similarly saved for political rationality.

He thus did not believe, like McCarthy, that the old Roosevelt coalition had gone forever, though he wanted to reinforce that coalition with the new men of Galbraith's technostructure in their natural habitat of suburbia. But he did not suppose, like Humphrey, that the Roosevelt coalition could be reconstituted from above by men whose names appear on organization letterheads. His effort was to reconstitute the coalition from below—through his own intense and effective communication with the excluded groups in American society, through urging programs on their behalf and through increasing their own direct participation in the political and administrative process. Out of all this he hoped to form a coalition of innovation and justice for the seventies. He showed last spring that this approach might still work. His success, for example, in both Negro and backlash districts, far from demonstrating (as the McCarthyites used to say) that there must be something unworthy about his tactics, showed that he had the personal power to rally disparate groups behind rational policies—as Franklin Roosevelt had rallied disparate groups behind rational policies a generation ago.

For this reason Kennedy believed, as McCarthy did not, in a strong and purposeful Presidency. No doubt President Johnson had abused his power in foreign affairs, but a general retrenchment in Presidential power would only increase the nation's incapacity to deal with its problems. Kennedy understood that we are heading as a nation into perilous times, that the ties which had precariously bound Americans together are under almost intolerable strain and that cutting back presidential authority could be a disastrous error in an age when only a strong President can enable us to meet our most difficult and urgent internal issue: racial justice. As never before, the President had to be the tribune of the disinherited and the dispossessed.

So the Democrats must make their choice after 1968—whether to follow the Old Politics of the Humphrey way, the elitist politics of the McCarthy way, or the national politics which I trust will continue to move forward in the spirit of Robert Kennedy. As a Democrat, I believe that we will succeed if we see our party not as a collection of obsolescent power blocs nor as a semi-precious alli-

of college men but as a truly national party, embracing the poor as well as the rich, the black as well as the white, the young as well as the old, the uneducated as well as the educated, in a common fight for a just and liberal America.

I trust that what I have said makes it clear that the Republicans, with the inestimable advantage of presidential leadership, have quite as good a chance as the Democrats to build a truly national party and construct the new framework for American politics. Whichever party assumes the task, the message is the same. The indispensable need is to unify our tormented nation and bring the alienated groups at last into the national community. I see no other way of restoring the moral energy of American politics and of incorporating the grave forebodings and desperate urgencies of our time into the constitutional process. John F. Kennedy said in his first State of the Union message, "Before my term is ended, we shall have to test anew whether a nation organized and governed such as ours can endure. The outcome is by no means certain." People ignored this remark at the time; it has a terrifying relevance now; for, if the American government renounces the obligation to be the active champion both of racial justice and of civil peace, it is by no means certain that our nation will endure.

The next four years will test many things: the intelligence and vision of our new administration, the resilience of our party system, the patience, generosity and clear-headedness of our people. It marks, I am sure, the exhaustion of an older conception of politics; it demands the insights and values appropriate to new problems and a new age. It calls for a creative political genius on the order of Jackson, Lincoln and Roosevelt. We must hope that the historians of the future will view this time not just as an end but as a beginning. For, if we can jettison the stereotypes and cliches of the past, if we can confront the realities of the present and comprehend the necessities of the future, we may begin to put the fantastic achievements of contemporary science and technology to the services of a greater society than we have ever known. In the short run, perhaps, the answer depends on our leaders. In the long run, the answer depends on us.

Mike Mansfield (1903–) was elected to the U.S. Senate in 1952 after serving in the House of Representatives. He was selected by Lyndon Johnson to be party whip, and in 1961 when Johnson became Vice President, he was elected Senate Majority Leader. He exercised his power quietly and continuously. By 1966, he was a strong opponent of the war in Vietnam, and he tried to persuade President Johnson that a military victory was impossible. He continued as one of the leading Democratic critics of President Nixon's prolongation of the war, especially arguing against the President's usurping the war-making prerogative of the Congress. His long-time interest and expertise in Asian affairs led President Carter to appoint him as Ambassador to Japan in 1977.

A Pacific Perspective

Mike Mansfield

In the first two decades of the Landon Lecture Series only two individuals have appeared twice—Ronald Reagan, first as Governor of California and later as President, and U.S. Senator Mike Mansfield of Montana. In both his lectures, Senator Mansfield directed the attention of his listeners to Asia and the Pacific, a part of the world too often neglected by the people of our "Atlantic-minded nation." He invited his audience to look beyond the trauma of Vietnam to its future relations with Japan, China, Indonesia, the Philippines, and the other countries of the region. Included here is his 1969 lecture, which sets forth the broad outlines of his "Pacific perspective."

MARCH 10, 1969

I

We have been an Atlantic-minded nation and understandably so. Fourteen of the states border the Atlantic. The majority of our ancestors reached America via the Atlantic. Most of us follow religions of trans-Atlantic origin. The languages that are learned in our schools are primarily those of the nations across the Atlantic. Americans who travel abroad usually begin their journeys by crossing the Atlantic. Fashions, architecture, routines of living in this nation all show strong influences from the opposite side of the ocean. We are, in short, preponderantly "Atlantic" by heredity, tradition, and proclivity.

However, the authority as well as the territory of the United States stops at the western edges of the ocean. The Atlantic has been a kind of sea barrier for us in the sense that the Pacific has not been. In the Pacific, not only do five states reach the ocean, but one of them—Hawaii—literally emerges from it. In addition, we have territories of various sizes, shapes, and legal relationships spread through its distant reaches. The Aleutian Islands which project towards the Soviet Union and Japan are part of the State of Alaska. American Samoa, Guam, Wake, Johnston, Midway and the Howland, Baker and Jarvis Islands are far-flung dependencies. The Canton and Enderbury Islands are an American-British condominium. The Trust Territory of the Pacific Islands has been administered by the United States since the end of the Second World War; it comprises over 2,000 islands and atolls which together total only 678 square miles of land but which are dispersed over three million square miles of ocean. World War II left a provisional American administration in Okinawa and the other Ryukyu Islands; there it has remained for a quarter of a century, almost within sight of the Asian mainland. More than a frontier, more than an avenue of communication and trade, the Pacific is a vast marine-arena within which lie states, territories, and dependencies appertaining in large part to the United States.

I would like to make clear that in referring to the Pacific, I do not include the Asian mainland or the waters immediately adjacent. On that mainland, there are no American possessions but there are more American forces than anywhere else in the world outside the United States. Not only is there the immense consignment in Viet Nam but large American military contingents are also stationed in Thailand and South Korea. For the first time in history, we have deployed military power in mass along the whole arc of the Asian mainland.

In this matter, almost without realizing it, we have cast ourselves in the role of Asian power. We have extended the outposts of our Pacific power to China's borders. We have done so on the assumption that China is bent on military expansion and that it is essential for the United States to contain that expansion. That we have erred in the form of our response, even if the assumptions are accurate, is illustrated, in my judgment, by the war in Viet Nam. The war has not contained China in any sense. Nor has it even decreased Chinese influence in Viet Nam. If anything, it may be having the opposite effect.

What needs most to be learned from the tragic experience in Viet Nam is that there is no national interest of the United States which requires us to perform the functions of an Asian power. On the contrary, it is as self-damaging as it is futile to presume that that role can be exercised by an outside power anywhere on the Asian land-mass. The fact is that the nations of Asia are going to develop along economic and political lines which are determined by themselves. The development will spring from their history, philosophy, and tradition. It will be based on their human and material resources. It will reflect the political realities of their surroundings.

Nations outside the region, perhaps, can participate economically in limited ways in this process, but they cannot control the social evolution of Asia. What applies to other outside nations applies to us. We have never been a part of the Asian continent. We are not now. We will not be in the future.

However, we are a part of the Pacific, as I have already observed, and we will continue to be. Whether we will remain a Pacific power is not in question; we have no choice. What is at issue is our future role with respect to Asia. On that score, it seems to me, the character of our commitment is largely a matter of our choice. We were not forced, for example, into the present involvement in Viet Nam. Largely by a pyramiding of successive unilateral declarations and acts, the commitment was built to its great dimensions. The choice was ours. By the same token, this nation, through the President, still retains, in my judgment, the capacity to increase, reduce, or even to dismantle that commitment by its own calculated decisions.

Whatever else may prove true of our future role in Asian affairs, I am persuaded that it will differ from the role we have played in the past. The postwar World War II era has ended, whether or not we recognize it. Whether or not we realize it, we are in a period of transition in our relations with the nations of the Western Pacific.

II

That such is the case is best illustrated by reference to Japan. Our relations with that nation have been relatively quiescent for many years. Time has brought changes in Japan which have now reached a point just short of crisis.

The cloud on the horizon is the U.S.-Japan security treaty. Under the terms of the treaty, beginning in 1970 either party may announce an intent to amend or terminate the agreement. As this date has drawn closer, the political debate in Japan over the treaty has grown in intensity. It has centered on two specific points.

The first is the question of the American bases in Japan—number, location and use. Among the Japanese, there has been a growing resentment of these bases. They are not uniformly regarded as sources of a benevolent American protection. Often, they are seen as symbols of excessive foreign influence as well as hazardous nuisances. Furthermore, U.S. military airfields, on occasion, act to disturb the populace, not only because they occupy scarce land, but also because they pose dangers of accidental explosions and crashes. In the case of naval bases there is, in Hiroshima-conscious Japan, the additional concern with the assumed danger of radiation whenever nuclear-powered U.S. vessels call at these facilities.

The second specific issue around which the debate has centered in Japan is the question of the Ryukyu Islands (notably Okinawa), which were an integral part of Japan before World War II. At the end of that conflict, the United States occupied these islands and has since administered them through the Defense Department. The Japanese peace treaty of 1951, however, left dangling, so to speak, certain matters pertaining to their final disposition. While the United States retained administrative control, Japan was not required to relinquish sovereignty. Moreover, this nation has since stated on more than one occasion that there is no question that Japan possesses "residual" sovereignty over the Ryukyus.

Nevertheless, the United States has converted Okinawa into a great military depot. Bases on the island are specifically exempted from certain restrictions which are in effect on similar U.S. installations in Japan proper. In 1960 the United States agreed that bases on the Japanese main islands cannot be used for "military combat operations" without the agreement of the Japanese government but by contrast the same inhibition is not in effect in Okinawa which has served as a staging area for the war in Viet Nam and for B-52 bomber operations. Finally, there is a most fundamental difference: we have agreed not to store nuclear weapons in Japan proper; there is no such agreement respecting Okinawa.

The military bases relate to the larger issue of Japan's future military role in the Pacific. What is involved in this question is the continuance of a situation in which the primary responsibility for defending Japan, and indeed the entire Western Pacific, falls to the United States. Over the years, this state of affairs has cost us untold billions of dollars. Its persistence is now beginning to appear somewhat anachronistic a quarter of a century after World War II and with a Japan that is the third greatest industrial power in the world.

Many Japanese are restless under U.S. military surveillance of their homeland and adjacent waters. On the other hand, there is also a conflicting factor of Japanese anxiety that American military protection may be withdrawn. Out of the dichotomy has come a view that Japan should rearm beyond the modest "self defense" forces which it possesses and assume a part of the defense functions which are now being discharged by this nation. The view has adherents not only in Japan but in certain quarters in the United States.

All of the issues which I have discussed so far have a significant characteristic in common: they are military matters. There are, of course, also non-military matters in dispute between Japan and the United States as, for example, certain barriers to trade and investment. The fact remains, nevertheless, that the main source of friction in U.S.-Japanese relations, today, is to be found in disagreement over military questions. I emphasize this point because there has been some tendency to avoid public consideration of these matters in connection with foreign policy. Yet, the questions are fundamental. The future of the U.S.-Japanese relationship will be very shaky, indeed, if we proceed to try to base it preponderantly on our military convenience in the Pacific, notwithstanding the irritation and hostility which may be caused thereby in Japan.

It seems to me there is a need for great alertness to changing Japanese attitudes respecting our military activities. While some sentiment already exists in Japan for the removal of all U.S. military bases, I do not think that that is the dominant view. There is, rather, a general desire to see a reduction in the number of U.S. bases in Japan. A prompt response to this desire, I believe, not only would meet Japanese wishes but would also correspond to the interests of this nation. Certainly, it would dovetail with our present effort to reduce federal expenditures and, in particular, expenditures abroad. In my judgment, it would also act, in timely fashion, to preserve an accommodating tone in U.S.-Japanese relations.

Indeed, I am persuaded that much of the growing controversy with Japan could be dispelled if it were simply stated that we are prepared to abide by Japanese desires respecting the bases. The installations are maintained at great cost to this nation on the grounds of the contribution which they make to Japanese security and, hence, indirectly to the security of the United States. If the bases have now ceased to have that function in Japanese calculations, how can they possibly serve a useful purpose in ours? They become, in fact, a growing liability if they cause mounting friction between this nation and the Japanese populace.

Whatever the sentiments on the question of American bases in Japan, Okinawa is the looming issue in Japanese-American relations. It is the lightning rod, so to speak, which has attracted most of the arguments, most of the protests, and most of the attention.

There is strong and growing pressure within Japan and Okinawa for the immediate repossession of full control over the Ryukyus. It seems to me that we have delayed a long time—perhaps too long—on this sensitive issue. Okinawa is Japanese; we have never claimed otherwise. I see no just or rational alternative other than to try to arrive at a fixed time-schedule for the progressive and prompt return of administrative control over the Ryukyu Islands to Japan. In restoring Japanese administrative control over Okinawa, moreover, it seems to me that there are also strong arguments against insisting on a "deal" which will permit the use of the military bases in ways which are not acceptable to the Japanese people.

There will be, I am sure, cries of anguish in some quarters at any significant modification of our right to unrestricted use of Okinawa. Nevertheless, entrenched parochial interests cannot be permitted to prevail in this critical matter. Okinawa is undoubtedly a great military convenience but it is by no means indispensable. The fact is that there have been enormous technological developments in the military field since World War II. We now have missiles which can carry nuclear weapons into space. We have planes which can carry them in the atmosphere over the ocean. We have ships which can carry them on the ocean, and submarines which can carry them under the ocean. We also have other bases in the Pacific—bases which are under unchallenged American sovereignty—where nuclear weapons can be stored and where Strategic Air Command planes with nuclear weapons may be based without question or complaint.

As I have already noted, the issues of the bases and Okinawa relate to the larger question of Japan's future military role. Here, too, it seems to me, that a greater sensitivity to Japanese popular sentiment is essential. It would appear particularly ill-advised for the United States to try to push the Japanese towards a new and expanded military role in the Western Pacific. To be sure, the Japanese may one day raise the present level of their self-defense forces. They may even, one day, amend their constitution in order to possess other than self-defense forces. Any such decisions, however, should result from Japanese political processes which reflect Japanese judgments of Japanese needs—judgments for which the Japanese accept full responsibility. They should not result from American pressures reflecting American judgments of American needs and, for which, this nation in the end will have to bear responsibility.

III

If the Japanese do not assume the military burdens which the U.S. would relinquish when the bases in Japan are reduced in number and those in Okinawa are restricted in use, some will ask: who will defend the Pacific? Presumably, it is fear of China which gives rise to this question. It does not follow, however, if the Chinese are bound on expansion, that they are capable of trans-Pacific aggression. Indeed, President Nixon has made it clear that he does not buy the contention of some defense advisors that a "thin" anti-ballistics missiles system is needed because of the Chinese threat.

A thrust of military power across the Pacific is quite a different matter from expansion on the Asian continent. Even in the latter use there is a difference of view as to the nature of Chinese continental pressure and what constitutes the principal danger to orderly progress in Asia. Among the nations of Southeast Asia, for example, it is commonplace to find that the threat of Chinese military aggression is rated a more remote menace than the immediate problems of economic underdevelopment and political instability which, in some cases, stem from internal economic disparities and in others from conflicts between two or more countries within the region.

These latter problems can hardly be met by U.S. defense outposts in the Western Pacific. Rather, their solution requires cooperation for constructive purposes among the Southeast Asian nations and with other nations outside the region. In fact, such cooperation has begun and it is taking two forms. First, there are groups of states within the region, such as the newly formed Association of Southeast Asian Nations. Second, there are regional organizations with outside members, such as the Asian Development Bank. The Bank includes European and North American subscribers whose modern resources can play an important, if peripheral, part in the progress of the Asian nations.

In this connection, there seems to me to be considerable merit in Japanese suggestions that the United States, Canada, Australia, New Zealand, and Japan should form a "Pacific" community to help developing countries. I should add, that in a grouping of this kind, Japan can play a most significant part. Indeed, in my judgment, it is in the sphere of economic development wherein lies Japan's principal potential for a contribution to the peace and progress of the Western Pacific.

IV

I have talked of several facets of the situation in an effort to place the needs of our Asian policies in clearer perspective; of the distinction between a Pacific power which we have no choice but to be and an Asian power which we can and should choose not to be; of our military relations with Japan and the heat which is rising from the issues of the bases, Okinawa, and the over-all Japanese role in the security of the Western Pacific; and, finally, of economic development in the Asian countries and the possibilities of cooperative aid. There are several other related questions which need to be touched on to complete this discussion. One concerns our relations with mainland China.

Strictly speaking, China is not of the Pacific but of Asia. Yet, the very vastness of China projects its relevance not only over the Asian mainland and the Pacific but, in fact, throughout the entire world. It is not possible to talk about the future of international peace, let alone about our future in the Pacific, without reference to the great nation which lies on its farther shore.

China will not remain forever, as is now the case, in substantial isolation. Its proper role is as a leading nation in the councils of the world. Sooner or later China will assume that place. It seems to me the Japanese have long since come to recognize that prospect. And there are indications that they are seeking to bridge the gap with China. Even if we could, there is no cause for this nation to impose obstacles of any kind—either spoken or unspoken—to increasing Japanese contacts with China. On the contrary, such efforts— whether in the economic, cultural, or political fields—might well be encouraged. They can serve not only Japan's needs for trade, they can contribute to clearing up a whole range of enigmas involving China and the security of the Western Pacific. In that fashion, they can be helpful in bringing about an enlightened approach to the building of a stable peace in that region.

For our part, and for much the same reasons, I see no purpose in imposing any special restrictions on the travel of Americans to China. Nor do I see any reason not to place trade with China in non-strategic goods on the same basis as trade with the Soviet Union, Poland, and other Communist countries. For a decade and a half we have sought to maintain a rigid primary and secondary boycott of Chinese goods. The effort is unique in our history and it finds no parallel among the present practices of other nations with respect to China. In my view, we would be well advised to abandon this antiquated pursuit of China's downfall by economic warfare and treat the Chinese in matters of trade as we treat European Communist countries—no better and no worse.

It seems to me, the Nixon Administration's announced intention to reopen previous offers to exchange journalists, scientists, and scholars with China is well founded. The cancellation of the meeting in Warsaw on February 20, at which these offers were to be reiterated, is regrettable. One can only hope that another opportunity will soon present itself and, hopefully, that the official offers will be made and accepted.

Trade, travel, and cultural and scientific exchanges are relatively tangible issues in our relationship with China. Hence, they seem to be more readily amenable to solution; perhaps, that is why current discussion of the relationship with China tends to concentrate on them. Similarly, the present debate is intensive on the questions of Chinese admission to the United Nations and U.S. diplomatic recognition of Peking. These issues, too, seem susceptible to clear solution. They are not, however, at the root of the difficulties. To try to resolve them at this point may be a useful intellectual exercise but it also tends to put the cart of the difficulty before the horse.

The fundamental problem of U.S.-Chinese relations is the status of Taiwan. It is a problem which is as complex as it is crucial. It is not an either-or issue. It is not really soluble, in an enduring sense, in terms of two Chinas as has been suggested in recent years because there are not two Chinas and the attempt to delineate them is synthetic. The fact is that China is a part of Taiwan and Taiwan is a part of China. Both Chinese governments which are agreed on little else are agreed on that score. The question is not whether the twain shall meet but when and in what circumstances. While we are not aloof from this question, the decisions which appertain thereto involve primarily the Chinese themselves—the Chinese of the mainland and the Chinese of Taiwan. Sooner or later the decisions will have to begin to be made. Only then will the other part of the Chinese puzzle—such questions as U.S. recognition and U.N. admission—fall into a rational place in our policies.

V

While I have spoken today principally about the United States, Japan, and China, two other major nations are of immediate concern. I refer to the Republic of the Philippines and to Indonesia.

There are signs of difficulties in our relations with the Philippines principally in the field of trade and investment and with respect to U.S. military bases. In my judgment, however, none of the problems which confront us is of a nature as to be beyond reasonable solution in the light of the general cooperation which we have

78

long enjoyed with the Philippines. Yet it is precisely this basic cooperation which seems to me now to be in jeopardy. It is adversely affected by a vestigial tendency—a hang-over from pre-independence days—to continue to think almost automatically in terms of special economic privileges and concessions. Similarly in the field of foreign relations there is an inclination to expect that the policy of the Philippines government, inevitably, will mirror our own attitudes. Therefore, such departures as the recent Philippine initiation of contact with Communist countries seems somehow inimical to continued warm U.S.-Philippines relations. That is ironic inasmuch as we have long since had contact with most of these countries.

It is not a law of nature—it is an Aesopian fable—that familiarity must always breed contempt. A half century of familiarity which was crowned with the common sacrifices of World War II laid the basis not for a mutual contempt but for an enduring friendship between the Filipino and American people. It seems to me that we need to bestir ourselves now if this mutually valuable tie is not to be lost. Indeed, it would be my hope that the new Administration would give prompt attention to this matter.

To allow barriers of estrangement to be raised, by negligence or nonsense, is to admit a serious disability in our capacity to order our relations with other countries, notably those which have gained independence since World War II. After all, if we cannot hold the confidence, the friendship, and the respect of a people with whom we have been intimately associated for half-a-century, what can be expected with regard to other nations in Asia with which we have had little or no historic connection?

Indonesia is one such nation. Formerly the Dutch East Indies, this immense island chain was largely unknown to Americans during the colonial era. In the post-independence period, there has been a considerable contact but it has been uneven and unpredictable. In recent years, there has been a deterioration which, at times, has reached almost the point of outright mutual hostility. The pendulum apparently is now swinging and hope exists once again for a more agreeable situation.

It will take time, however, for us to form a balanced view of this enormous island-nation which in terms of population is the sixth largest in the world. It will take time, too, for Indonesia to emerge from its accumulated political and economic ills. The burden of the past is heavy and pervasive.

The United States can do little to speed up the development of a better association with Indonesia. Indeed in present circumstances the best policy is to accept our own limitations in this regard. To be sure, there are the gestures of goodwill which can be made in the form of technical, scientific, and educational cooperation. Moreover, through regional aid channels, such as I have already discussed, some assistance can be provided to Indonesia for economic development. That is a far cry, however, from self-delusive assumptions that by sending Americans to fight in Viet Nam we have somehow saved Indonesia from Communism or that the astute efforts of U.S. agencies and enough money in some miraculous fashion can act to delineate the emerging structure of the Indonesian nation.

VI

Having described the problems which confront the United States in the Pacific, I feel that I have an obligation to close with a few general words of prescription. Almost fifty years of association with the Pacific—as a student, Marine, teacher, and frequent visitor—prompt me to do so. A quarter of a century of political experience, on the other hand, impel me in the other direction. In these years of specializing in foreign relations both in the House of Representatives and in the Senate I have come to recognize the general absence of finality in the disposition of major international problems.

Nevertheless, I did remark at the outset that whatever our future in the Pacific, that future will be unlike the past. I am now under some compulsion to fill in details which sustain the general observation. The most fundamental new factor in the situation, as I see it, is the appearance of at least one new generation since my generation began to grapple with the post-World War II Asian situation and, in particular and with a singular lack of effectiveness, with the monumental upheaval of the Chinese revolution. This new generation is a source of hope for the future. It is a hope which derives largely from the interest young people now take in the affairs of the other side of the Pacific. That interest is more profound and far better informed than was the case two decades or more ago.

It used to be that in an "Atlantic-minded" nation the consideration of Asian questions was left largely to a relative handful of Americans, to "old Asian" or "old China hands," whose attitudes were churned out of a mixture of 19th century religious altruism, political idealism, cold-cash imperialism, and unscrupulous adventurism. World War II altered this mixture; the Korean War modified it further; and now Viet Nam has changed it greatly. The attitudes which once held sway in this nation with respect to our relations with Asia and the Pacific have lost most of their relevance and much of their potency.

If there is to be a worthwhile future in the Pacific, it seems to me that U.S. policies for the problems of the Asian littoral will not be left in "old Asian hands." Rather they will take on the sense and sensitivity of "young American hands." The problems will be dealt with in a new spirit of cooperation and collaboration, free of attitudes of dominance or condescension. The keynote of a new policy for contemporary Asia, as I see it, is mutuality. Its characteristics will be mutual respect, mutual appreciation, and mutual forebearance.

For us there is no choice. We must make the effort to put our policies into that perspective. We will not only continue to live in the Pacific, we will also have to learn to live with the Pacific and the nations of its western reaches, basing our relations with its peoples—with the Chinese, Japanese, Filipinos, Koreans, Indonesians, and others—henceforth, on a profound respect for the equal dignity and worth of all.

Hubert H. Humphrey (1911–1978), after serving two terms as mayor of Minneapolis, was elected to the U.S. Senate in 1948. He was an avowed anti-communist and ardent supporter of the welfare state. One of the many bills he introduced was for medical care for the aged. It was finally passed in 1965. His first attempt at the Presidency ended in defeat by John Kennedy in the West Virginia primary in May of 1960. He was Senate Majority Whip during the Kennedy administration and helped enact legislation establishing the Peace Corps and the nuclear test ban treaty. After Kennedy's death, he was floor manager of the historic Civil Rights Act of 1964. He was elected Vice President in 1964 and, until late in 1968, was a zealous supporter of President Johnson's Vietnam policy. In 1968, he lost the presidential election to Richard Nixon. After a two-year stint at university teaching, he was reelected to the senate in 1970. In 1972, he lost his bid to be the Democratic candidate for President to Senator George McGovern. He was found to have cancer in 1976 and died in January, 1978.

How We Can Make Our Government Work

Hubert Humphrey

Hubert Humphrey's Landon Lecture, the eleventh in the Series, was delivered in Ahearn Fieldhouse on January 9, 1970. From the vantage point of the first month of the new decade, he reviewed the 1960s and offered prescriptions for the 1970s. His call for public solutions to the problems of poverty, urban growth and pollution, and his charge "that we ventilate the clogged channels of political participation and of social opportunity" convey some of the reformist spirit of the times, much more akin to FDR's New Deal and Lyndon Johnson's Great Society than to the antigovernmental spirit of the 1980s. Similarly, Humphrey's optimism for the 1970s seems in retrospect to have been misplaced.

JANUARY 9, 1970

I want to talk today about our social order, our government, this country, its role in the world. I've said that the topic would be "How We Can Make Our Government Work"—or perhaps I should say work better. I want to talk to you about the federal structure of our government. I realize this isn't the most soul-gripping topic. It isn't politically sexy, but it is terribly important.

Decade of Discovery

Let us take a look at the 60s. I don't want to spend too much time on them—but let's take a quick look and then we will look ahead to the 1970s. The 1960s could well be described as the decade of dissent and discovery . . . the decade of war and worry. It was a period in which we—in a sense—discovered ourselves.

Everybody is trying to do that these days. And when you try to

83

discover yourself—your individual identity or your national identity—you have to be prepared to discover some things you may not like.

The 1960s saw us, 15 years after World War II, with vast changes that had taken place worldwide—and yet with many habits in the American political and social structure that had not changed.

The 1960s found us with unprecedented economic prosperity—and yet with a poverty of spiritual resources—with no real satisfaction out of our affluence, even though that's what most of the people of my generation thought was most important.

We were the sons and daughters of the depression, and to us economic security was vital. We learned the hard way. There were no jobs; the nation was prostrate. The leaders that were in power—in business, in government, in labor, in every institution in our country at the beginning of the 1960s with few exceptions—were men and women who had suffered the anguish and the pain and the disaster of war—world war—, of depression—worldwide depression.

Our Major Objectives

Therefore our major objectives were to see, number one, that never again would a depression level this nation and this world. And we spent our time trying to create the economic mechanism that would assure the production of goods and services to guarantee economic health for the nation.

Perhaps we forgot that man does not live by bread alone.

But we did learn—also learned the hard way—that isolated as a nation, there was no security. We learned it from Hitler and Tojo; we learned it from the tragedy of World War II. We learned that isolation was dangerous and that aggression likewise was dangerous, and therefore we bound together in many pacts and alliances called collective security.

I think maybe we failed to recognize that you can overdo that as well.

Too Much Confidence; Too Little Understanding

So the 1960s could be described as a time when we had too much confidence in our wealth, too much confidence in our power—thinking that wealth was goods and services and that power was military might and alliances. There was far too little emphasis, I suppose on real power, namely, reason and understanding, knowledge directed to action, a knowledge with commitment.

Let me say as I speak to you that knowledge without commitment may be wasteful, but commitment without knowledge is dangerous. So we were treading on wasteful and dangerous ground.

We had a little too much confidence in our science and technology. We were overwhelmed—awed—by computers, by electronics, by the Space Age—thinking that these things would somehow or other bring us the millennium. We failed to recognize that science must be a tool for man; that it must be his servant, not his master.

The 1960s taught us that we should make science and technology our servants and this requires that we have political conviction, political decision, and social decision.

To Achieve Our Goals

What I am saying is that we have created the material means to do the great things that need to be done. The question is whether we, as individuals, have the willingness to do what the founders of this republic said we would have to do if we wanted life, liberty, and the pursuit of happiness: namely, to pledge our lives, our fortunes, and our sacred honor to the achievement of these goals.

In the 1960s, a great deal of self-analysis took place. For the first time, we began to appreciate the ugliness, the sin, the immorality, and the indecency of racism—and may I say to this campus that this is still a central problem in our society. But at least we have come to grips with it, at least we have faced it.

The first sign of health is recognizing your sickness. A strong nation and a great people do not run away from their problems, they confront them head on—and recognize that they can be solved.

We came face to face with the fact of hunger in our midst at a time of unbelievable production of foodstuffs. We came face to face with the fact of poverty in the richest nation on the face of the earth. I am not talking about people just being poor. To be poor is one thing; to be the victim of poverty is an entirely different thing.

Victims of Poverty

People who are poor can have their troubles remedied by money; but the victims of poverty have suffered defeat and failure. They are hopeless and helpless. They have lost motivation and self-respect, and they are sick in a very serious and fundamental way—and it takes more than just income or income maintenance to bring them out of that sickness.

We are coming to grips for the first time with the hidden poor and with the victims of poverty.

An Urban Population

And we found in the 1960s that we were a nation of cities. Demographers tell us that by the year 2,000, ninety percent of our people will live in cities of over 200,000 people each. As a matter of fact, seventy-five percent of our people already live in such cities. And all at once, the problems of noise, of congestion, of slums, of overlapping governmental jurisdiction, of the inadequacy of social services and resources were right on our doorstep.

Polluters and Pollution

And we began also to realize that our environment, our physical environment, was being destroyed. In fact, that environment was becoming more dangerous to our well-being than the weapons of our military arsenals. The young men and women of today understand that—at least they are beginning to understand it. Pollution—the polluters and pollution—came into focus.

And I believe, too, that out of the agony of a tragic and costly, painful, festering war we have begun to understand our role in the world—that we cannot be the world's policeman. We must act as a partner and a scholar, as a doctor and a healer and a technician. The role I hope we will play is that of a good neighbor. We cannot decree that America must have its way and that other people must do our bidding.

The Right to be Different

I think one of the greatest statements made in the sixties was made by the late President Kennedy when he said that our purpose is to help make the world safe for diversity—for the right to be different—and he coupled that with the right to be different in peace, without violence.

There is no guarantee, you know, that democracy, this fragile strategy of human relations, can endure. Many democratic systems are short-lived because we believe that all we need to do is to legislate, write, ordain, and it happens.

We're privileged as a people to have grown in the traditions of Anglo-Saxon law. We are privileged as a people to have had forebears who were unique and scholarly students of social structure. They were the scholars of Locke, and they were the scholars of Rousseau. They were the scholars of the Greeks and the Romans and the great philosophers of the Middle Ages.

And at the time that our Constitution was written, it was written for all generations yet to come—and the key to the federal system in this country is that our Constitution is written in the present tense.

The preamble of the Constitution of the United States says "we the people of these United States do ordain and establish"—at this hour, today, here in Manhattan, Kansas—it did not say "did ordain and establish" in Philadelphia.

It is in the present tense. It is a contemporary document. It is a living instrument; and because it is that, it changes just like the human body and the human mind and the emotions of human beings, and all living organisms.

How Government Changes

The government of the United States draws its powers from that Constitution and the Constitution draws its powers from the people—so that government must change and the social structure must also change.

And what we seek is change with order and order with change. It's a tremendous assignment. And it requires that we understand the difference between dissent on the one hand and violence on the other; the difference between liberty and license; the difference between rights and privileges.

Now, we all know that in the early days of our country, communication didn't amount to much. And the government most responsive and responsible to the people was local government.

If I asked a student of mine at the University of Minnesota or Macalester College to write a paper on the government of the United States in the year 1825 and he spent over one paragraph on the government in Washington, I would flunk him—because the government of the United States in 1825 was in the townships and in the villages and in the cities (and small cities they were), in courthouses and possibly in the statehouses.

And when I hear people today talking about governments in other lands—whether it be a government in New Delhi or whether it be a government in Peking, or whether it be a government in Saigon or wherever else it may be—I think it is important that we remember that in developing countries or in agricultural countries, government that really affects people's lives is close, local.

A Multi-racial Society

But communication changed that in our country. And communication has brought us together as one people from many, a pluralistic society, a multi-racial society, seeking common purposes. It is not too difficult to govern a homogeneous people, but remember that this is one of the few free countries in the world—one of the few countries with representative government—with free elections. This is one of the few countries—and the only major one—that has a multi-racial base.

Our people are drawn from every area of the world. And the task of bringing about responsible, responsive, representative, broadly participating government in such a society is no small task—and there are no instant ways to achieve it. But we've had presidents who have been talking to us about these things. President

Kennedy and President Johnson talked about what they called Creative Federalism. One of them talked about a new frontier, one of them about a great society. President Nixon has talked about the new federalism. What they are all saying is that things have changed, and that federalism today is no longer a limitation on the powers of the federal government, but a positive assertion of the cooperative relationships between federal government, state governments, city, county, and other local government units; between universities and governments; universities and hospitals, and voluntary agencies, professional and trade associations, labor associations, and the whole spectrum of the private sector.

Now why do I give you that broad description? Because today there isn't a single problem that confronts this country that can be handled successfully by any one of these governmental structures or any one of these groups. No problem. Racism cannot be handled by the trade unions or business or the churches or the universities. It requires both legal sanctions and a change of heart and attitude and perspective.

New Partnerships

The congestion of our cities, of our highways, of our traffic lanes, cannot be handled by any one level of government.

So what we are talking about is a great new partnership. Possibly the greatest contribution of the space program, into which we poured great resources, is not that man set his foot on the moon and took that great stride for mankind, but that the space program demonstrated that modern society requires a partnership of private and public sectors, a partnership of the university with the private economic community and the government and all other segments of society.

And it requires new management methods. The space program was more than science and technology. It was a demonstration of the mobilization of resources and of commitment to a goal—with the willingness to pursue it relentlessly.

Ladies and gentlemen, while I know you cannot always translate the facts of science and technology into the social sciences, you can concentrate the commitment, the national decision, the mobilization of resources, the national goal, and in these ways, the space program told us what we can do.

Any nation that can do what we did in less than a decade of space science and technology can surely help put a man on his feet right here on earth.

And that's exactly where the action needs to take place. We can't escape this planet—this is our space—this is our space satellite. We're on it together, and we are either going to keep it together and preserve it together, or we will destroy it together.

A Time of Decision and Dissent

The 1960s have shown us these possibilities. That's why I call it a time of decision and dissent—there was dissent against the inadequacies of the moment, dissent against old practices which no longer work; but there was also great discovery, discovery of what we could do, the possibilities that are ours.

This new federalism, therefore, wasn't so much a delineation of power between national and state government as it was a pattern or description or formula of cooperative partnership of all levels of government in concert with private resources, the partnership of creative federalism.

Your government—and that's what we're talking about—was designed to maximize and mobilize the nation's resources for the achievement of national goals and the solution of increasingly complex problems. This is the only modern industrial nation in the world that lacks a system to establish our priorities.

Goals Are Needed

We do not have unlimited resources. We need to have goals, we need to set priorities. If I were to go through this audience and ask you to list our priorities according to what you believe their significance should be, there would be as many ideas about priorities and goals as there are people.

This is not the way you direct the energies of a nation. I had some awareness of and some participation in the new legislation of the fifties and sixties, legislation that for the first time carried broad statements of national purpose.

In a whole basketful of categories, the federal government made clear its determination to improve the conditions and opportunities of life for all the citizens in our society. This new federalism emphasizes one vital point: the citizen is not only a citizen of the state or locality, he is above all a citizen of the United States of America, and therefore is entitled to every protection and every guarantee of the Constitution.

The emphasis of the sixties—which will carry forward for the rest of this century—is upon that citizenship, that national citizenship, and the federal policy is to emphasize that United States Citizenship.

Congress once and for all has asserted the primacy of the national interest in a broad range of activities. There are obvious reasons for this dramatic change. We've become a mobile nation, we are on the move. State loyalties have diminished. Our ties are to country, to family, and often, to a corporation. Provincial local loyalties are vanishing. No longer do families remain in the towns of their forebears. No longer do children live in the cities where they were born or raised.

A Mobile America

Migration to our cities—and particularly to the sea coasts and to the sunny states of Florida and California—are in large part the result of improved communication.

Rural families, once isolated from the general culture, were able to see New York and Chicago and New Orleans and Los Angeles close up on their television screen. These places looked good to many Americans, and many migrated before there were services to meet their needs. The poorly schooled boy from South Carolina began showing up as a welfare statistic in New York City. The malnourished child from Appalachia showed up in a hospital in Detroit.

This mobility among our people made health and welfare, the physical environment, education and economic development matters of national, rather than just local, concern. There was recognition that no city can protect itself from pollution by itself.

There was recognition of the inability of minority groups to achieve first-class citizenship after a century of struggle. There was clear need for a legal statement of national conscience, and federal enforcement of national standards.

Major Legislation of the 60's

Four major pieces of legislation in the 1960's revolutionized American politics and the social order, and we are yet to really sense their impact.

The first is the Civil Rights Act of 1963, which for the first time put the power of the Federal government on the side of the citizen. This did not eliminate prejudice, but it made acts which flow from prejudice illegal. Our job for the future is to eliminate the residual prejudice that results from two centuries of depredation and segregation.

The Civil Rights Act of 1964, the Voting Rights Act of 1965—which uses the power of the federal government to protect the right to vote—these will change the American political structure far beyond what we sense today.

The Economic Opportunity Act of 1964 said that the government of the United States is going to wage war on man's most ancient enemy—poverty. And with the Economic Opportunity Act came the often criticized Community Action Program.

Ladies and gentlemen, the Community Action Program, the community council concept, is built around the premise that those who are to be affected by programs should have something to say about them. Maximum feasible participation by the poor—we haven't done it yet—there is always a gap between man's pronouncements and his performance. But I can tell you that it has set a pattern, and the avenues of participation have been opened.

The last Act I want to mention is the Elementary and Secondary Education Act which, for the first time, permitted the federal government to pump billions of dollars into the educational system of this country—not nearly as much as we need, but a beginning.

Now we are looking not only at the need for financial resources for education, but at the need for change in the methods and the technology of education.

These four legislative enactments represent a whole new dimension in the revolution of American democracy—a peaceful revolution, and a continuing revolution. And in this series of acts the federal government identified national goals and committed federal funds to achieve them.

New "People Programs"

Now the central premise of all these new "people programs" is that they are designed to meet local needs, but local needs that are in the national interest.

No longer does the government just pump in money. It also establishes programs and standards to achieve what is established by statute as a national policy.

But it is in the county courthouse, the city hall, the state capitol, the thousands of town meetings across the country, that the success or failure of these programs will be determined.

You can't legislate good administration; and you can't legislate creative government. But you can provide the resources and the direction that make it possible. This is a complex subject, and our time is limited today.

I can only tell you that we must find ways to coordinate and to eliminate duplication in this huge and complicated government structure, so that we maximize the purpose of government as never before. With thousands of governmental units, with hundreds of federal grant programs, coordination is essential.

Coordination is Necessary

This is why in 1968 when I sought the highest office in this land I recommended that the next President of the United States have a Domestic Policy Council to coordinate every domestic program just as the President has a National Security Council to coordinate issues of national security.

I also suggested that there be at a regional level a presidential ambassador who would be the President's personal representative to the multitude of federal agencies within that region—just exactly as an ambassador to a foreign country represents your nation in all of its aspects abroad. This kind of coordination in policy structure could help us to achieve some of our goals, for government is a tool to be used, not an enemy to be abused.

We can't afford to isolate any level of government if we are to succeed in our great national undertakings. In our growing and demanding United States, we need the wisdom to create, to control, and to support a government that is sufficiently strong to achieve its objectives and to protect our liberties, and a government that is sufficiently sensitive and concerned to meet the needs of all our citizens.

A Look Toward the 70's

I look to the decade of the seventies with optimism. For, just as war has its own built-in escalation, so does the process of peace have its built-in escalation, and the first priority of this nation must be the search, and not only the search, but the attainment, of peace.

It is my view and my conviction that until we are able to obtain peace and disengagement—obtain it not in a sporadic outburst of emotion, but with full consideration of our responsibilities—until then, many of our domestic priorities will be set aside.

Our First Priority Is Peace

Therefore, peace must be the first priority; and there is good reason to hope that this will be achieved in the early days of the seventies. But America must have a broader vision than that. If we were out of Viet Nam this afternoon, we would still face great problems.

Let us not use Viet Nam to escape from the realities of our time. We need to build in America an open society in which people of every race, creed, and color can move freely without prejudice and without discrimination. We need to cleanse ourselves of every vestige of racism. That's our number one problem in this country, ladies and gentlemen.

We can't have two Americas. We need a positive program to set priorities for the development of human resources.

Strength In Our People

The strength of this nation is not in its arms or in its industry, it is in its people. And the wealth of this nation is not in its banks or its insurance companies, it is in its people. We must develop these human resources.

And we must conserve the physical resources we are abusing and ruining at an unprecedented rate, not only in our nation, but throughout the world. When six percent of the people of the world, which we represent, consume forty percent of the produce of the world, which we do—six percent of the people consume forty percent of all that the world produces—then I think the rest of the world might consider us overindulgent.

Protection of Our Environment

And surely if there is one focus for the seventies, it must be survival and the protection of our physical environment.

I'm not here to talk on ecological matters, per se, but, ladies and gentlemen, don't underestimate the danger that is before us. Our danger is not merely nuclear weapons and it's not merely the poor man's atom bomb—the bacteriological, biological, and chemical weapons—all of which should be abolished. The danger that faces us today comes right out of the exhaust pipe of our automobiles and our busses, and out of the water that flows from an industrial plant into the river, and out of the smoke stacks that spew their poisonous gases into the air and out of a jet engine.

And if young America will become as excited about this kind of contamination as it has been excited about violence abroad and about nuclear proliferation, maybe we can save ourselves.

These are the central problems. We must promote the conditions that are conducive to peace—and that includes curbing the arms race. We must halt the arms race before it halts the human race—and we can.

Confidence and Understanding; in Proper Measure

It isn't a matter of whether we can trust the Russians, because we have developed alternatives for trust—sophisticated detection systems. So it is a question of whether we have the confidence and the will to understand that we are all together on this planet—and we're going to live or die here.

I recall Adlai Stevenson's words as I leave you today. Adlai Stevenson was defeated for the presidency twice. But he was, in a greater sense, a winner. There's a lot of difference between failure and defeat, you know.

Failure is when you are defeated and neither learn anything nor contribute anything.

"Democracy is not Self-Executing"

Alfred Landon was defeated for the presidency, but he was not a failure. He has given a great deal to this country, even out of office. Adlai Stevenson was one of the noble men of our times, and, like this good former governor of yours, Adlai Stevenson gave much to his nation without ever having the trappings of office. This noble man of the fifties—that great spirit—reminded us again and again that "Democracy is not self-executing. We have to make it work. We have to understand it. Not only external vigilance but unending self-examination must be the perennial price of liberty because the work of self-government never ceases." Adlai Stevenson didn't want to destroy the system, he didn't want to tear it down.

He said "unending self-examination is the perennial price of liberty." He said "the work of self-government never ceases."

And he said we have to make this democracy of ours work— and that's where you come in. In order to make it work, we have to understand it. That's what I've been trying to say today—that we must understand our government, and we must not lose faith in it.

The Challenge of Change

So, therefore, with a sense of urgency, I suggest that we ventilate the clogged channels of political participation and of social opportunity. These refreshing winds of change, which are everywhere about us, must be directed to constructive purposes—but not through violence, not through hate, not through bitterness, not through ugly passion, but through responsible debate and dissent, through reason and discussion, until decision and direction are clear.

This, my friends, is the meaning of government by the consent of the governed. This is what we mean when we say a wholesome and decent respect for the opinions of others. This is what we mean by a social contract among equals.

And this is what creative federalism means—a government that never stands still, a society that sees change as a challenge not as an enemy, a social structure that constantly expands and opens its doors because we, the people, know that there are new people to be heard from, new ideas to be discovered, and new ways of life to be found.

Richard M. Nixon (1913–) became President of the United States in 1969 after narrowly defeating Hubert Humphrey in a hardfought race which also included third party candidate George Wallace. He began his political career as a member of the U.S. House of Representatives. In 1950 he was elected to the senate and served as Vice President under President Eisenhower from 1953–1960. In 1960 he lost by a slim margin to John F. Kennedy in the race for President. In 1962 he lost again in his bid to become Governor of California but made his political comeback in the 1968 presidential election, defeating Hubert Humphrey. His policy of "Vietnamization" of the Vietnam war was designed to reduce the number of U.S. combat troops while stepping-up the bombings of both North Vietnam and Cambodia. In 1972, Nixon easily defeated Senator George McGovern, in part on the claim by Henry Kissinger that a peace treaty with the North Vietnamese was at hand. Shortly after the election, he began the intensive "Christmas Bombing" of North Vietnam. In January of 1973, a cease-fire was proclaimed.

In February of 1973, the Senate established a special judiciary committee to investigate illegal campaign practices, including the break-in of Democratic National Headquarters in the Watergate Hotel. In July of 1974, the Senate Judiciary Committee passed three Articles of Impeachment. Nixon resigned from the Presidency, August 9, 1974, before the House of Representatives could consider the charges. Since his resignation, he has remained active as a writer and commentator on political matters, especially foreign affairs.

It's Time to Stand Up and Be Counted

Richard M. Nixon

Richard Nixon was the first United States President to speak in the Landon Lecture Series. He was also the first speaker, and one of only two or three in the first two decades of the series, to encounter verbal protest during the course of his lecture. Like some of the other lectures in this series, the Nixon speech was a political event in itself, regardless of its content. In a period when America's continued military presence in Southeast Asia was being protested on campuses across the country, the Landon Lectures provided the President an opportunity to demonstrate that his policies had broad public support, especially among the youth. By the same token, local opponents of Nixon administration policies saw the lecture as an opportunity to voice that opposition, which they did by unfurling banners and by heckling during the Nixon speech. The President responded by exhorting his audience to "stand up and be counted." Their applause, and the acoustic assistance of the public address system, effectively overpowered the protest. Writing to KSU President James McCain on September 18th, President Nixon asserted that Kansas State's students had "demonstrated dramatically that the mindless disrupters are not the voice of America's youth, and not the voice of the academic community." He went on to note that "at Kansas State there are many and diverse views about the great issues that confront our country today. But these are questions about which rational people can argue rationally. Only those who fear the process of reason have cause to shout down those they disagree with."

The protesters, comprising students, faculty, and at least one campus chaplain, argued however that a campus lecture by the President of the United States was not a rational debate of the issues, and that they had taken their protest inside Ahearn Fieldhouse only after being denied any opportunity to protest outside. When President Ronald Reagan spoke in the series twelve years later, peaceful protests were permitted outside the fieldhouse, and the lecture inside proceeded without disturbance.

SEPTEMBER 16, 1970

99

Governor Landon, President McCain, Governor Docking, Senator Pearson, Senator Dole, all of the distinguished guests on the platform, and all the distinguished guests in this audience for this Landon Lecture Series:

I want to express first on behalf of both Mrs. Nixon and myself our warm appreciation for your welcome. It is good to be on the campus of one of America's great universities. And for the benefit of our television audience, I should explain this tie. As we were flying out to Kansas on Air Force One, Senator Pearson, Senator Dole, the Members of the Congressional Delegation, and others presented this tie to me and they said, "You must wear it when you speak at Kansas State."

So, I put it on. And then the television director for today saw it and he said, "You can't wear that tie." I said, "Why not?" He said, "Because purple doesn't go with a blue suit."

All I can say is I am proud to wear the purple at Kansas State.

And incidentally, I also want to thank those who made the arrangements for this meeting for having as the waiting room before we came into the auditorium here, the dressing room for the Kansas State basketball team. It is nice to be in a room with a winner, believe me.

At this great university, in this very distinguished company, I cannot help but think about the twists of fate—and of how we learn from them.

I think of the fans of Wildcat football here today who have known what it is to lose—and then who have known what it is to win.

I think back to 1936. You were not born then. But I think then, when Governor Landon—who already knew what it was to win— the only winner among governors on the Republican side in 1934— a man who knew what it was to win up to that time, learned what it was like to lose.

And I think, too, of some of the moments of my own career: as a football player who spent most of his time on the bench; as a candidate who knew the great satisfaction of winning—and then as a candidate who learned what it is to lose.

Having won some and lost some, I know—as you know—that winning is a lot more fun.

But I also know that defeat or adversity can react on a person in different ways.

Inspiration For Another Try

He can give up; he can complain about "a world he never made"; or he can search the lessons of defeat and find the inspiration for another try, or a new career, or a richer understanding of the world and of life itself.

When Alf Landon lost to Franklin Roosevelt in 1936, he was not a man to waste his life in brooding over what might have been. In the 34 years since then, the world has been transformed. And enriched by his experience, Alf Landon has continued to grow with the world—until now he is one of the great elder statesmen of America, a man whose wisdom and common sense, and whose outspoken concern for the welfare of this nation, have inspired and aided generations that have come thereafter.

We applaud him and commend him today for that distinguished career.

Or in a completely different field, but related, take Kansas State and its football team.

As some of you may have noted, I am somewhat of a football buff. Just three years ago, the Wildcats had a dismal seven-year record of eight wins and 60 losses. But there was a dogged spirit here, a determination, a readiness to learn new ways—and when Vince Gibson came to the campus it was that spirit, that determination, that "Purple Pride" that he helped translate into the "Purple Power" of today.

As for myself, I doubt that I would be President today if I had not learned from the lessons of defeat in 1960 and 1962—and I hope that I can be a better President because of those lessons.

I cite these examples not only to suggest that we here today have something in common—but also because this pattern of playing by the rules, of losing some and winning some, of accepting the verdict and having another chance, is fundamental to the whole structure on which our liberty rests.

There are those who protest that if the verdict of democracy goes against them, democracy itself is at fault, the system is at fault—who say that if they don't get their way the answer is to burn a bus or bomb a building.

Yet we can maintain a free society only if we recognize that in a free society no one can win all the time. No one can have his own way all the time, and no one is right all the time.

A Study of Why

Whether in a campaign, or in a football game, or in debate on the great issues of the day, the answer to "losing one" is not a rush to the barricades but a study of why, and then a careful rebuilding—or perhaps even a careful re-examination of whether the other fellow may have been right after all.

When Palestinian guerrillas hijacked four airliners in flight, they brought to 250 the number of aircraft seized since the skyjacking era began in 1961. And as they held their hundreds of passengers hostage under threat of murder, they sent shock-waves of alarm around the world at the spreading disease of violence and terror and its use as a political tactic.

The same cancerous disease has been spreading all over the world and here in the United States.

We saw it three weeks ago in the vicious bombing at the University of Wisconsin. One man lost his life, four were injured and years of painstaking research by a score of others was destroyed.

We have seen it in other bombings and burnings on our campuses, and in our cities; in the wanton shootings of policemen, and the attacks on school buses, in the destruction of offices, the seizure and harassment of college officials, the use of force and coercion to bar students and teachers from classrooms, and even to close down whole schools.

Consider just a few items in the news:

—A courtroom spectator pulls out a gun. He halts the trial, gives arms to the defendants, takes the judge and four other hostages, moves to a waiting getaway van—and in the gunfight that follows four die, including the judge.

—A man walks into the guardhouse of a city park and pumps five bullets into a police sergeant sitting quietly at his desk.

—A Nobel Prize winner working on a cancer cure returns to the cages of his experimental rats and mice to find them vandalized, with some of the animals running loose, some thrown out of windows into the sea, hundreds missing.

Just think, years of research which could have provided some progress toward bringing a cure to this dread disease destroyed without reason.

—A police patrolman responds to an anonymous emergency call that reported a woman screaming. He arrives at the address. He finds the house deserted but a suitcase is left behind. He bends over to examine it. It explodes, blows off his head and wounds seven others.

These acts of viciousness all took place not in some other country, but in the United States, and in the last five weeks.

America at its best has stood steadfastly for the rule of law among nations. But we cannot stand successfully for the rule of law abroad unless we respect the rule of law at home. A nation that condones blackmail and terror at home can hardly stand as the example in putting an end to international piracies or tensions that could explode into war abroad.

Violence and Terror Have No Place

The time has come for us to recognize that violence and terror have no place in a free society, whatever the purported cause or whoever the perpetrators may be. And this is the fundamental lesson for us to remember. In a system like ours, which provides the means for peaceful change, no cause justifies violence in the name of change.

Those who bomb universities, who ambush policemen, who hijack airplanes and hold their passengers hostage, all share in common not only a contempt for human life, but also the contempt for those elemental decencies on which a free society rests—and they deserve the contempt of every American who values those decencies.

Those decencies, those self-restraints, those patterns of mutual respect for the rights and feelings of one another, the willingness to listen to somebody else, without trying to shout him down, those patterns of mutual respect for the rights and the feelings of one another—these are what we must preserve if freedom itself is to be preserved.

There have always been among us those who would choose violence or intimidation to get what they wanted. Their existence is not new. What is new is their numbers, and the extent of the passive acquiescence, or even fawning approval, that in some fashionable circles has become the mark of being "with it."

Commenting on the bombing three weeks ago at the University of Wisconsin, the *Wisconsin State Journal* recently said:

". . . it isn't just the radicals who set the bomb in a lighted, occupied building who are guilty. The blood is on the hands of anyone who has encouraged them, anyone who has talked recklessly of 'revolution,' anyone who has chided with mild disparagement the violence of extremists while hinting that the cause is right all the same."

What corrodes a society even more deeply than violence itself is the acceptance of violence, the condoning of terror, the excusing of inhuman acts in a misguided effort to accommodate the community's standards to those of the violent few.

When this happens, the community sacrifices more than its calm and more even than its safety. It loses its integrity and corrupts its soul.

The Rule Of Reason

Nowhere should the rule of reason be more respected or more jealously guarded, than in the halls of our great universities.

It is the rule of reason that is the most important.

Yet we all know that in some of the great universities small bands of destructionists have been allowed to impose their own rule of arbitrary force.

Because of this, we face today the greatest crisis in the history of American education.

In times past we have had crises in education. I remember them.

We faced shortages of classrooms, shortages of teachers, shortages that could always be made up, however, by appropriating more money.

These material shortages are nothing compared to the crisis of the spirit which rocks hundreds of campuses across the country today. And because of this, to put it bluntly, today higher education in America risks losing that essential support it has had since the beginning of this country—the support of the American people.

America and Americans, from the time of our foundation, and particularly those that did not have the opportunity to go to a great college or university, have been proud of our enormous strides in higher education. They have supported it.

Quality Of Education Threatened

The number of students in college today has doubled in the past 10 years. But at a time when the quantity of education is going dramatically up, its quality is massively threatened by assaults which terrorize faculty, students and university and college administrators alike.

It is time for the responsible university and college administrators, faculty and student leaders to stand up and be counted. We must remember that only they can save higher education in America. It cannot be saved by Government.

If we turn only to Government to save it, then Government will move in and run the colleges and universities, and so the place to save it is here among the faculty, the administrators, the student leaders. To attempt to blame Government for all the woes of the universities is rather the fashion these days. But, really, it is to seek an excuse, not a reason, for their troubles.

Listen to this: If the war were to end today, if the environment were cleaned up tomorrow morning, and all the other problems for which Government has the responsibility were solved tomorrow afternoon—the moral and spiritual crisis in the universities would still exist.

The destructive activists in our universities and colleges are a small minority. But their voices have been allowed.

My text at this point reads: "The voices of the small minority have been allowed to drown out the responsible majority." That may be true in some places, but not at Kansas State.

As a result, there is a growing, dangerous attitude among millions of people that all youth are like those who appear night after night on the television screen shouting obscenities, making threats or engaging in destructive and illegal acts.

An Unfair Reflection

One of the greatest disservices that the disrupters have done, in fact, is precisely that, to reflect unfairly on those millions of students, like those in this room, who do go to college for an education, who do study, who do respect the rules, and who go on to make constructive contributions to peaceful change and progress in this country.

But let us understand exactly where we are. I would not for one moment call for a dull, passive conformity on the part of our university and college students, or an acceptance of the world as it is. The great strength of this nation is that our young people, the young people like those in this room, in generation after generation, give the nation new ideas, new directions, new energy.

I do not call for a conformity in which the young simply ape the old or in which we freeze the faults that we have. We must be honest enough to find what is right and to change what is wrong in America.

But at the same time we must take an uncompromising stand against those who reject the rules of civilized conduct and of respect for others—those who would destroy what is right in our society and whose actions would do nothing to right what is wrong.

Automatic Conformity Wrong

Automatic conformity with the older generation—and I say this as one of the older generation—automatic conformity with the older generation is wrong. At the same time, it is just as wrong to fall into a slavish conformity with those who falsely claim to be the leaders of the new generation, out of fear that it would be unpopular—or considered square—not to follow their lead.

It would be a tragedy for the young generation simply to pursue the policies of the past, and it would be just as great a tragedy for the new generation to become simply parrots for the slogans of protest, uniformly chanting the same few phrases—and often with the same four-letter words.

Let us take one example—one example that deeply troubles, and I understand why it does deeply trouble, many of our young people today: the war in Vietnam. We know the slogans. I have heard them often. Most of them simply say end the war.

Ending The War

There is no difference between Americans on that. All of us want to end the war. And we are ending this war.

Ending the war is not the issue. We have been in four wars in this century. We ended World War I. We ended World War II. We ended Korea. The great question is how we end the war and what kind of peace we achieve.

If it were a peace now that would encourage those who would engage in aggression and would thereby lead to a bigger and more terrible war later, it would be peace at too great a price.

As we look back over the 20th century, as we look at that whole record of this century, only 70 years, we in America have not yet in this whole century been able to enjoy even one full generation of peace.

So, the whole thrust, the whole purpose of this administration's foreign policy—whether it is in Vietnam, or in the Middle East, or in Europe, or in our relations with the developing countries or with the Communist powers—is to meet our responsibilities in such a way that at last we can have what we have not had in this century: a full generation of peace. I believe we can have it.

That is why, in Vietnam, we are carrying out a policy that will end the war. It will do it in a way that will contribute to a just and a lasting peace in the Pacific, in Vietnam, and, we trust, also in the world.

There are those who say that this is the worst of times in which to live.

What self-pitying nonsense that is.

I am perhaps more aware of the problems this nation has at

home and abroad than most of you. But we in America, I say proudly today, have a great deal to be proud of—and a great deal to be hopeful about for the future.

Let us open our eyes. Let's look around us. We see, as we look at the whole sweep of history, that for the first time in the whole history of man, it is becoming possible here in America to do things that nobody even dreamed could be done, even 50 years ago.

Cleaning The Environment

We see a natural environment, true, that has been damaged by careless misuses of technology. But we also see that the same technology gives us the ability to clean up that environment, to restore the clean air, the clean water, the open spaces, that are our rightful heritage. And I pledge we can do that and shall do it.

I know the fashionable line among some: Wouldn't it be great to live in a country that didn't have all these problems of material progress?

Not at all. I have been to them. I have seen them. And I simply would like to say to you that great as our problems are as a result of our material progress, we can do things for ourselves and for others that need to be done, and we must see it in that way.

Look at our nation. We are rich, and sometimes that is condemned because wealth can sometimes be used improperly. But because of our wealth, it means that today we in America cannot just talk about, but can plan for a program in which everyone in this nation, willing and able to work, can earn a decent living, and so that we can care for those who are not able to do so on some basis.

We see a nation that now has the capacity to make enormous strides in these years just ahead, in health care, in education, in the creative use of our increasing leisure time.

Nation Poised To Progress

We see a nation poised to progress more in the next five years, in a material sense, than it did in the last 50 years.

We see that because of our wealth, because of our freedom, because of this much maligned system of ours, we can go on to develop those great qualities of the spirit that only decades ago were still buried by the weight of drudgery, and that in 75 percent of the world today are still buried by the weight of drudgery.

We see that we can do this in America, lift that weight of drudgery, allow the development of the qualities of the spirit, and we can do it not just for an elite class, not just for the few, but for the many. All this can happen in America. The question is: How shall we use this great opportunity? Shall we toss it away in mindless disruption and terror? Shall we let it wither away in despair? Or shall we prepare ourselves, as you are preparing yourselves, and shall we conduct ourselves in a way that this will be looked back upon as the beginning of the brightest chapter ever in the unfolding of the American dream?

Making its promise real requires an atmosphere of reason, of tolerance, and of common courtesy, with that basic regard for the rights and feelings of others that is the mark of any civilized society.

Defending The Pursuit Of Truth

It requires that the members of the academic community rise firmly in defense of the free pursuit of truth—that they defend it as zealously today against threats from within as they have defended it in the past against threats from without.

It requires that the idealism of the young—and indeed, the idealism of all ages—be focused on what can be done within the framework of a free society, recognizing that its structure of rights and responsibilities is complex and fragile and as precious as freedom itself.

The true idealist pursues what his heart says is right in a way that his head says will work.

But the first test of his idealism lies in the respect that he shows for the rights of others. Despite all the difficulties, all the divisions, all the troubles that we have had, we can look to the future, I believe, with pride and with confidence. I speak here today on the campus of a great university, and I recall one of the great sons of Kansas, Dwight David Eisenhower. I recall the eloquent address he made at London's famous Guildhall immediately after victory in Europe.

On that day, a huge assemblage of all the leading dignitaries in Britain was there to honor him.

The Heart Of America

In his few remarks, one of the most eloquent speeches in the history of English eloquence, he said very simply, "I come from the heart of America."

Now, 25 years later, as I speak in the heart of America, I can truly say to you here today you are the heart of America—and the heart of America is strong. The heart of America is good. The heart of America is sound. It will give us—you will give us—the sound and responsible leadership that the great promise of America calls for—and in doing so, you will give my generation what it most fervently hopes for: the knowledge that your generation will see that promise of the American dream fulfilled.

Earl Warren (1891–1974) was Chief Justice of the U.S. Supreme Court from 1953 to 1969. He began his political career as a county district attorney and then was attorney general of California. He was the Republican vice-presidential candidate in 1948 and, was instrumental in 1952 in getting the California delegation to support Dwight Eisenhower. In September of 1953, President Eisenhower appointed him Chief Justice. In 1954, he handed down the Court's unanimous decision in *Brown vs the Board of Education* that racial segregation in public schools is unconstitutional. Other important decisions of the Warren court involved federal and state legislative reapportionment ("one-man, one-vote"), increased rights for criminal defendants, prohibition of prayer in public schools, and expanded freedom of speech and of the press. In 1963, he chaired the commission which investigated the assassination of John Kennedy. He died in Washington in 1974.

The Alternative is Chaos

Earl Warren

Chief Justice Earl Warren presided over the most activist Supreme Court in American history. The most controversial and far-reaching of the Warren Court's decisions was that in the 1954 case of Brown vs the Board of Education of Topeka, *which declared "separate but equal" schools to be unconstitutional. The decision was a major step in the long and halting march toward racial equality in America. In this Landon Lecture, delivered fourteen years later, Chief Justice Warren reflected on how far this country still had to go before the full rights of citizenship could be enjoyed equally by Americans of all races. Warren's central point, that failure to make progress on these issues would result in chaos, had special meaning to an audience which had just experienced, in the previous three years, the riotous devastation of several American cities and, on the Kansas State campus, the destruction by arson of Nichols Gymnasium.*

OCTOBER 21, 1970

This is a thrilling experience for me to be at your University for a number of reasons, not the least of which is the fact that this series of lectures is named for my long-time friend, Governor Alf Landon, with whom I labored decades ago in the vineyards of politics. But our trails have not crossed often in recent years because I have been immured in the Supreme Court for the past 17 years where constant attendance is a matter of necessity. But I have always retained my admiration for his integrity, his wisdom, and his down-to-earth philosophy of life and politics throughout the years. I am happy to be with him today in these inspirational surroundings.

I like universities, and I have always liked university life—in my day, through the intervening years, and today, in spite of the vicissitudes of the moment. I am happy to be in this free market place of ideas. This forum appeals to me particularly because, in visiting with students, one is where the action is. It is where the criticism of my generation largely and properly, I think, comes from. It is the proper place from which such criticism should emanate because these students and young people of our day are to be the residuary legatees of both the benefits and the burdens which are being left to them. They are the ones who are to live with both, and they must reappraise the values of life and reorder priorities for the society of their day.

In talking to them, I only wish I could approach my discussion with the same assurance of finality as a scientist or a technologist would approach subjects within his competence. However, neither my age, my temperament, nor my preoccupation in life would permit me to do so.

The older we become the less certain we are of our own conclusions. As has been so well stated by Justice Oliver Wendell Holmes, and I quote him, "But when men have realized that time has upset many fighting faiths, they may come to believe even more than they believe the very foundations of their own conduct that the ultimate good desired is better reached by free trade in ideas—..." In my experience, I, too, have seen many fighting faiths upset; and I also believe firmly in the free trade of ideas.

Inexact Sciences

My preoccupation throughout a long lifetime has been with pragmatic affairs which cannot be evaluated through scientific analysis or reduced to scientific conclusions. Thirty-six years of my adult life were devoted to the field of politics and governmental administration; the last 16 years to the judicial process. Neither politics nor the judicial process are or can become an exact science because they deal with the vagaries of human nature and the actions of human beings.

Politics have been broadly defined as the art of the possible, and that is a fair description. The complexities of our society, and the cross currents of economic and social interests are involved in almost every political act. The ideal is rarely, if ever, achieved. Although sometimes proposed, the ideal gives way to practicality on the theory that a half loaf is better than none. In the last analysis, it becomes a matter of bargaining between competing interests until a consensus is achieved or the entire proposal is abandoned. Too often the latter is the result, and no progress is made. The effect of these eventualities is to bring into play a myriad of devices, either for advancing proposals or for stifling them. Some are helpful; some are destructive. Some are designed for the sole purpose of avoiding responsibility.

A Lesson In Avoidance

Illustrative of this point, I was told a story by an old-time state senator from one of your neighboring states concerning a little town in his district. He said that the affairs in the town were so deadly that there was nothing to be discussed or argued about except one thing, namely, whether the town should or should not have a new church, there being only one there at the time. But whenever the proposal was made for a new church, the argument divided the town into warring factions, and the longer it continued the more bitter it became.

Customers boycotted businesses; the children fought in school; and the women of the community ostracized each other from social gatherings.

The Board of Deacons of the church, of course, was in the very center of this storm, and all of the members, except one, suffered the afflictions of the rest of the community. The lone member of the Board who was untouched by the controversy was a man of business, and had been on the Board for many years. Finally, he concluded that he would retire from his position, but he asked the Board to elect his son to succeed him. This was done.

However, in a very short time the younger man was in the center of the controversy. His children came home from school with black eyes; his wife was not invited to church parties; and his business was boycotted. Finally, at the end of his wits, he went to his father and said, "Dad, I am in deep trouble. You got me into this trouble, and you must help me to get out of it." The old gentleman asked what the trouble was, and when the son told him, he said, "Oh, don't worry about that, my boy. I will tell you how you can avoid all those difficulties. Whenever there is a proposal to build a new church, you vote for the new church, but whenever a site is proposed, no matter where it is, you vote against the site. Then you will be out of trouble."

The story ended there, but I suppose that one might add that the young man followed his father's advice, and lived happily with his family ever after without assuming responsibility either for building or not building the new church. I add this because I have experienced the reenactment of this story hundreds of times in politics. People will often say to controversial proposals they wish to avoid deciding, "Oh, I agree with the principle, but I cannot agree with the proposed remedy."

Giving Judicial Meaning Not Easy

We even encounter this in the judicial process. There, in interpreting the often ambiguous or even contradictory laws of the legislative branch of the Government, the courts are required to divine from the legislative history, consisting of proposals, counter proposals, desultory argument, explanation of votes, etc., what judicial meaning should be given to the statute. Then, according to the meaning ascribed to it, it must be checked with some broad, general language in the Constitution to see if it conforms. When that has been done, the interpretation must be applied to the facts as developed in a courtroom, usually controverted and often not precise, in order to arrive at a final decision. And, of course, in the process, the foibles of the judge must also be accommodated. Few solutions could be less scientific than this. But in the judiciary we can only do our best under the circumstances.

But most of our problems of today stem from human relationships, and their solution must be achieved through human reactions. In more than a half century of experience in dealing with such problems, I have naturally, and almost of necessity, formed some conclusions, both as to the importance of the major problems and of the priorities which should be accorded them.

Many of them have been developing since the birth of our nation, and largely because our advances of recent years in science and technology have been so rapid that all of them are surfacing at about the same time. Certainly, they are all plaguing us today. It is not easy to assign relative importance to them, but I suppose that most people would agree today—not a few years ago but only recently—that warfare and particularly the undeclared war in Indochina is one of the most pressing. However, being something of an optimist, I am persuaded that because most people are so minded our participation in the Asiatic war will end in the foreseeable future—not speedily enough to satisfy all of us, but that it will end. We will then be free to focus our attention, our money, and our energy on taking care of the many domestic needs which have been starved during the 25 years we have been almost constantly engaged in warfare.

Rehabilitate Our Resources

In the rapid development of our country from ocean to ocean, and with the burgeoning of our population from four million to more than two hundred million, we have neglected to protect our natural resources, until deterioration of the environment of land, sea, and air is said to be approaching a question of the survival of plant, animal, and even human life. But I believe that with the public realization of the danger involved, and particularly realization on the part of the young people of our nation, we will have the capacity to turn the tide and rehabilitate our air, our water, and our soil. As a layman, and again as an optimist, I believe that the scientists who have made it possible for us to fly to the moon, to transplant human organs from one body to another, and to transmit vision as well as sound instantaneously throughout the world, will be able to find solutions, provided there is a national commitment to that objective and a dedication of the forces of science to it comparable to that which took us to the moon.

Also, during these same years of development, we have forgotten to preserve some of our human values, and have failed in our obligation to protect the health of our people until we now find, to our distress, that among the developed nations of the world we stand thirteenth in infant mortality; seventh in the percentage of mothers who die in childbirth; eighteenth in life expectancy for males; eleventh in life expectancy for females; and sixteenth in the death rate for middle-aged males.

Educational System In Trouble

Although we have developed a great system of both elementary and higher educational institutions, we are in trouble with the system at the present time. We do not appear to be satisfying the students, the faculties, the administrators, or the public. However, with as many people as we have dedicated to that cause, I have no doubt that it, too, will soon reoccupy its rightful place in the sun where truth can be freely pursued in peaceful surroundings with the co-operation of all who have a thirst for knowledge.

Poverty also can be wiped out in a country which is renowned for having the most affluent society in recorded history. It is difficult to believe that in a bountiful country such as ours, where the Government pays farmers not to plant staples of life and where a portion of an overabundant crop is required to be left on the tree, vine, or ground to rot, that one out of seven of our people, as has been widely reported recently, should go to bed hungry every night. Certainly, if our agricultural scientists and the industry of our farmers can make our land that productive, our technologists and the Government can distribute crops in a way to prevent hunger and avoid waste.

But the one thing that has the badge of insolubility on it is the problem of how we are to live together in harmony and mutual respect. We have boasted for almost 200 years that we are a plural society wherein we achieve unity through diversity and accommodate diversity through unity.

The Greatest Problem

But again the sins of former years are upon us, and it is my belief that the question of whether we can permanently have such a society is the greatest problem before the American people today. We started wrong, of course, by tolerating the cruel institution of human slavery which was in direct contradiction of the noble phrase in our Declaration of Independence to the effect—

> ". . . that all Men are Created equal, that they are endowed by
> their Creator with certain unalienable Rights, that among these are
> Life, Liberty, and the Pursuit of Happiness . . ."

It took almost a hundred years for us to absolve ourselves from the curse of slavery through the Thirteenth, Fourteenth, and Fifteenth Amendments to our Constitution after a bloody fratricidal war in which one out of every ten young Americans of military age gave their lives. And I believe that Kansans are, or at least should be, more aware of that than any other state in the Union because during that Civil War, Kansas had the highest percentage of casualties of any state in the Union. That ultimately was not the end of our problems, and today, after a hundred more years of our national life, we are still paying the price for that slavery.

We have in the nation today about 22 million Negroes who still bear vestiges of that badge of slavery, and they are still struggling to be out of the class of inferior citizenship. The emotions engendered by hundreds of years of discrimination and cruelties have welled up in them to the point of deep bitterness.

Demanding Rights And Privileges

They are, for the first time in our history, demanding en mass the rights and privileges of citizenship which have been denied them for so many years—the right to live where they desire; the right to a decent education without discrimination; the right to vote; the right to participate freely in their government; and the right to be treated in accordance with human dignity. The violence implicit in these denials, as exemplified all along the line by lynchings and other unlawful injuries to them, has now provoked counter violence in many quarters, and the time has come when the nation must restore good will and cooperation regardless of race or color if we are to be a healthy nation.

Because of the indignities which have been showered on them, like indignities, if not in degree, have been put on others within our borders who also do not have the same pigment in their skins as do the majority of us. There are a half million American Indians who also are chafing openly about their ill treatment through the centuries. We have a million and a half Asiatics and several millions of the ancestry of our Latin American neighbors living largely in the southwestern part of our nation, and they, too, have felt many of the indignities which were so prevalent against the Negroes because indignity to one person brushes off on another as well. Together—possibly 30 million—they constitute a large percentage of our total population, and are becoming more divided from the vast majority day by day.

The results of these disaffections have come to plague us in a myriad of ways. Without education, without training in keeping with automation and advanced technology of all kinds, they have been deprived of a livelihood, and at the present time are largely mired down in the slums of our great cities. In the cotton industry in the southern states alone, 900,000 illiterate cotton pickers have been displaced by recent cotton picking machines, and they, with their families aggregating two and one half or three million people, were thrown out of their livelihood. This number does not take into consideration a similar loss of employment in the important cotton-growing states of Arizona and California, nor does it take into consideration the loss of employment in the western states because of the mechanical fruit, nut, and field crop pickers which work was done by the same people, most of them illiterate.

An Army Of Unemployed

Other millions of illiterate and untrained people, largely black, have lost their jobs through other kinds of automation, and are in a similar predicament. Together they constitute an enormous army of the unemployed. Without education or mechanical or technological skills, or there being no other employment in the rural areas where they have always lived, millions have moved to the cities in desperation to find places in the industrial world.

Degradation Is Rampant

Without skills or the education to learn them speedily, and without even hospitable treatment in their newly found home, they drift into the already congested slums where unemployment is out of all proportion, where housing is deplorable, and where degradation of every kind is rampant. There they stay as if they were imprisoned. With rare exception, there is no place for them to go except from one slum to another. They wait from month to month, therefore, for a relief check, completely frustrated and eventually become embittered.

They are looked down upon by people in affluent circumstances who flee from them to the suburbs and leave them a people apart from the mainstream of American life. These slums contaminate every city where they exist, and weaken them in the same manner as a diseased lung, a diseased heart, or a diseased liver weakens the human body. And cities can die as do human beings. History is replete with examples, but as someone has said, our problem is that the only thing we learn from history is that we do not learn. All of us must recognize the plight of our great cities and the problems they have in maintaining a viable society. Poverty, crime, degradation, and complete frustration are the result of these great mistakes of the past.

Slum Dwellers Mostly Minority Groups

All of the slum dwellers, of course, are not black or yellow or tan, but a fast growing majority of them are. About ten million of our people were born in a foreign country, and the vast majority of them are white. On the other hand, millions of them were poor and often landed in a slum when they arrived in this country. They, too, suffered the indignities of slum life, but if they were literate and white they could more easily work their way out of their sordid surroundings. However, many of them are still there under conditions that belie the invitation on the Statue of Liberty at the entrance to the harbor of New York where eighteen million immigrants have thrilled and even cried as they entered our country.

That invitation reads—

> "... Give me your tired, your poor,
> Your huddled masses yearning to breathe free.
> The wretched refuse of your teeming shore.
> Send these, the homeless, tempest-tost to me.
> I lift my lamp beside the golden door!"

The hard core of all slums is made up of these unfortunates who have been discriminated against all their lives. It is difficult for those of us who have always been able to enjoy our freedoms to understand the feelings of those who have never had them, but who are now at long last determined to have them. This is not an unaccountable phenomenon. From 1941 to 1945, we fought a war, according to the solemn promises of our Government and her allies, to assure the four freedoms for all people throughout the world. American white and black boys fought and died, side by side, and in Korea, as they are now doing in Vietnam.

Burial Denied

Only a few weeks ago in one of our southern states, a soldier who was killed in action in Vietnam was denied the right of burial in a cemetery with other soldiers who were killed in action merely because he was black. And the tragedy of his death in greater intensity was visited upon his parents.

And only a few years before that a North American Indian was denied burial in a northern state for a similar reason, even though he had died in battle in Korea. And it seems to me that those who live together in life, and certainly those who are joined together for the preservation of our nation should at least be entitled to be buried in the same burial ground regardless of color, race, or creed.

Is it unrealistic or premature for them to now demand equal rights under the law?

There can be no other answer to our problem than to wipe out the discrimination for which we have now become so notorious, and to treat everyone in the nation with the consideration that we have always demanded and received for the majority of our people. Nothing else, it seems to me, will restore amity to our country; nothing else will bring harmony to our educational system, to our cities, and the political life of the nation.

I suppose I am particularly sensitive to this situation because during the years when I was active on the Supreme Court, and when these minority groups were coming to us to achieve their constitutional rights, many people would say to me, "I agree with you that there should be no discrimination and that everybody should be treated equally under the laws, but don't you think that we are moving too fast? The Negroes have improved their situation in the United States more in the last hundred years than they have in any part of the world." Now, this was said, not in anger, but as an escape from responsibility, very much like the old deacon in the building of the church. However, the question assumed that the Supreme Court had the right to ration freedoms, and that it should go slow enough so as not to offend anyone in doing so. Of course, no such power exists for the courts either in law or in morals.

Either all rights of citizenship belong to the minorities in our country or they are entitled to none, as was said of them in the *Dred Scott* decision which precipitated the Civil War. The plain words of the Constitution now answer that question.

Bitterness Born From Discrimination

When the basis of problems is bitterness, the solution is impossible until the bitterness is removed. The bitterness in this situation is born of the discrimination of centuries, and can only be removed by elimination of that cause.

It, therefore, seems clear to me that if we are ever to have a placid nation again at least during the lifetimes of our children and their children, it will be necessary for us to set aside our prejudices on account of race or color, and be willing to live in a plural society where American citizenship means, in fact as well as in precept, that all men are created equal, and as such are entitled to Life, Liberty, and the pursuit of Happiness.

There is only one other alternative, and that alternative is—chaos.

William Fulbright (1905–) served in the U.S. Senate for thirty years. A former Rhodes scholar at Oxford, he taught law and later became president of the University of Arkansas. After one term in the U.S. House of Representatives, he was elected to the Senate. He introduced, in 1946, the bill to establish the international educational exchange program which bears his name and became Chairman of the Senate Foreign Relations committee in 1959. From 1965 on, he was a critic of U.S. involvement in Vietnam. Under the Nixon administration, he continued to criticize U.S. foreign policy, especially the anti-ballistic missile system and the Pentagon's involvement in lobbying on foreign relations issues. He was a leader in securing passage in 1973 of the War Powers Act which limited the President's ability to commit U.S. troops to foreign combat without Congressional approval. In 1974, he was defeated in the Democratic senatorial primary by Governor Dale Bumpers.

Energy and the Middle East:
Interests and Illusions

J. William Fulbright

The Middle East has been a major trouble spot for most of the past half-century. During the 1970's the importance of the region was magnified and made more complex by the energy crisis and, later, by political successes of militant Islam. In his Landon Lecture on February 13, 1975, Senator J. William Fulbright, longtime Chair of the Senate Foreign Relations Committee, articulated his perception of American national interests in this key foreign policy arena. In doing so, he suggested policy alternatives which still merit consideration.

FEBRUARY 13, 1975

There is a profoundly important difference between our current deep involvement in the Middle East and our lingering half-involvement in the wars of southeast Asia. The difference is that American interests are at stake in the Middle East—access to oil, the survival of Israel, and the avoidance of conflict with the Soviet Union—making our involvement important, if not indeed inevitable. In Vietnam and Cambodia, by contrast, nothing of surpassing consequence for the United States is or ever was at stake, and for that simple but compelling reason our involvement has been, and remains, a mistake, rooted in illusions about our national interest.

The term "national interest" is an imprecise one, and it begs the question to invoke it as a guide to policy unless we have a fairly clear conception of what an "interest" is and what it is not. I would suggest the following distinctions:

A "vital interest" is anything which pertains directly to our national survival, or short of that, something materially and discernibly pertinent to the security and well-being of the American people.

Most of us would agree that the avoidance of nuclear war—which is the object of detente with the Communist powers—the NATO alliance and alliance with Japan, and access to oil and other essential resources belong in this category. I personally would put the development and strengthening of the United Nations in the "vital" category at the top of the list, but I am painfully aware of being in the minority on this matter.

We also have interests which are less than vital—not really matters of life and death for our society, but matters of strong preference to many or most Americans, whether for reasons of idealism, humanitarianism, or ethnic or religious affiliation. I would place in this category such objectives as the development of India, democracy in Latin America, and the survival and prosperity of Israel. The distinguishing characteristic of these goals is that they are things which we want very much, and would make certain sacrifices for, but which are necessarily secondary to our *vital* interests.

Although there may be gradations on the way, we come at last to the category of illusions, of infatuations about the national interest—or if you like, the "arrogance of power." Here we are dealing with matters of national prestige, imperial presumption, or the vanity of leaders who do not care to admit that they have made a mistake. The distinguishing characteristics of our many national enterprises of this kind are that they usually involve great cost, great risk and no discernible benefits to the American people. Honorable mention in this category goes to the $30 billion we might have spent on energy research in the 1960's but instead spent to put a man on the moon so as to avoid the horrible disgrace of letting the Russians get there first. Even more honorable mention goes to our gigantic defense expenditures for exotic and unnecessary weapons systems, such as the F-111 bomber, the C-5A transport, the Trident nuclear submarine, or most recently, something called the "cannon-launched guided projectile," an artillery shell whose course can be changed in mid-flight like a guided missile. Like politicians experimenting with ideas in their speeches, the military experiment with weapons systems, not because we need them for our defense but just to see if they will work. The difference of course is the cost: a politician's oratory may be superfluous but it is usually provided free of charge—or at least at moderate price: missiles and bombers may be equally superfluous, but at a cost of billions.

The gold star in this category of foreign policy illusions goes of course to the war in Indochina. It is not my purpose here to revive the old arguments about Vietnam but only to point out that there is no more justification for our continuing heavy expenditures to sustain the regimes in South Vietnam and Cambodia than there was for our own direct military involvement. Our security is not threatened; there are no essential resources involved; the cost is exorbitant. And from a humanitarian viewpoint, it is exceedingly cruel to subject the Indochinese peoples to endless civil war, perpetuated by our military assistance. Nonetheless, despite high unemployment,still rampant inflation and gigantic budget deficits here at home, the Ford Administration is asking Congress for sizable new military appropriations for Indochina, including $300 million in emergency assistance for South Vietnam, $222 million for Cambodia, and a projected $1.3 billion of military aid to South Vietnam for the fiscal year 1976. Congress, in my opinion, would be well-advised to reject these requests, for reasons of compelling national interest.

I make these observations by way of preface to my major theme for today, which is the Middle East. The point to be borne in mind is that our foreign policy cannot be based across the board on general principles of involvement or non-involvement, idealism or *realpolitik*. The guiding principle must be the national interest in its various gradations and components, and in the way these relate to each other. The American people do not engage their public servants to conduct foreign crusades or adventures, even idealistic adventures, but rather to advance their own security and welfare. In a report of several years ago the Senate Foreign Relations Committee noted that "Foreign policy is not an end in itself. We do not have a foreign policy because it is interesting or fun, or because it satisfies some basic human need; we conduct foreign policy for a purpose external to itself, the purpose of securing democratic values in our own country."[1]

The Middle East

There is nothing illusory about our interest in the Middle East, but we do suffer from certain illusions about the character of our interests, and the way in which they relate to each other.

The catalyst, if not the cause, of our current, mounting difficulties was the Middle East war of October 1973. Like the assassination at Sarajevo in 1914, the October war set loose a chain reaction of events. The war precipitated the oil embargo, and the embargo, combined with Arab military successes, gave the Arabs a whole new sense of their own power and capacity. The oil-producing countries, non-Arab as well as Arab, became suddenly and belatedly aware of the power they had in their hands. United in OPEC (the Organization of Petroleum Exporting Countries), they set out to redress the imbalance between cheap oil and costly imports, and also, in a psychological sense, to redress centuries of colonialism and exploitation.

They did this through huge and precipitous increases in the price of oil. In the long run, as the finite supply of fossil fuels in the world runs down, the price of oil was bound to rise anyway. It is true too that until 1973 oil was artificially low in price owing to unbalanced terms of trade between raw materials and manufactured products. And it is also true that oil price increases are by no means the sole cause, or even the major cause, of current high inflation rates in the industrial countries. Nevertheless, the suddenness and extent of the oil price increases, more than four-fold in a single year, have had a devastating effect upon the economies of the consumer countries, especially in their international payments. In 1974 the United States had a trade deficit of $3.07 billion, the second largest deficit of this century; but if oil imports had cost the same as in 1973, we would have had a trade surplus of $14 billion. The World Bank estimates that by 1980 the oil producing countries will hold $600 billion in unused monetary reserves. If producer country imports continue at their current unexpectedly high level, the imbalance will be reduced, but not sufficiently to eliminate the threat of the collapse of the world monetary system. If that is to be prevented, a great deal more will have to be done.

First and most urgently we must take steps to save the international monetary system. That means that ways must be devised to keep the money which is flowing into the oil-producing countries flowing back as well; which is to say, it must be "recycled." That is the first requirement, regardless of what else is done, now or later, to bring down the price of oil. The most populous oil-producing countries—Iran, Venezuela, Nigeria and Indonesia—are already recycling most of their earnings, by spending them on foreign goods and machinery for their national development programs. Some too, especially Iran, are spending large amounts of money on foreign arms. Though unevenly distributed, money spent for foreign manufactured products enables the recipients of these funds to finance their oil imports.

The problem arises with respect to the underpopulated oil producers—Saudi Arabia, Kuwait, Libya and the United Arab Emirates. With their small populations there is only so much these countries can usefully buy from abroad, with the result that huge money surpluses accumulate and are in effect put out of circulation. With no way to earn their money back, the industrial countries are threatened with international bankruptcy and domestic depression. To correct this dangerous imbalance, I would propose that urgent steps be taken, both by government and by private groups, to induce large-scale oil-country investment in the United States and other oil-importing countries. Just putting their money in our banks as demand deposits does no good—the money can be taken out at any time and is therefore unavailable for income-producing investments. Perhaps a high-level committee of private citizens who are expert in banking and investment, and who also have the confidence of the oil-exporting countries, could be formed to advise and assist these countries in channeling their funds into safe, profitable and productive long-term investments in the importing countries.

At present there is widespread fear of "Arab takeovers" of our industries if we allow them to invest heavily. Aside from the ill-grace of such complaints coming after two decades of heavy American investment in European industry, the fear of Arab investment is rooted in both prejudice and unspoken political assumptions. The prejudice is against the Arabs as people—it is the old stereotype of the Arabs as not quite civilized desert riders who ought not to be trusted, like Europeans, with serious responsibilities like the management of money. The unspoken political assumption, which one detects in the atmosphere, is that extensive new economic ties with the Arab countries will undercut our commitment to Israel, all the more if these ties are in fact mutually rewarding.

For these reasons we are urged against initiatives which are clearly in the national interest. We are urged to erect obstacles to the inflow of funds which we badly need to overcome our foreign payment deficits. The prejudice against the Arabs is as ignorant as it is cruel—Americans who have done business in the Arab world almost always find their counterparts cordial, knowledgeable and reliable. The connection of Arab investment with our commitment to Israel points up two facts: first, that the issues are indeed connected and must be dealt with in relation to each other; second, that when two national interests seem to conflict, the task of leadership is to reconcile them, not to pretend that the conflict does not exist, or to devise rationalization for sacrificing the greater interest to the lesser.

In addition to "recycling" we must conserve energy. Conservation will not only lower our total oil bill; it may induce lower prices by lowering overall demand in relation to the supply. And, for reasons to which I will return, energy conservation may be a boon to the quality of life in our society.

The amount and means by which we shall have to cut back our oil imports is currently in hot debate. At present we consume 17 million barrels of oil a day, of which 7 million barrels a day are imported. The Ford Administration says we must reduce imports by 2 million barrels a day by the end of 1977. Others say the cutback must be much greater—on our part and also on the part of other oil-importing countries—if overall demand is to be reduced sufficiently to bring about a lowering of prices. Still others contend that with discoveries of oil—in the North Sea, Alaska, and off our own east coast there will soon be a glut on the world market, which will knock prices down, and that therefore the current alarm is unwarranted.

Nor is there any more consensus as to the means of cutting imports and consumption. The Administration proposes a program of tariffs combined with the decontrol of our domestic oil and natural gas prices. Some members of Congress deplore this approach as inflationary, preferring import quotas and either a stiff increase in gasoline prices or outright gasoline rationing. At the same time, with unemployment at 8.2 per cent, the highest since the end of the Great Depression in 1941, certain reputable economists are contending that we should postpone cutbacks on oil imports and consumption lest we further deepen the already deep recession.

With these observations I hope that I have clarified for you exactly what must be done to solve the energy crisis and end the recession. More likely I have merely added to your confusion, in which event you have joined company with our leaders and with the experts. The trouble with economics—so appropriately termed the "dismal science"—is that it is replete with propositions which, though equally plausible, are quite contradictory. I do not wish to be unduly alarmist or pessimistic, but one gets a picture these days of a government, and of experts, in confusion and conflict with one another. It would seem almost as if the Marxian prediction of breakdown resulting from the "contradictions" of capitalism were about to become a reality. Mr. Brezhnev himself said in a speech last fall that inflation and economic crises were "speeding up the disintegration of the political machinery of capitalist rule," and that this indeed was "unavoidable" because it stemmed from the "very nature of capitalism."[2]

My own belief is that things are bad but not that bad. I feel reasonably hopeful that through tax cuts and other means of "pump-priming" we will gradually pull out of the current recession—although probably at the cost of rekindling inflation. I also believe that we should not allow either the recession or the prospect of new oil strikes to deter us from a stringent program of energy conservation. I have no great objection to the President's proposal for reducing imports through tariffs, although the same result could be achieved quickly and effectively by import quotas. Similarly, I think that the decontrol of domestic oil and natural gas prices makes long-term economic sense if we are to bring demand into balance with supply and also create incentive for new explorations and drillings.

We must also proceed with a carefully balanced but sizable national program for the development of new energy sources. This would include offshore oil drilling, with all possible care being taken to prevent pollution of the sea, and the development of improved technologies for mining coal and for its liquification and gasification at manageable cost. We must also proceed with research and development of the exotic new energy possibilities, including nuclear fusion and solar and geothermal energy. To encourage this it will be necessary, despite our desire to bring oil prices down, to keep them from coming down *too much*. The reason for this is that if oil prices were to drop, say, to their 1973 level, we would lose our incentive to conserve, while industry would lose its incentive to invest in the new energy sources which we are absolutely certain to need within the next decade or so. To deal with this problem Secretary Kissinger has suggested that the major oil importers agree to use tariffs or other means to maintain a "common floor price" on oil imports, considerably lower, we would hope, than the current price, but high enough to encourage the development of alternate energy sources.

Devising the best means of conservation at home requires us to go beyond immediate economic considerations and take into account the long-term necessities of our society and environment. I would suggest, therefore, that we focus our conservation measures on that most energy-wasteful, environmentally destructive, and socially obsolete feature of American life, the heavy, over-powered private automobile. Here on the broad plains of Kansas the pressures of over-crowding and urban pollution may seem remote, but they are real and pressing in the great urban centers. At the same time we have come into a period, at least for the next decade or so, of costly energy. Both of these factors combine to make the big private automobile a kind of dinosaur in modern America. In our urban areas we are going to have to rely increasingly on mass public transport. And both in and out of the cities we are going to have to trade in our gas-guzzling limousines and sports-cars for smaller, lighter vehicles which can go 25 to 30 miles or more on a gallon of gasoline. To encourage this I would recommend the following: an excise tax on new automobiles steeply graduated according to fuel efficiency; a legally imposed limit on automobile horsepower; and an increase in the federal gasoline tax of whatever amount is necessary to curb consumption substantially, with a system of rebates for individuals whose livelihoods depend upon their car or trucks or tractors.

As I suggested earlier, energy conservation could bring unexpected benefits to our society and life-style. With our current, energy-intensive life-style we Americans are not only living beyond our economic means; we are living beyond our environmental means as well, depleting not only the world's fossil fuels but also many other renewable raw materials. We are also consuming renewable resources such as fish faster than the earth's natural processes can replace them, and fouling the rivers and oceans beyond their natural capacity for cleansing themselves.

We have fallen into what may be called a "technological illusion" about the good life. The more machines and gadgets we possess, and the more energy we therefore consume, the better we think our lives are—as if living affluently were the same as living well. In fact they are not the same. Living well requires a certain harmony with nature, a sense of pace about time, the taking of pleasure in simple things—the view of a mountain or the sea, a fine day, the company of family and friends.

The average American today consumes twice the energy he consumed thirty years ago, twice as much as is now consumed by a European, and perhaps 50 times as much energy as a Chinese. Do you suppose for a moment that the average American is now twice as happy as he used to be, or twice as happy as the average German or Frenchman, or fifty times as happy as a Chinese farmer? There is certainly no visible relationship between our greatly increased energy consumption of recent years and, say, the quality of our architecture, or of our literature, or of urban life in general. The thought arises that such improvements in our civilization might be encouraged by *diminished* energy consumption. The philosopher and microbiologist Rene Dubos suggests that intensive use of industrial energy frees us of the necessity to make creative and adaptive responses to environmental challenges. It "makes for an easier life," he writes, "but it impoverishes our experience."[3] It may be, therefore, that the end—or interruption—of the age of cheap energy may give us incentive to redirect our creative powers from growth and gadgetry to a renewed concern with the quality of life and culture and the environment, freeing us from the illusion that technology is progress.

The Arab-Israel Conflict

There is another whole aspect to the energy crisis, and that is its close relationship to the Arab-Israel conflict. Our efforts to deal with both have been blunted, in large part indeed thwarted, by the illusion, or pretense, that they have nothing to do with each other. In fact, as I suggested earlier, they have a great deal to do with each other, not only because the oil price revolution was precipitated by the war of October 1973, but because the principal Arab oil producers, notably Saudi Arabia, perceive and act upon two issues—oil and Israel—in relation to each other.

As I also suggested earlier, I believe that access to oil is the greater of our interests in the Middle East, a *vital* interest, whereas our commitment to Israel is a less-than-vital interest. I believe too that the all-out supporters of current Israeli policy in Congress and elsewhere are well aware of this priority of interests, and precisely because they do recognize it, contend that the two issues are unrelated. Only by denying the connection can support of Israeli policy be given precedence over our national energy requirements. The issue is further obfuscated by the invocation of "idealism" on Israel's behalf. To this I would suggest that there are other ideals involved besides Israel's democracy and vitality—impressive though these are—including the ideal of self-determination for the Palestinian people. But even more I would stress again that our Government is not an *eleemosynary* institution: its first obligation is to the security and welfare of the *American* people, not perhaps to the extent of exclusiveness but certainly to the extent of primacy.

In practice I do not believe it is necessary to sacrifice oil to Israel, or Israel to oil. Indeed, I believe it to be perfectly feasible to achieve both an equitable settlement which will assure the survival and security of Israel and also solidify our good political and economic relations with the Arab countries. In order to do this, however, it is necessary to appreciate the convergence of the two issues—oil and Israel—and also to appreciate the central importance of Saudi Arabia in this linkage.

Within OPEC the countries most insistent on repeated price increases have not been the Arab states, but two of the principal non-Arab producers, Iran and Venezuela. The largest oil exporter with the largest reserves, Saudi Arabia, has shown a keen awareness of the dangerous disruptions threatened by the four-to-five-fold increase in the price of oil, and Saudi officials have made known—both publicly and privately in unmistakable terms—their strong desire to lower prices and to work out long-term supply arrangements for the industrial nations, especially the United States. The Saudis are motivated by strong feelings of friendship and also of reliance upon the United States. Greatly fearing communism and Soviet and Chinese influence in the Arabian peninsula, Saudi Arabia looks to the United States as its mainstay against communism in the Middle East.

But the Saudis are caught in a dilemma. It is exceedingly difficult, if not impossible, for them to accommodate the United States while the United States provides the money and arms which enable Israel to occupy Arab lands. Further—and this is the heart of the matter—King Faisal feels a special responsibility—indeed a stewardship—for the holy places of Islam. Second only to Mecca in sanctity to Muslims is Jerusalem, where the Dome of the Rock is located, scarcely a hundred yards from the Wailing Wall, which is Judaism's holiest site, and within a half-mile of the Christian shrine, the Church of the Holy Sepulchre.

As a city sacred to three religions, Jerusalem warrants a special status. Exactly what the status is is less important than that it be acceptable to all parties. It might be feasible to re-partition the city between the "old" Arab sector and the "new" Israeli city as before 1967, but providing for free access to all the religious shrines, and perhaps redrawing the boundary to include the Wailing Wall within the Jewish sector. Or, as has often been suggested, Jerusalem could be internationalized in accordance with the original United Nations partition plan of 1947.

Equally as important as Jerusalem for a just and durable settlement is the provision for self-determination by the Palestinian people. Forcibly expelled from their homes and country, and subjected for over a quarter-century to the harsh privation of refugee camps, the Palestinian people are deserving of restitution just as the Jewish people were deserving of restitution after World War II. They have as much right to a homeland as do the Jewish people, and they have shown, moreover, that they can and will persist in their guerrilla warfare until they get one. Accordingly, a reasonable settlement must allow of a Palestinian state being established in the territories now occupied by Israel on the West Bank of the Jordan River and the Gaza strip. Alternately, the Palestinians might form a confederation with the Kingdom of Jordan, but the choice must be theirs and, by all current indications, that would not be their choice.

Far from "selling out" Israel, a settlement based on Israeli withdrawal to the approximate borders of 1967, along with explicit great power guarantees, would call upon Israel to do nothing more than she ought to do anyway, even if there were not a drop of oil in the Middle East. Indeed it would be to Israel's advantage—probably her salvation—because there can be no lasting security for that small, beleaguered community without a settlement, and there can be no settlement without withdrawal. For the United States the occasion—if we rise to it—is one of those rare and happy ones in which justice and self-interest coincide.

Five years ago, in a remarkable but little-noted article, the President of the World Jewish Congress, Dr. Nahum Goldmann, raised the question of whether an Israel armed to the teeth and repeatedly at war could fulfill the Zionist ideal of a homeland for Jewish culture and religion. Noting too that the long-term balance of power would inevitably swing to the Arabs with their vastly greater numbers, their oil wealth, and their growing technological capacity, Dr. Goldmann concluded that Israel should seek to become a neutralized state, somewhat like Switzerland, guaranteed by the nations of the world, including the Arab nations. "I was always a political

Zionist," Dr. Goldmann wrote at that time, "in the sense that I believed that Jews must have a state of their own to secure their identity and civilization. More and more, however, I am coming to the conclusion that Israel cannot be one of the more than a hundred so-called sovereign national states as they exist today and that, instead of relying primarily and exclusively on its military and political strength, it should be not merely accepted but guaranteed, de jure and de facto, by all the peoples of the world, including the Arabs, and put under the permanent protection of the whole of mankind."[4]

Is such an arrangement remotely feasible from the Arab point of view? "Whoever knows the Arabs," Dr. Goldmann also wrote, "their history and character, agrees that pride is one of their most excessive virtues. But an appeal to the generosity of the Arabs, to be guarantors with the rest of the world for a Jewish state in a tiny part of the tremendous territories at their disposal—however unrealistic it may sound at the moment—may be more effective in the long run for an Arab-Israeli co-existence than one Israeli victory after another."[5]

How, as a practical matter, should American and other statesmen proceed toward the achievement of so desirable an arrangement? I would suggest two essential changes of approach: we must accept the Russians as full partners in the making and guarantee of a Middle East peace; and the Israelis must accept the Palestinians, represented by the Palestinian Liberation Organization, as negotiating partners with a right to form a state of their own.

Although Secretary Kissinger has made admirable progress with his disengagement agreements, and may on his current trip secure another Sinai disengagement, there are limits to the progress that can be made through the current "step-by-step" approach. Welcome and impressive as the withdrawals in Sinai and the Golan Heights have been, they do not deal with the central, crucial issues of Jerusalem and the West Bank. As the noted Egyptian journalist Mohammed Heykal notes, this is a policy of "pacification" rather than of "seeking a solution," and it is insufficient because "You cannot pacify forever."[6]

Nor can the Soviets be expected to acquiesce in a process, or a settlement, from which they have been excluded. If and when peace is finally made, the guarantee of the Soviet Union will be hardly less important than our own. One hopes that American diplomats will not succumb once again to what Mr. Heykal calls their "hunter's instinct," the old geopolitical impulse to "expel" Soviet influence from the Middle East while detaching Egypt from the other Arab countries.

We should, therefore, proceed as quickly as possible after Mr. Kissinger's current mission to convene the Geneva conference under the co-chairmanship of the Soviet Union and the United States, and to negotiate through that forum a general settlement based on Israeli withdrawal to the 1967 borders, self-determination for the Palestinian people, and a special status for Jerusalem, all under the guarantee of the great powers as members of the Security Council of the United Nations. I would also hope that consideration might be given to Dr. Nahum Goldmann's proposal for a neutralized Israel. And as I have suggested on numerous occasions for the last five years, I would think it appropriate for the United States to re-enforce the general guarantee of Israel with an explicit, bilateral American guarantee through a treaty ratified by the Senate.

Through these means we can, I believe, reconcile our three major interests in the Middle East—access to oil, the security of Israel, and the avoidance of confrontation with the Soviet Union. An Arab-Israel settlement will not solve our energy crisis or assure the reduction of oil prices. It would, however, eliminate the major irritant in relations between the United States and the Arab states— especially Saudi Arabia—and in so doing create a much improved environment for negotiations on oil supply and prices. A settlement making just provision for the old city of Jerusalem and for the other occupied territories would greatly increase the political influence of Saudi Arabia, and therefore its weight as a force for moderation within OPEC. Saudi Arabia would be liberated, in effect, to do what King Faisal and his ministers want very much to do: cooperate to keep the West, and especially the United States on which Saudi Arabia relies, prosperous and strong.

There is not now—nor has there ever been—any basic incompatibility among our interests in the Middle East. Our difficulty in reconciling them has been the result of our own illusions about the priority of those interests in relation to each other. These illusions of course are not entirely accidental; they have been fostered and promoted by ardent and skillful lobbying. Of late, I note with satisfaction, some serious reassessment seems to have been taking place. The new Chairman of the Senate Foreign Relations Committee, Senator Sparkman, recently expressed his support for a Palestinian state and for a settlement guaranteed by the Soviet Union and the United States in cooperation with the United Nations Security Council.[7] Similarly, Senator Percy of Illinois, a sincere friend of Israel, gained a new impression of the Palestinians in the course of a recent visit to the Middle East, stating upon his return that the PLO leader, Mr. Arafat, is "relatively speaking, a moderate." Senator Percy also advocated Israel's withdrawal to the approximate borders of 1967 and suggested, most sensibly, that "we cannot support Israel indiscriminately."[8]

Interests, it appears, are being recognized, and illusions dispelled—slowly and belatedly to be sure, but that is the way of statecraft. "Common sense," as Voltaire noted, "is not so common." By contrast with our prodigies of technology, we do not seem to advance very quickly when it comes to the running of nations, the reconciling of interests, or the sensible conduct in general of human affairs. But we do sometimes manage it, and in that we can take hope. As Dr. Johnson said of the dog walking on his hind legs, "It is not done well; but you are surprised to find it done at all."

Notes:

1. "National Commitments," *Report Prepared for Committee on Foreign Relations,* April 16, 1969, p. 9.

2. Quoted by Victor Zorza in "Kissinger's Global Scenario," *The Washington Post,* October 15, 1974, p. A20.

3. "Less Energy, Better Life," *New York Times,* January 7, 1975, p. 33.

4. Nahman Goldmann, "The Future of Israel," *Foreign Affairs,* April, 1970, p. 453.

5. *Ibid.,* p. 454.

6. Mohammed Hassanein Heykal, former editor of *Al Ahram,* "Pulling Back from the Mideast Precipice," *New York Times,* January 16, 1975, p. 41.

7. "Palestinian State is Proposed," *Philadelphia Inquirer,* January 10, 1975.

8. "Percy Sees Limits to American Aid for Israelis," *New York Times,* January 29, 1975.

David S. Broder (1929–) is a journalist and author on political issues. He has written for the *Congressional Quarterly, Washington Star, New York Times,* and the *Washington Post,* where he has been an editor since 1975. His books include *The Republican Establishment, The Party's Over, The Failure of Politics in America, Changing of the Guard, Power and Leadership in America.* He received the Pulitzer Prize for journalism in 1973.

American Politics in the Carter Era

David S. Broder

David Broder, Pulitzer Prize-winning columnist for the Washington Post, *offered in his 1977 Landon Lecture a perceptive analysis of the presidency of Jimmy Carter. His analysis is interesting in comparison with Arthur Schlesinger's discussion of the 1968 election. Like Schlesinger, Broder places the election in the context of longer-term trends in American society. Some of the trends, as Broder observes, are mutually contradictory: most notably the pressures to reduce "big government" and the demand for continued governmental responses to social and economic problems in America. Both of these themes have appeared repeatedly in other Landon lectures over the years. The speeches by Hubert Humphrey, Ronald Reagan, Ted Kennedy, and Tip O'Neill, all reprinted in this volume, touch on various aspects of the issue. Broder's analysis is also interesting in retrospect, given Jimmy Carter's subsequent problems as president and his loss in 1980 to Ronald Reagan. Broder accurately defined inflation as a problem which Carter would fail to solve only at his political peril.*

DECEMBER 9, 1977

Governor Landon, may I say to you here what I said to you backstage, that while I have had the opportunity to shake your hand only once before, the letters that you have written me over the years when something that I had written came to your attention have been the source, I think, of as much pleasure and pride for me as a journalist as anything that has come my way. I am honored deeply, sir, to be here as a participant in this lecture series that bears your distinguished name.

What I want to try to do in these formal remarks is to relate the Carter presidency, at least as much of it as we've had a chance to see so far, to some of the broader themes and more basic trends in our politics, in our country, and to some extend even in the world.

This is a risk, because I think the hardest thing journalists do is to step back far enough from the day-to-day events which are the grist for our mill to get perspective on some of these long range trends. So there are no guarantees at all that go with this analysis.

The proposition that I would like to examine with you, is this: I think that it is possible to describe much of what has been happening in the Carter presidency as the product of his efforts to cope with three sets of opposing forces that operate in the contemporary world. Each of them, interestingly, was important to Carter's election and each now poses serious problems for his performance as president.

By examining these three sets of opposing forces, I hope that we may gain a few insights not just about the character of this president and this presidency, but about this time in American politics.

The first set of forces that I think we have to try to describe and analyze are those that we shorthand in journalism very conveniently and very inaccurately when we talk about conservatism and liberalism. As Governor Landon, I hope, will not be displeased to hear, even the *Washington Post* and its political reporter have come to understand in recent years that the basic political trend in this country has been in the conservative direction. I think that trend is traceable back almost with an unbroken line to the mid term election of 1966. That was, for some of you younger people in the audience, not really a referendum on Vietnam, although it has often been described in those terms. It was the public reaction to the great rush of legislative activity which President Johnson pushed through the Congress after the 1964 landslide—the creation in rapid-fire order of the major elements of what he called "The Great Society."

The message that the voters were delivering in that mid term election, when they gave the Republicans their biggest victory in a congressional election in a very long time, was that they felt that process had gone far enough, fast enough. They were about choked on the amount of new social legislation increasing the size of government, that had been passed in very rapid order.

From 1966 on, probably the most significant development in our internal politics, it seems to me, has been the embedding of inflation as the major concern of the American people. There have been some variations in the polls; there have been times when the Vietnam war displaced inflation as the major concern; there have been times when unemployment has come close to rivaling it as a concern. But even in the depths of the last recession more people said they were worried about inflation than said that they were worried about unemployment.

Along with that change has come a growing belief—as measured by the polls and as measured by everything that I can see in American politics—a growing belief that the root cause of inflation in our society is not the greediness of big business, or the insatiability of the demands of big labor. Rather, people have come to identify inflation as being caused principally by excessive spending on the part of the federal government.

Now, how does this relate to Jimmy Carter? I think, the growing conservative political atmosphere in this country was more easily realized by Democratic politicians operating outside of Washington than by the Congressional Democrats who make Washington their home.

In a long career of serious political misjudgments one of the few recent things that I can look back on and say, "Well, for once you were on target, Broder," was an article I wrote for the *Atlantic Monthly* in the spring of 1974 about the condition of the Democratic party. In it I said that the strongest prospects among the Democrats' presidential possibilities, in terms of electability, although at the time not the likeliest to be nominated—were their southern governors.

And I mentioned specifically Reubin Askew of Florida, Dale Bumpers of Arkansas, and Jimmy Carter of Georgia. I said those men in their states had had to learn something which few of the northern liberal presidential hopefuls in Congress had had to learn—namely, how to develop public support for progressive policies in an essentially conservative political climate.

Carter, who was the only one of the three who took the chance on running for the presidency, exploited that insight, and exploited it very effectively, particularly in the primaries against other Democrats. He ran as a more conservative Democrat in the primaries than most of his opponents—George Wallace probably being the major exception to that. I don't want to minimize the importance of the tactical skill, the timing, the concentration of resources, that was part of it. But I think essentially what underlay the Carter victories in the spring of last year was his realization that there was a growing constituency, even within the Democratic party, for a more conservative approach to fiscal and economic policy. He kept almost all the other liberal candidates out and had George Wallace almost to himself except in Florida. In the key victories that marked Carter's path to the nomination—New Hampshire, Illinois, Wisconsin, Pennsylvania, Ohio—his vote came from the conservative side of the party. It came from the small towns and the rural areas, including traditionally Republican areas. It did not come from the big cities which had been the traditional base of Democratic presidential candidates and presidential victories.

On the other hand, and this is where the opposing force comes in, once Jimmy Carter became the nominee of the Democratic party, opposing Gerald Ford, he had to come to terms with other constituencies and other forces. Organized labor, the teachers, minorities, big city mayors, the activists of the consumer movement, and the environmental movement, all raised their issues and their demands with this man who was going to be the nominee of their party. They raised issues that were on their agenda and, if you will, I think you can think about those issues as being the leftovers from the New Deal-Great Society agenda.

The most important of those are: civil rights, which in our times has been translated into a question of affirmative action; the issue of welfare and income support; the issue of national health insurance; the issue of pollution; the issue of consumer protection; and concentrating all of these in one place, the question of the future of the old central cities with their decaying housing and fiscal structure.

Carter had to recognize those forces and he began to give them acknowledgment. The first sign that he knew of their power and potency was in his choice of the vice presidential candidate, Walter Mondale, who was probably the favorite of those traditionally liberal forces inside the Democratic party. But if you remember also in the period right after the the convention, he made a number of visits and speeches to union conventions; he held a well-publicized meeting with Ralph Nader, and took other actions symbolizing his sympathy to the liberal agenda.

The man who had in his earlier primaries been opposed to a federal bail-out of New York City, reluctant to endorse the Humphrey-Hawkins Bill, opposed to federal control of natural gas prices, reversed and revised his positions or modified them substantially on all those issues.

And immediately in the Carter entourage you began to see the tension that was going to result from that. Rosalynn Carter, then as always a terribly important force in her husband's political career and political views, said to him very bluntly, "You have forgotten why people voted for you in the primaries. They weren't voting for you as the traditional Democratic advocate of all of those big federal programs. They were voting for you because you were more conservative than those other Democrats."

But Jimmy Carter knew that if he was going to be elected against an incumbent Republican president, he had to appeal to those core Democratic constituents. As Pat Caudell, his pollster, said in his post-election memo, Carter won essentially because he was able, in a policy of deliberate ambiguity, to get southerners to vote for him as a southerner and northerners to vote for him as a Democrat.

Jimmy Carter defeated Gerry Ford, I think in large part, because he won the unemployed and those concerned about the unemployed, who believed that he would do more on that problem, because the blacks believed that he would do more on the issues of welfare and poverty and education and the plight of the cities; and because those big city mayors, some of whom remembered that famous headline in the *New York Daily News* which ascribed incorrectly to Ford the view "Drop Dead, New York," came to Carter's aid. The cities, which had not supported Carter in the primaries— New York, Philadelphia and Pittsburgh and the rest—came through for him in the general election.

The tension that was visible in that period before the general election has not dissipated since he became president. It is there today. It is there acutely today in the current struggles between the demands from the Department of Health, Education and Welfare, Housing and Urban Development, and others, for expanded social programs, against the efforts of the president and the Office of Management and Budget to exert budget discipline.

The clearest way you can express that tension is this: if Jimmy Carter succumbs and allows the kind of increase in federal spending that his domestic department chiefs are pushing for and the result of that excessive spending is a return to severe inflation—double digit inflation in this country—then his own political advisers believe that he has sealed his defeat in the 1980 election.

On the other hand, to the extent that he denies those constituencies and governs in terms of what he assumes to be the general conservative mood of the country; to the extent that he alienates labor, the teachers, the blacks, the mayors, the environmentalists, the consumer advocates, he guarantees himself a serious challenge for renomination from the "Candidate of the Left" in the Democratic party. So that is one tension that I think operates within this administration.

The second that I would mention is the tension between the forces of centralization in our government and decentralization. Here it seems to me we are dealing with one of the major shifts that has taken place in American society and American politics in recent years. For years, from the time of the New Deal through the time of the Great Society, there was a prescribed pattern to national politics. When the Democrats in power discovered that there was a problem out there in the country, they invented a program in Washington to deal with that problem and they created an agency in Washington to administer that program. The beneficiaries of that program then became the clientele of that agency, and the political supporters of the party and government that brought that program and agency into existence. This was the characteristic pattern of Democratic administrations from Franklin Roosevelt through Lyndon Johnson. I have to say that I think it was not a bad thing for this country, because it did deal to some extent with some real problems that were there in our society. But it is now the victim of its own success.

As Americans have become more affluent, and particularly as

Americans have become more educated, we have reached the point where most of us are no longer satisfied to be part of a client-patron relationship with our government. We have a citizenry now that wants to have a very direct and immediate sense that they have a voice themselves in those decisions that affect the quality of their own lives. Particularly, they want to have a direct voice in those institutions which make a major difference in the quality of their own neighborhoods and communities, schools, police—all of the factors that make a difference as to whether you live comfortably, safely, and securely in your own community.

Republicans recognized, I think, this secular change in our society. They had no doctrinal difficulties in accepting it because they had been skeptics and critics of big federal government for a very long time. With Richard Nixon they began a program called New Federalism. The landmark, perhaps the only major achievement of that program, was the general revenue-sharing program. It was a first step in redirecting resources and control away from Washington and back to states and local communities. It was not a full and evolved theory of devolution in the Nixon administration. I don't think they had worked out even theoretically the question of which functions ought to remain in Washington and which ought to be turned over to the states and which ought to be turned back to local communities. But they started in this direction.

Now once again, one finds an interesting and a direct connection with Jimmy Carter. He was one of the few Democrats who engaged himself seriously in the debate about general revenue sharing, and the rest of the New Federalism program. He was a critic of much of what the Nixon administration was attempting to do, but he did not share the point of view of those Congressional Democrats who said, "It is wrong to take any of this power away from Washington." On the contrary, Charlie Kirbo, one of Carter's closest friends—one of his few friends of his own age—once said to a group of us, "It's important to remember when you're talking about this president, this man, that the most frustrating experiences of his adult life did not come in his dealings with the big banks or the big businesses. They came in his dealings with big federal government, looking at it from the perspective of a local official, a state senator, a governor." Carter was interested in effective moves to decentralize power in this country and his criticism of the Nixon program was not that it was headed in the wrong direction, but that it was not traveling the right path at the right rate of speed. He recognized, as very few Democrats operating in Washington did recognize, the extent of the public disillusionment with that big federal bureaucracy. And again if I may quote Pat Caudell's studies in his post-election memo, he said that the single issue which most clearly identified and distinguished Carter from the other candidates in 1976 and which contributed significantly to his victory was his pledge to reorganize and reduce what he always called the "bloated federal bureaucracy."

Along with that was a pledge that he would make that a matter of high priority by becoming a domestic president. As you remember he said, "I do not plan to travel overseas in my first year as president." He said he thought the problems that we have to deal with are the problems here at home and many of those problems are right here in Washington, where we have a government structure which interferes with the efficient operation of our private economy and our private society.

There is in this case as in the other, however, an opposing and countervailing force at work. It is a force that is increasingly making it impossible for a president, or anyone else, to distinguish and to maintain a sharp line of demarcation between domestic and foreign policy. Because there can be no such distinction made, there is an inevitable tendency to push, not for decentralization of power, not for tearing down the federal bureaucracy, but for more centralized government and increased bureaucracy.

In the past when we talked about the foreign involvements of the United States, what we tended to think of were principally the issues of war and peace and national defense. When Franklin Roosevelt moved from being Dr. New Deal to Dr. Win the War, we understood that there was a clear shift from a domestic to an international priority. But as you know, defense spending has been shrinking as a percentage of the gross national product and as a share of the federal budget, and the concern with issues of war and peace as measured by public opinion polls has been diminishing as a factor in the psychology and thinking of American voters. What is now pulling us—and pulling us strongly—into the international orbit are not defense issues but economic issues. And the reason that is happening, of course, is that with every passing day, this world becomes more interdependent as an economic unit. It is increasingly difficult for a president to be domestic, because almost every domestic issue that he wants to tackle turns out to have important international dimensions. It is significant as a sign of this that the first Carter trip abroad, the one on which he broke his promise, was to—what—an international economic summit in London. The growth of the US economy, which has to be his major concern, is tied ineluctably to the decisions that are being made in Germany and in Japan. If there is unemployment in the steel mills in Youngstown, the answer has to be sought—where—in Tokyo, in Bonn, in Cologne. What is true of steel is equally true of agriculture and what is true of industry and agriculture is also true of the consumer's worry about inflation. The pattern of international trade, the availability of goods in the international market has a major effect on consumer prices. And of course and most obviously, it is true of the issue that has been given top priority by this president, the issue of energy.

What we are seeing here is the internationalization of what we used to think of as domestic problems. And as an iron law, when domestic problems become internationalized, it produces an inevitable effect of bringing those issues to the national government, expanding the power, the responsibility, the scope, and the bureaucracy in the national government. Thus this president, who had as his central pledge an effort to reduce the size and the complexity of the national government, has, as the landmark achievement of his first year—what—the addition and creation of a brand new cabinet-level, department of energy, whose size is larger initially than that of five of the old cabinet departments. Does it mean that he is dishonest? No, it means in my judgment that he is pressured by forces that are operating beyond his own control.

It has also produced a clear shift in his priorities. He is not a domestic president. He is as much of an international president, in terms of his focus and his use of time, as any of his predecessors. A president has only limited time available. Time that is spent worrying about the Middle East or worrying about Japanese trade policies is not spent reorganizing the federal government. And just as Richard Nixon found China more compelling than the passage of General Revenue Sharing, so Jimmy Carter finds his international issues more compelling than reorganizing federal agencies.

The third set of tensions, and the last, deals with what I would call the pattern of entrepreneurial politics, individualized politics, versus the need for coordinated national policy. I have written and talked about it so much in recent years that I don't want to spell it out in great detail for you here. I don't think it's necessary. But clearly, one of the major trends of the last 25 years in American politics has been the decline of the political party as a basic institution for working through conflicts in our society. The root causes of that decline are many and fundamental. They range from the development of television as the principal means of mass communication to the decline of patronage, and the rise of civil service, as well as some historical accidents, such as Dwight Eisenhower and Lyndon Johnson and a few other people, each of whom made his own contribution to the decline of the role of the political party.

Suffice it to say that without the weakening of the political party, Jimmy Carter could never have become the nominee of the Democratic party. He was certainly not the choice of those who traditionally, in the past, had controlled Democratic party nominations. He was not familiar to, and certainly not originally very sympathetic, to major labor leaders. He was an unknown to members of Congress and to the intellectual community. And as for his position with his peers, I suppose one of the great ironies is that a man who could not have been elected chairman of the National Governors' Conference was nonetheless the choice of the Democratic convention for President of the United States.

But those insiders no longer control the nominations of the political parties, because the political parties' structure has become so weakened and diffused that that kind of centralized control is no longer possible or even, as viewed by most people, desirable.

Carter was a true outsider, and like most modern presidents chosen under this system, he is surrounded by his own political aides on the White House staff, men who tend to see the answer to governmental problems in doing the same sort of thing that they did in the campaign.

What is the offsetting force in this case? It is that this kind of autonomous president, who got there on his own by running his own campaign for a very long time with his own staff, and who says proudly, "I owe the special interests nothing," now comes to occupy an office where the ability of a president to get things done on his own has been substantially reduced.

The presidency is in a weakened condition as an agency of national leadership today. It has been weakened by important historical events—by the Vietnam war, by Watergate. It has particularly been weakened in its relationship to Congress, because the response of the Congress to these calamities of Vietnam and Watergate, that have overtaken the president, has been to assert its own claim to power very aggressively against the president.

Congress has a role in foreign policy now, greater than it has had in the past. Congress has a role in domestic policy now, greater than it has had in the past. Congress, for the first time, has given itself an effective institutional mechanism through its own budget process to exert a greater power in budget and fiscal decisions than it has in the past. The personalities and force of character and force of will of key congressmen has been greater than that of recent presidents. A Tip O'Neill, a Bob Byrd, a Russell Long, do not regard themselves as being in any way—constitutionally, institutionally, or politically—in an inferior position to the president. What resources of leadership does the president have? Is he really the leader of the Democratic party? Is he able through his own alliances with leaders of business and labor and other interest groups to mobilize those forces on his behalf? No, it is Jimmy Carter, the peanut farmer from Plains, still very much out there on his own, coping with the world as best he can, with whatever help he can get from those young men who have been his associates in this long and lonely struggle to the top.

Most of the Democrats in the Congress of the United States had never served with a Democratic president until the moment, last January 20, when Jimmy Carter raised his hand and took the oath of office. All their experience, all their skills, had come in a time of political combat with Republican presidents. They gave themselves heavy weapons for that struggle. They learned to use them effectively and they did use them effectively to challenge the power of presidents. The fact that a new man moved into the White House with a D in back of his name, instead of an R, did not change their inclination to exert that power to the full. What we have seen in this past year, in my judgment, is not a unique or unusual situation. It is probably a foretaste of American politics. With our weakened political party structure, with our autonomous but weakened president, it is now possible to have, literally, a situation in which you have an opposition Congress of the same party as the president.

Now what does all this mean? What I have been trying to say, at greater length than was necessary, is that the dilemmas that President Carter faces in his term in office stem from some of the basic forces that are operating on the modern presidency and on the modern American society: pitting the demands of special constituencies for increased governmental assistance and increased governmental intervention against the general resistance of the public to further growth of governmental power; pitting the powerful anti-Washington decentralizing tendencies in the public against the need for central government management of international economic issues: pitting our entrepreneurial, individualistic politics against the need for a mechanism for greater sharing of power, particularly between the executive and legislative branches.

All of these forces, in my judgment, essentially are destabilizing forces in their impact on our politics and on our governmental system. I think they explain why it is so hard, not just for this president, but for modern presidents generally, to avoid frustration at the personal level, at their inability to move government policy in the direction that they want it to go, and, at the public level, to avoid a sense of public disillusionment and disappointment in their performance of office.

Gerald R. Ford (1913–) was President of the United States from August of 1974 to January of 1977. Elected to Congress in 1948, he was subsequently reelected twelve times and became Minority Leader of the House of Representatives in 1965. He was a supporter of the Nixon administration and a defender of its Vietnam policies. In 1973, he was named Vice President by President Nixon when Spiro Agnew was forced to resign. His appointment was confirmed by wide margins in both the Senate and the House. On August 9, 1974, he became the 38th President upon the resignation of Richard Nixon. In September, he provoked a public outcry by pardoning Nixon of all federal crimes he may have committed. In 1976, he was narrowly defeated in the presidential election by Jimmy Carter.

The War Powers Resolution

Gerald R. Ford

President Gerald Ford spoke in the Landon Lecture Series on February 20, 1978, approximately a year after his departure from the White House. Like many of the lectures in the series, his topic was both specific to the era in which it was given and indicative of a more fundamental issue in the American political system. The narrower, more specific, question was the War Powers Resolution, passed by Congress in 1973. The more fundamental issue was the separation of powers and the check-and-balance system built into the American Constitution, especially the Presidential-Congressional struggle for dominance. Having served in leadership positions in both the legislative and executive branches—as House Minority Leader, then as Vice President and President—Ford was in a unique position to comment upon this issue. Unlike Presidents Nixon and Reagan, whose Landon Lectures were delivered during their presidencies, Ford was under no political compulsion to defend either his record or the office of president in his public comments. Although his final position, on balance, favors the presidential side of the issue, his argument is both well-reasoned and reflective of his long and varied experience in government.

FEBRUARY 20, 1978

President Acker, Governor Landon, Governor Bennett, distinguished state officials, my former colleague in the House of Representatives, Keith Sebelius, members of the faculty, student body and guests. It's a great privilege and a very high honor to have the opportunity of being on the Kansas State University campus. I'm especially honored to have the privilege of giving a Landon Lecture on public issues.

I thank Governor Landon, I thank the University, and I thank all of you for this wonderful experience. I was looking over the list of people who have previously given the Landon Lecture and it's a very prestigious group. There was one that struck me because of my long-standing personal friendship with him, a person on the other side of the political aisle, an individual who was sworn into the United States Senate the same day that Jerry Ford became a member of the House on January 3, 1949. I speak of Hubert Humphrey.

Even though we had many differences and even though we discussed issues from a different point of view, over a long period of time, Hubert Humphrey and Jerry Ford became very close friends as did his wife, Muriel and my wife, Betty. I could tell you many wonderful stories about Hubert, but one comes to mind, because it was the last. I was in the nation's capitol in December of last year, and there was a ceremony honoring Hubert.

He had been the author of certain legislation. I, as president, had approved the legislation, signed it into law, so I was asked to participate in the ceremonies. They were held in the Senate caucus room with foreign dignitaries, members of the House and Senate and the press. I was asked to make a few remarks and I paid tribute to a great senator and statesman of this era, and it came from the heart because of our personal relationship.

Hubert then had the opportunity to make some observations and comments. I was sitting to the right, as Governor Landon is at the present time, and Hubert got up and said he had just seen Betty as a commentator on the Bolshoi ballet, when they were performing the *Nutcracker*. He said, "My, she's beautiful, my, she's attractive," and then he turned to me and he said, "Yes, and some people always marry above themselves."

But, it's wonderful to be here on your campus. A fine facility for basketball. I understand that you had a certain victory a week or so ago against a team from the Soviet Union. I congratulate you. I hope the United States is as competitive and as successful against the Soviet Union in our wide variety of contacts as the Wildcats were a week or so ago.

It goes without saying that Governor Landon is one of my favorites in public life. You know probably better than I that Alf Landon has always stood for constructive, affirmative action for those involved in the political arena. He has always worked for the best interests of the United States regardless of partisanship or political philosophy. And all of us are deeply indebted to Governor Landon and wish him the very, very best for a good many more years of good health and good happiness. Alf, it's nice to see you.

Despite my retirement, I've had a rather hectic schedule lately. Last week I was privileged to be a visiting professor on the campus of UCLA in Los Angeles. The weather in southern California, was, how can I say it kindly, a little different from Manhattan.

But it's nice to be here with the students. I enjoyed the one class this morning, and I'll have another this afternoon. I've been to 25 college universities and campuses since leaving office January 20, 1977, and I find regardless of the area that I visited or the college or university campus where I was privileged to be, that the students are bright, optimistic, inquisitive, respectful, and they're deeply concerned as to what is right and what is wrong in our government and our government's policies.

With the thought of those kinds of questions, I would like to discuss the quest or the challenge for a proper balance of power, particularly in foreign policy between the executive and legislative branches of the federal government. This fascinating, frustrating search is as old as our Constitution with roots much deeper in the history of governments. It has, at various times, concerned the Roman Senates and Caesars, the English kings and Parliaments. It has concerned others fully as much as it concerns American presidents and the United States Congress at the present time.

The framers of our Constitution, well-schooled in the history of governments, recognized the need for separate powers as checks and balances among the executive, legislative and judicial branches. They gave the Congress the power to coin money, collect taxes, appropriate funds; to regulate commerce; to establish courts; to raise and support an army; raise and support a navy; to declare war; and to make all the laws necessary and proper for executing the powers of government.

The president on the other hand was assigned the powers of commander-in-chief of the Army and Navy; the appointment of ambassadors, the appointment of judges and other public officials; the veto of congressional legislation; and the power to convene the Congress in special session.

With powers thus divided, neither branch was intended to dominate the other. Yet each has established a clear dominance at stages in America's history. In 1885, a young Woodrow Wilson published his doctoral dissertation on the subject of "Congressional Government." He concluded that the Congress was the dominant branch of government and that the president, and I quote, "was nothing but an ineffective figurehead."

He advised and again I quote, "We think less of checks and balances and more of coordinated power," and that we achieve that coordinated power through "the encouragement of presidential leadership." But the question remains, "how should those powers of the executive and legislative branches be coordinated, especially in the field of foreign policy?"

And I address this question today as one who has been honored to serve at both ends of Pennsylvania Avenue over the past 28 years. As a member of Congress, I often wondered if the presidents with whom I served weren't going too fast in making important decisions and commitments for the United States. I wondered if the White House didn't isolate them too much from public opinion and from the free expression of competing views.

Later, like many modern presidents, I occasionally displayed a certain impatience with the painstaking, deliberative process that is the heart and soul of the legislative branch. The pace of this modern age, however, has been so fast, its problems filled with such urgency, that the parliamentary rules and customs so deeply rooted in our tradition often seem antiquated, petty, agonizingly slow when viewed from the Oval Office in the White House.

So the problems of coordination can be troublesome and they are magnified a thousandfold when foreign policy is involved. In the years just following World War II, while a very junior legislator named Ford was just learning his way around Washington, there was a remarkable degree of national consensus about the role America should play throughout the world. Americans held the very noble conviction that since the United States alone had emerged virtually unscathed by the destruction of war—since the war in fact had made us the most formidable military and economic power on earth—we as Americans had a special responsibility to build a new and better world from the ruins of the old.

We knew, too, that we had been dragged into two world wars we did not want by the collapse of the world political system in 1917 and 1931, and that we could not sit by and let that system collapse again.

This national consensus was made possible by such men as Senator Arthur Vandenburg of Michigan, my own political mentor, who championed bipartisanship in foreign affairs and helped cement, with President Harry Truman, a common bond of purpose in international relations between the legislative and executive branches of government.

Working together, the president and the Congress, it was an easy and rewarding task to guide public opinion and mandate government resources for such monumental efforts as the Marshall Plan, the Point Four Program and NATO. Consensus was also made possible by the recognition of a growing threat from the Soviet Union.

In that early post-war era, the Soviets under Stalin were consolidating their power and authority over the nations of Eastern Europe. They were also probing for footholds in the Middle East, first in Iran and Turkey. Today they are in Africa, especially in Angola and Ethiopia. No one knew how far their aggressive designs might reach, and none denied that if the Soviets in their march were to be stopped, the United States would have to assume the active leadership of the free world.

The nations which had guided European diplomacy for so long no longer had the power to do so, especially before the massive threat of Soviet expansion.

These goals for a new and better world, and these challenges of the cold war, established a foreign policy consensus that endured well into the 1960's.

It is the presidential drama of this period we remember best: Eisenhower pledging to go to Korea; the dramatic summit conferences; Kennedy's courage in the Cuban Missile Crisis.

But underlying every presidential initiative was a broad foundation of support in the United States Congress.

Even in the case of Vietnam, the SEATO treaty was approved by the Senate 82 to 1 in 1955, and the Gulf of Tonkin Resolution was passed in 1964 in the Senate by a vote of 88 to 2, and in the House of Representatives by a vote of 414 to 0.

But as that frustrating war went on year after year after year, our national unity was shattered, and with it the essential foreign policy coordination between the president and Congress. Old assumptions were challenged. Long-standing commitments were called into question. Bipartisanship in foreign policy gave way to deep divisions within the two parties themselves.

Members of Congress who came to oppose the war would also come to oppose the presidents who prosecuted the war. In the end, they would argue that the presidency itself had grown too powerful, that a usurpation of the powers by the president from the Congress was chiefly to blame for our disillusionment and our involvement in Vietnam.

These concerns found legislative expression in the War Powers Resolution of 1973. This resolution claimed for the Congress, in my opinion, unprecedented power in the conduct of foreign policy.

A major and crucial section of the resolution provided that any troop commitment must be terminated within 60 days unless Congress has declared war, specifically authorized the commitment, or has been unable to convene because of an armed attack on the United States. The legislation also specified that, by passage of a concurrent resolution, the Congress can direct the president to remove U.S. forces before the 60-day period expires.

"No more Vietnams" was the theme sounded over and over again in the debate in both the House and Senate on the War Powers Resolution. Senator John Sherman Cooper, a cosponsor of this legislation, reminded his colleagues that "The Congress, particularly since World War II, has not only acceded to, but has supported 'executive requests for congressional authority' to use the armed forces of the United States, if necessary, in hostilities."

"These are settled facts of history," Senator Cooper said. "We can change our course but we cannot revise and rewrite American history."

While the debate on the resolution was underway in 1973, a new and distressing chapter in American history was being written across the front pages of our nation's newspapers. Day after day, new allegations of excessive and misused presidential power were being unveiled. It was in this highly charged atmosphere in the boiling passions of Vietnam and Watergate, and in defiance of President Nixon's veto, that the Congress finally passed the War Powers Resolution.

The debate was framed by constitutional issues. As Professor Eugene Rostow of the Yale University Law School has noted and I quote, "The battle cry of 'constitutional usurpation' quickens the blood of every congressman, indeed of every American. We find it easy," he said, "to conclude that whatever we dislike intensely must therefore be unconstitutional, as well."

But as John Sherman Cooper's good friend in the United States Senate, Senator George Aiken of Vermont has written, the War Powers Resolution was "largely a political effort, an attempt to amend the Constitution by congressional resolution."

The arrangements which the Constitution makes for the conduct of foreign policy involve a complex interplay between the legislative and the executive branches of our federal government. Congress is given the power to declare war and to raise an army and navy. The Senate is given the additional power of advise and consent in the ratification of treaties, the appointment of ambassadors and other officials, including the secretaries of defense and state.

The president, on the other hand, under the Constitution was made commander-in-chief, and head of state. By fundamental definition, certainly by tradition, the chief executive is also given the power to execute American foreign policy. It is not intended that these powers be consolidated in the interest of efficiency, but rather that they be separated in the interest of democracy.

Coordination between the two branches was obviously to be encouraged. The brilliant system of checks and balances which the founding fathers devised was not meant to breed constant, paralyzing confrontation between the president and the Congress of the United States.

But as former Undersecretary of State, George Ball, testified in hearings on the War Powers Resolution: the War Powers Resolution "represents an attempt to do what the founding fathers felt they were not wise enough to do." It seeks by simple legislation to codify the military powers of the president, spelling out exactly what he can and cannot do, and how, and under what circumstances, to defend the United States and its citizens from international danger.

The resolution also grants to the Congress powers which tend to make it superior to the executive branch, as in the provision, for example, that Congress may order the withdrawal of troops within 60 days by a concurrent resolution not subject to presidential veto.

I ask, where are the constitutional checks and balances in such a system? The resolution requires consultation by the president with congressional leaders in military emergencies. Of course, consultation by the president and congressional leaders is a wise and normal feature of our constitutional and political life.

No president with any common sense would dream of neglecting this aspect of his obligation. But can it be mandated by law, and if so, what does it mean as a practical matter? Can the president satisfy the law by having breakfast with three or four or even a dozen if he decides they are the key people? Does the law mean that the leaders of both Houses, both sides of the aisle, key members of relevant committees, can speak for or bind the Congress?

Finally, there is a question of how closely this resolution would involve the Congress in the actual execution, as opposed to the general direction, of foreign policy, particularly in times of crisis. Does the consultation provision require the approval of Congress before executive action is taken? What if the president and the Congress disagree? Which of these separate but equal powers would prevail in such a confrontation?

These arguments, serious as they are, can be more than matched, I might say, by other arguments of workability. The United States was involved in six military crises during my 30 months as president: the evacuation of US citizens and refugees from Da Nang, Phnom Penh and Saigon in the spring of 1975; the rescue of the Mayaguez in May 1975; and two evacuation operations in Lebanon in June of 1976.

In none of these instances did I believe the War Powers Resolution applied. Many members of Congress also questioned its applicability in cases involving protection and evacuation of American citizens. Furthermore, I did not concede that the resolution itself was equally binding or legally binding on the president on constitutional grounds. Nevertheless, in each instance, I took note of its consultation in reporting provisions and provided certain information on operations and strategies to key members of the House as well as the Senate.

Let me stress in my administration it was customary to communicate with the leaders of Congress when an important executive action was about to be taken, particularly any action involving foreign policy. As a former member of Congress and as the minority leader for over nine years in the House of Representatives, I knew from first-hand experience that congressional understanding and support developed with such communication. It is my view that when the president as commander-in-chief undertakes such military operations he would inevitably take the Congress into his confidence in order to receive its advice, and if possible, insure its support.

This type of consultation, as Keith Sebelius knows, makes common sense and certainly strengthens the trust between the executive and the legislative branches. But it is to be distinguished—and I emphasize, "to be distinguished"—from the detailed information and time limits imposed by the War Powers Resolution.

The role of the president in these critical situations is clearly defined by the traditions, if not by the laws. As commander-in-chief and chairman of the National Security Council, my job, as any president's job, was to concentrate on resolving the crises as expeditiously and as successfully as possible. As you might expect, it's a full-time job.

When the situation permitted, as in the case of the Mayaguez, I consulted personally with the bipartisan leadership in the House as well as in the Senate. However, the nature of most of these crisis situations was such that the consultation process with the legislative branch had to be delegated to others, primarily my Congressional Relations staff at the White House.

In the interest of absolute accuracy, a summary of actions that I proposed to take or had taken was drafted by the National Security Council staff. This summary was reviewed by senior officials at the departments of State and Defense and by me at the White House. This careful attention to detail was absolutely essential. But let me assure you it was also time-consuming for senior officials who were at the same time acting as my advisers in a fast-moving international situation.

The information summary often went through two or three drafts to insure, as nearly as possible, that there would be no mistakes, no confusion of highly sensitive information. Once the consultation process began, an inherent weakness of the War Powers Resolution from a practical standpoint was conclusively demonstrated.

When the evacuation of Da Nang was forced upon us during the congressional Easter recess of 1975, not one of the key bipartisan leaders of Congress was in Washington, D.C. Without mentioning names, here is where we found the leaders of Congress at that time: two were in Mexico, three were in Greece, one was in the Middle East, one was in Europe, and two were in the People's Republic of China. The rest we found in 12 widely scattered areas of the United States.

This, one might say, is an unfair example since the Congress was in recess. But it must be remembered that critical world events, especially military operations, seldom wait for the Congress to convene. In fact, most of what goes on in the world happens in the middle of the night Washington time.

On June 18, 1976, we began the first evacuation of American citizens from the tragic civil war in Lebanon. The Congress was not in recess but it had adjourned for the day. As telephone calls were made by my top staff people, we discovered among other things, that one member of Congress had an unlisted number which his press secretary refused to divulge.

After trying and failing to reach another member of Congress, we were told by his assistant that the congressman didn't need to be reached. We tried so hard to reach a third important member of Congress that our resourceful White House telephone operators—and believe me they're the best—had the local police leave a note on the congressman's door, "please call the White House."

When a crisis breaks it is impossible to draw Congress into the decision-making process in an effective way. It's impractical to ask them to be as well-versed in the fast breaking developments as the president, the National Security Council, the Joint Chiefs of Staff, who deal with foreign policy and national security situations every hour of every day.

It is also impossible to wait for a consensus to form among those congressional leaders as to the proper course of action, especially when they are scattered literally around the world when the time is one thing that we cannot spare. The potential legal consequences of taking executive action before mandated congressional consultation can be completed may cause a costly delay. The consequences to the president, if he does not wait for congress, could be as severe as impeachment. But the consequences to the nation, if he does wait, could be far, far worse.

There is absolutely no way American foreign policy can be made or military operations commanded by 535 members of Congress on Capitol Hill, even if they all happen to be on Capitol Hill when they are needed.

Domestic policy for housing, health, education or energy can and should be advanced in the calm deliberation and spirited debate that I loved so much as a member of the House for 25 plus years. The broad outlines and goals of foreign policy also benefit immensely from this kind of meticulous Congressional consideration. But in times of crisis, decisiveness is everything and the Constitution plainly puts the responsibility for such decisions on the shoulders of the president of the United States.

In other cases, in recent years, there have been attempts to introduce the Congress into sensitive negotiations with foreign nations—and in my opinion, all ill-advised.

And let me cite one or two examples. The Jackson-Vanik amendment to the Trade Act of 1972, in effect, sought to liberalize

Jewish immigration from the Soviet Union by legislative decree. But the fact is, that amendment had precisely the opposite effect, the Jewish immigration in '75 and '76 from the Soviet Union went down significantly instead of being increased.

The congressional restrictions on military assistance to Turkey after the Cyprus crisis of 1974 proved how determined and how wrong the Congress can be, and how cumbersome diplomacy by rigid legislative dictate can be.

Where then does the balance of power lie in our system of government at the present time? It cannot lie in a constant rivalry for power. As Professor Rostow has written, this "would tend to convert every crisis of foreign policy into a crisis of will, of pride and of precedence between the president and the Congress." Nor, obviously, does the balance lie in the dominance of one branch of government over the other. The Constitution makes that plain enough and our own history proves that.

Woodrow Wilson refused to involve the Congress in his plans for a League of Nations and saw his noble dream crushed on Capitol Hill. The balance must lie in a frank recognition of the basic strengths and weaknesses of both the executive and legislative branches of our government, in the institutional capabilities as well as limitations imposed by the Constitution and by common sense.

As I said in my last State of the Union Address in January of 1977, "In these times, crises cannot be managed, and war cannot be waged by committee; nor can peace be pursued solely by parlimentary debate. To the ears of the world, the president speaks for the nation. While he is ultimately accountable to the Congress, the courts and to the American people, he and his emissaries must not be handicapped in advance in their relations with foreign governments."

The notion that the president must sometimes use the armed forces of our nation on his own ultimate responsibility comes very, very hard to Americans because we are, and always have been, deeply concerned about democratic control. But this power has been recognized as necessary, even as inescapable, since the earliest days of our Republic. Pirates attack our ships off the coast of Tripoli, the president must respond. The Soviet Union blockades Berlin, or places missiles in Cuba, we must respond. An American ship is seized off the coast of Cambodia, we must respond. And if the nightmare danger of nuclear attack becomes a reality some dread future day, we must respond.

For such challenges, which vary from year to year, and generation to generation, there is no substitute for presidential leadership. But there is always democratic control in the electoral process and in legislative action.

The bitter experience of Vietnam and the national atmosphere in the last decade have encouraged, in my opinion, too much tampering with basic machinery by which the United States government has run successfully for the past 200 years. We must not abandon the wisdom of ages in the passion of a moment. If we have disagreements of policy let us resolve them as matters of policy rather than escalating them into constitutional confrontations.

Tragically, in recent years, the basis of trust, cooperation and civility between the legislative and executive branches of our government have been eroded. In their place there have been attempts to build new and permanent structures on the shaky ground of mutual suspicion.

This is no way for the government to serve the American people. It is, instead, the sure way to division at home and danger abroad. What we need, as Wilson said, is "more coordinated power."

We need to seek, once again, a common ground on which the president, the Congress, and the American people can proudly and firmly stand through crisis as well as calm. We must decide again as a nation what is important to us. What goals will we set, what dangers will we risk, what burdens will we bear in our dealings with a wider and more interdependent world?

The Congress has a responsibility to do what it does best—meet these great issues openly, freely, thoroughly—and help us find a new path on which we may all travel together. The new administration, free of the burden of war, unfettered by the mistakes of the past, has an historic opportunity to lead America to a new age in foreign policy, an age in which the goals and commitments we hold precious as a nation may be fulfilled through the quiet, beneficient strength that commands respect and invites cooperation.

All this will not be easy, as President Carter has discovered. The world is very different now from what it was 30 years ago. We are different. Our problems and aspirations are far more complex, but we are still Americans who love our country, who cherish peace and freedom throughout the world.

Let is us in the months ahead open a constructive dialogue among the American people, the Congress and the president, leaders past as well as present, so we can preserve the bulwark of our strength—the Constitution—and find the mechanisms to combine with spirit, a spirit that has made America what it is today, free and dedicated to a better world for all people. Thank you.

Milton Friedman (1912–) is a leading theorist in economics and a professor emeritus at the University of Chicago. In 1976 he won the Nobel Prize in economics. He is one of the foremost critics of Keynesian economic theories and a vigorous proponent of completely free markets. His books include *Capitalism and Freedom, The Monetary History of the United States,* and *Price Theory.* He is currently at the Hoover Institute at Stanford University.

Free Trade: Producer versus Consumer

Milton Friedman

Several leading economists have spoken in the Landon Lecture Series, including John Kenneth Galbraith, William Simon, Walter Heller, and Paul Volcker. Among the most articulate and influential was Nobel Laureate Milton Friedman, whose free-market theories have been propagated in his books, lectures, and television series. In his Landon Lecture on April 27, 1978, Friedman focused upon the issue of free trade, arguing with his typical clarity and good humor that the free international market is both the most efficient· and the fairest system of trade among nations.
Friedman's argument should be compared with Sheikh Ahmed Zaki Yamani's Landon Lecture, also in this volume. Yamani's equally forceful defense of market controls provides a direct antithesis, at least in the specific instance of the international oil market, to Friedman's free trade doctrines.

APRIL 27, 1978

Thank you, President Acker and all of you on the platform. I observe from the tie which Dr. Flinchbaugh wears, and from several other things around here, that if I am going to be in Kansas State tradition, I must speak purple prose. I shall try to do so without offending you.

There's a standard cliché, which I am sure you have all heard, that if you have two economists in one room you are bound to have at least three opinions.

The subject I am going to talk about today, however, is one subject with respect to which that is not true. With respect to the area of international trade, with respect to the question whether it is desirable for a country to have free trade or to have tariffs and other restrictions on imports and exports, in that particular area economists have spoken with almost one voice for some two-hundred years. Ever since the father of modern economics, Adam

Smith published his great book, *The Wealth of Nations,* in 1776, the same year in which the Declaration of Independence was issued in this country; ever since then the economics profession has been almost unanimous on the subject of the desirability of free trade. Of course, complete unanimity is hardly ever possible, and every once in a while there have been some deviations from the straight and narrow path. Almost always those deviations have reflected not a disagreement with the fundamental message of Adam Smith, not a disagreement that in the good world free trade would be best of all possible courses, but they have tended to reflect special circumstances of the time.

Perhaps the most famous such deviation was by the most noted and some would say notorious of modern economists, John Maynard Keynes, the English economist who gave his name to the Keynesian Revolution. In 1931 in the course of the depression, John Maynard Keynes, who had been a free trader all his life, came out in some articles in Britain in favor of departing from free trade and of introducing tariffs. He did so not because he thought that was in and of itself the best policy, but because he thought that the best policy was politically infeasible. In his view, the right policy for Britain at that time was to go off the gold standard, end a fixed exchange rate, allow the pound sterling to be a free market currency whose price would be determined in the market, as it now is, of course, in a world of floating exchange rates today. But Keynes, an economist, made the political judgment that it was not politically feasible for Britain to go off the gold standard. Tariffs can be an alternative to devaluation. If on the one hand the price of the pound sterling was changed from the four dollars and eighty some cents, which then was its price, to let's say four dollars, that would make British goods cheaper to foreigners; it would make foreign goods more expensive to British residents. In that way, it would redress the problem of the balance of payments they were facing. That's one way to do it and the best way. But Keynes thought that was politically infeasible and it comes to the same thing, to introduce a tariff on imports and a subsidy to exports. That's an indirect and concealed form of devaluation. And so Keynes came out for that concealed form.

His political judgment was like that of many economists, flawed. About three weeks after he came out for a tariff on these grounds, Britain went off the gold standard. I may say that this is not an isolated story. Time and again, economists, in my opinion, have erred when they have proposed second-best solutions in the area where they are experts, namely economics, because of predictions they make about political feasibility in an area where they are not experts. At any rate, Keynes had a very flexible mind and one week after Britain went off the gold standard he retracted his support for tariffs. He published an article saying, now that we have gone off the gold standard, there's no longer any point to tariffs; I return to my free trade principles.

Later when he reprinted that retraction in a book of essays, he appended a footnote, which is a very revealing footnote because it shows how much damage can be done by the tendency for people to preach second-best solutions. He said in his footnote, "Not all my free trade friends proved to be as prejudiced as I had thought, for after a tariff was no longer necessary, many of them were found voting for it." In other words, it's often easier to turn people in the wrong direction than it is to reverse that and get them back on the right line.

It's often argued that the reason we have bad economic policy is because the experts disagree; that, if only the experts would agree, if only all economists were of the same mind, we would have an excellent and fine economic policy. The case of free trade and the tariff is a clear counter example. Here is one case where economists have all agreed, or essentially so. As I say, you have the very minor deviations like Keynes, but very few others. Yet, except for the case of Great Britain from the repeal of the Corn Laws in 1846 to the First World War when, for nearly a century, Britain had complete free trade with no tariffs whatsoever on anything, tariffs have been widespread. The United States had tariffs throughout the nineteenth century. One of these measures, the infamous Smoot-Hawley Tariff Bill of 1930 which raised tariffs sharply, has been given some of the responsibility for the subsequent difficulties in the United States and the world.

Today, we have a widespread move for protection: pressures

from the steel industry, I am sorry to say successful, to have the government take measures to restrict the imports of steel; so-called voluntary agreements to restrict the imports of TV sets from Japan, and of textiles from Hong Kong, Korea, and I know not where else; and of shoes from Italy. We have a growing pressure for quotas on imports of oil and of other products. We have widespread concern that somehow or other a weakening dollar—the decline in the price of the dollar in terms of the mark or in terms of the Swiss franc or the yen—that a weakening dollar in that respect, requires the government to impose restrictions on imports or to subsidize exports.

The interesting question, and the question I want to explore with you today, is why is it that interference with international trade has been so widespread, despite the almost uniform condemnation of such measures by economists? Why is it that you have the professional agreement on the one side, and observe practice on the other which departs so sharply from that agreement? The political reason is fairly straightforward. The political reason is that the interests that press for protection are concentrated. The people who are harmed by protection are spread and diffused. Indeed the very language shows the political pressure. We call a tariff a protective measure. It does protect; it protects the consumer very well against one thing. It protects the consumer against low prices. And yet we call it protection.

Each of us tends to produce a single product. We tend to buy a thousand and one products. If we impose a tariff on steel, or restrict imports of steel in other ways, the people who benefit are visible and clear and available and apparent. They have a very strong interest to press for restraints in that respect. The interests of the rest of us are very diffuse. Each of us will pay a few pennies more. We don't have the same interest to oppose it.

Let me take a much more extreme case that you may think does not come under the heading of protection but yet it does. We have a program of subsidizing the merchant marine, the maritime industry. That is really protection because what we are doing is taking measures to prevent the use of foreign ships, that is, of importing the services for transporting goods. Those measures to benefit the merchant marine through ship building subsidies, through operating subsidies and so on, involve a total expenditure each year of roughly $600 million. That amounts to about $15,000 per year for each of the 40,000 people who are affected. You may be sure that they have every incentive to spend a lot of money on lobbying, on giving contributions to political candidates, and so on to see that continued. But $600 million with a population of two-hundred million people, that's three dollars apiece for each of us. Which one of us is going to go to Washington and lobby our congressman to avoid that extra three dollars of taxes?

While, on a superficial level, it's very easy to see why we have had tariffs and other restrictive measures such as the maritime subsidies, such as the recent import quotas, because producer interest is concentrated and consumer interest is diffused, that alone is not really a fully satisfactory answer. Let me take another example of exactly the same thing. Why have we had price supports of farm products—to take up a subject of special interest here where there are special interests? (We're all of us special interests; it's only the other fellow who's a special interest.) Why have we had farm price supports? You will find it very hard to find any economists who will support farm price supports. This is another case in which the consumer is simply being protected against low prices. Why do we have them? Because the agricultural interest has been concentrated and the consumer interest diffused and widespread. Because you have a relatively small group of people who regard themselves as having much at stake and therefore they are able to be more effective politically than the diffused consumer interest.

We often think that this is a country in which we have a majority rule. That's true, it is a democracy. We do elect people to Congress. We do have majority rule. But it is a very special kind of majority. It's a majority that is formed by a coalition of minorities. If you want to get elected to Congress the way to do it is to find 3 percent of the people who will say to you, "If you vote for this, we'll vote for you whatever else you do." Then you find another 3 percent and another 3 percent, and you build up a 51 percent majority consisting of a coalition of special interests. And yet, that overstates the case. Because it's also true that special concentrated groups of that kind have never been able to get their way unless they could make a plausible case that it was in the general interest of the country as a whole to promote their special interest. The maritime interest could not have gotten their way unless they had been able to persuade at least a large fraction of the public that there was a genuine national security reason for maintaining a merchant marine. The agricultural interest, the farm price support proponents, could never have gotten their way unless they had been able to establish a case that appeared plausible to a large fraction of the people that there was a national interest in preserving family farms or in some other aspect of agriculture.

So if we go below this superficial level to a deeper level, the question is, why is it that the economists have not been able to persuade the public of the virtues of free trade policy? After all, the argument for free trade is basically a very simple argument. Let me give you the argument which Adam Smith made two-hundred years ago. It's as persuasive now as it was then. And I quote, "In every country it always is and must be in the interest of the great body of the people to buy whatever they want of those who sell it cheapest. The proposition is so very manifest that it seems ridiculous to take any pains to prove it. Nor could it ever have been called in question had not the interested sophistry of merchants and manufacturers confounded the common sense of mankind. Their interest is in this respect, directly opposed to that of the great body of the people." That was the argument as he put it two-hundred years ago. And there is very little that needs to be added to it.

The basic reason I believe why economists have not been able to persuade the public is the one that I have already alluded to. It is suggested by the title of a famous essay which was written many years ago by a great economist, Wesley Mitchell. The title of his essay was "The Backward Art of Spending Money." And he asked, "Why is it that we are all of us so sophisticated about the activities in which we earn our living and tend to be so unsophisticated and backwards in the ways in which we spend our money?" And his answer was the one I have already mentioned: that each of us tends to be involved generally in only one kind of productive activity. We spend our working life, forty hours a week or sixty hours a week, whatever it may be, as a worker producing a product, as a merchant distributing a good, as a professor—well, forty hours a week teaching is a little long, but we're supposed to be putting in that much time on related ancillary activities and most of us do. On the other hand each of us buys a thousand and one things and it's perfectly understandable therefore that we devote far more attention and far more interest to the way we get our income than to the measures that affect how we spend it.

Unfortunately, this backward art of spending money leads to erroneous views in many directions and not only in the area of the tariff and of protection. For example, public discourse tends to be carried out in terms of jobs as if a great objective was to create jobs. That's not our objective at all. There's no problem about creating jobs. You can create any number of jobs by having people dig holes and fill them up again. Do we want jobs like that? No. Jobs are a price; we have to work to live, whereas if you listen to the terminology you would think that we live to work. Some of us do. There are workaholics, as there are alcoholics, and some of us do live to work. But in the main what we want are not jobs; we want productive jobs. We want jobs which will enable us to produce the goods and services we consume at a minimum expenditure of effort. In a way, the appropriate national objective is to have the fewest possible jobs, that is to say, the least amount of work for the greatest amount of product.

In the international trade area, the language is almost always about how we must export and what's really good is an industry that produces exports. If we buy from abroad and import, that's bad. But surely that's just upside down as well. What we send abroad we can't eat, we can't wear, we can't use for our houses. The goods and services we send abroad are goods and services not available to us. On the other hand, the goods and services we import provide us with TV sets we can watch, with automobiles we can drive, with all sorts of nice things for us to use. The gain from foreign trade is what we import. What we export is the cost of getting those imports. The proper objective for a nation, as Adam Smith put it, is to arrange things so we get as large a volume of imports as possible for as small a volume of exports as possible.

This carries over to the terminology we use. I have already referred to the misleading terminology of protection. But when people talk about a favorable balance of trade, what is that term taken to mean? It's taken to mean that we export more than we import. But from the point of view of our well-being that's an unfavorable balance. That means we are sending out more goods and getting fewer in. Each of you in your private household would know better than that. You don't regard it as a favorable balance when you have to send out more goods to get less coming in. It's favorable when you can get more by sending out less.

The tendency to concentrate on the productive side of our lives and to neglect the side of consumption is reinforced by the fact that even for the productive side of our lives the visible effects of tariffs are good; the invisible effects of tariffs are bad, even on the productive side. I have already referred to the steel case. It's perfectly clear that if you restrict the imports of steel, there are some workers in the steel industry who will have jobs they otherwise would not have. The beneficial effects for them of a tariff are perfectly clear. But if we import less steel, foreigners earn fewer dollars. They have fewer dollars to spend in this country. There are people around the country who will not have jobs, not have productive jobs because exports do not develop.

I should not have to spell this out in great detail here in Kansas. This is a great agricultural state. Agricultural products are one of our major exports. The harmful effects of restricting steel imports are to reduce jobs in agriculture. But that is invisible. The people who might have been producing goods to sell abroad don't know they might have had that job. So out of sight, out of mind. As a result, on both the side of consumption and the side of production you have the concentrated special interests versus the diffused general interests.

But then you will say to me, what's wrong with all these fine arguments I hear? What's wrong with the arguments by George Meany at the AFL-CIO convention: that the high-wage American workers are being unfairly competed against by the low-wage foreign workers; that we have to protect our American workers and their standard of living from the competition of foreigners in Japan, or Korea, or somewhere else who are willing to work for much less than the American worker? What's wrong with that argument? In the first place, what does a high wage and a low wage mean? The Japanese worker is pain in yen, the American worker is paid in dollars. How do I know how many dollars equal how many yen?

Let me go at this a little more directly. You can see the fallacy in this argument I think most clearly by taking an extreme case. Let's take the most extreme case of all. Let's suppose that at the existing exchange rate, whatever it is, Japan, to take the example which is a favorite "whipping boy," could undersell us in everything, that the Japanese can produce whatever you name across the board from wheat and soybeans to television sets and automobiles more cheaply than we can. And let's see what would happen. We'd rush to buy them. The Japanese sellers would be paid for them in dollars. What would they do with the dollars? Nothing for them to buy in the United States, because by assumption everything is cheaper in Japan. What then would they do with the dollars?

If they would be willing to burn them up or to bury them in the Pacific Ocean, ah, that would be wonderful. After all, there is no product we can produce more cheaply than green pieces of paper. But of course, the Japanese are not going to do that. They are not going to work and produce goods and send them over here in order to get pieces of paper which they are going to burn up. They want to get goods and services and when they discover that there are no American goods and services that are cheaper than those in Japan, they will say, "Well, gee, I had better convert these dollars back into yen." But who is going to sell them yen? Why would anybody sell them yen? Because if I have yen I can buy the Japanese goods, by assumption, more cheaply, so nobody would be willing to sell yen.

Let's suppose, to begin with, that the rate of exchange between the dollar and the yen was, as it was for a long time, 360 yen to the dollar or one dollar would buy 360 yen. Then these people who had all these dollars that were useless to them would say, "If you'll sell me some yen, I'll give you a dollar for 300 yen." "No," says the owner of the yen, "even at 300 yen to the dollar American goods are too expensive. They're not worth it." "Okay, I'll give you a dollar for

200 yen." And you can see what would happen. The price of the yen would be bid up until what? Well, the fewer yen you get for a dollar, the more expensive Japanese goods are to Americans. The more dollars you get for a yen, the cheaper American goods are to Japanese. So the effect would be that the yen would rise in price until it was no longer true that all U.S. goods were more expensive than all Japanese goods. As the yen became more expensive, Japanese goods would become more expensive to U.S.citizens in dollars and American goods would become cheaper to Japanese in yen. That would continue until on the average the dollar value of the goods that the Japanese would buy in the United States would be roughly equal to the dollar value of the goods that the U.S. would sell. At that point, the price of the yen in terms of the dollar would be at an appropriate level.

I have simplified the story because over and above these bilateral transactions between the United States and Japan, of course, these flows of trade will take roundabout directions. The Japanese will spend some of their dollars in Brazil and the Brazilians in turn will spend their dollars in the U.S. and the dollars may flow in very roundabout circles. But the principle is the same. People want dollars not in order to have pieces of paper but in order to have U.S. or other goods. And again, the actual situation is complicated by the fact that, in addition to the flows of goods and services, there are also capital flows, also investments abroad. The United States throughout the nineteenth century, throughout the period when we were building up and getting to be the economically most developed country in the world, had a balance of payments trade deficit every single year almost. Why? Because the U.S. was a country in which foreigners wanted to invest capital. The British were producing goods and sending them over to us in return for pieces of paper, not those green peices of paper but different pieces of paper, bonds, promising to pay back a sum of money at a later time plus interest on it. The British regarded that as a good investment and they regarded it therefore worth their while to send us goods in order to get those pieces of paper.

There was nothing wrong with that. On the contrary, we benefited by having foreign investment here that enabled us to develop more rapidly and the British benefited by getting a higher yield on their savings than they could have gotten any other way. In the twentieth century that was reversed. We had what was called a favorable balance of trade because the U.S. citizens were finding that they could get a higher return for their money by investing abroad than they could at home, and as a result we were sending goods abroad in return for those pieces of paper.

Again, in the post-World War II world under American foreign aid and Marshall Plan programs we were making gifts abroad. We were sending goods and services abroad as an expression of our belief that that was a contribution to a peaceful world.

So the situation is more complicated, but the fundamental point is the same. So long as you have a free exchange rate which is free to determine in the market the price of the dollar in terms of the yen, there is no balance of payments problem. There is no sense in which American industry is in danger of being undercut by foreign industries and destroyed.

Let me put the matter to you a little differently. Suppose on the average an American worker is roughly twice as productive as the average Japanese worker. That's roughly what the situation is. On the average the American worker takes home from his work as pay for his activities a sum of money which will buy about twice as large a basket of goods as his Japanese counterpart can buy. If that's the case, we cannot afford—well that's a little exaggeration, we should not afford—we should not use any American worker in an activity in which he is less than twice as efficient. This is what was dubbed 150 years ago, in the jargon of economics, the principle of comparative advantage. We may be more efficient in everything than the Japanese. That doesn't mean it pays us to produce everything at home. We should concentrate our efforts on those activities in which we are the most efficient.

Let me put it to you in a simple way. In a domestic illustration, I have a lawyer who is a very good typist. Does that mean he should dispense with his secretary and type his own letters? He may be a better typist than his secretary but if he is only one and one-half times as good a typist but five times as good a lawyer, both he and his secretary are better off if he concentrates on doing the law and she concentrates on typing the letters—or in this day and age I should say she concentrates on doing the law and he concentrates on typing the letters. (As it happens, I have a daughter who is an attorney, so that's personal as well as general.)

In the light of all this analysis, let us consider some current issues. Take the case of steel. What about the argument of steel that we need a steel industry for our national defense? You know there was a famous statement by, I think it was Emerson, that patriotism is the last resort of the scoundrel. I don't want to call the steel people scoundrels, they're not. They're perfectly decent human beings. They're like you and me and like you and me they know very well that what's good for them is good for the country. We are all sincere about that. The greatest human capacity we have is not to reason

But what of the validity of that argument? Well, there are two things to be said about it. First, if we had complete free trade in steel, there is not the slightest chance in the world that the U.S. steel industry would disappear. The advantages of being close to sources of supply, to sources of fuel, and to the market could certainly guarantee that we would have a very large steel industry. It might be that foreign imports would amount to 15, 20, 30 percent of the total. But so far as our national defense needs are concerned, insofar as we cannot satisfy them by importing steel from abroad, we would always have a domestic steel industry. Second, ask a steel man whether before he builds a factory he gets estimates of the cost of building it. He'll look at you as if you're mad and say, "Of course, of course I get estimates." And I will say to him, well now tell me do you get estimates of building it just one way? "Oh no, we get estimates of building it in a variety of alternative ways and then pick the best." And my standard answer to the steel man who gives the national defense argument is to say that when the steel industry presents to this country cost estimates of alternative ways of providing for our national security I will believe that its argument is sincere and not simply an excuse for self-interest.

Because there are many ways. You can stockpile steel. It's the easiest thing in the world to stockpile. Some of it may rust but that's not a very serious problem. Aside from stockpiling it, you can maintain some steel plants in mothballs the way we maintain ships in mothballs, and so on. There are lots of alternatives. Have you ever seen a cost estimate by the steel industry of how much it would cost to protect our national security one way or the other?

The same thing has been true over the years of the continuous argument by the oil interests that we ought to have, at one point, an oil import quota, or percentage depletion, or all sorts of other things on national security grounds. I believe that is an excuse and not a reason.

What about the argument of unfair competition? What about the argument that the Japanese dump their goods below cost? As a consumer, all I can say is the more dumping the better. If the Japanese government is so ill-advised as to tax its taxpayers in order to send to us, at below cost, TV sets and other things, why should we as a nation refuse reverse foreign aid?

What about the problem of the price of the U.S. dollar, the weakening of the dollar abroad? It is an artificial problem to which we should pay no attention. The market will set a price, let it. So far as we as a nation are concerned, the important thing is to get our internal house in order. If we followed policies at home which would eliminate inflation, and provide the basis for sound and healthy economic growth, the price of the dollar in foreign exchange markets would take care of itself. If we follow policies as we have been that produce a steadily rising inflation, or unsteadily rising inflation, I should say, ups and downs, well then, of course, the dollar is going to become worth less at home and it will be worth less abroad than it otherwise would be.

I come again to the problem of farm policy here, agricultural policy. That is an area which has been very intimately related to foreign trade. You will remember some years back when there was a great scandal about the extent to which the American taxpayers subsidized the Soviet Union by selling agricultural products at a price below the domestic price. I have already expressed the view that there is no national interest whatsoever in farm price supports or in government attempts to manipulate the price of farm products any more than there is in government attempts to manipulate the price of steel, or of any other product. But it's much more fundamental than that. Agriculture is one of our major export industries. It is an area in which we have been incredibly efficient, in which we can produce goods and out-compete almost everybody in the rest of the world. There is nothing that would be in the greater self-interest of the agricultural producer than for the U.S. to have complete free trade. That would generate a greater supply of dollars abroad to produce a better market for U.S. products.

I submit to you that the movement toward having farm price supports is a very shortsighted movement. What will be its results? It can only have the effect of either destroying export markets or requiring the government once again to subsidize exports. If we have a high artificial price at home, which is above the world price, nobody in the world is going to buy American products unless somebody or other sells these to them at the world price. Hence, a system of artificially high domestic agricultural prices necessarily requires a system of government subsidies for the export of wheat abroad.

I submit to you that that's not in the interest of the American consumer, it's not in the interest of the American taxpayer, and in the longer run it is not in the interest of the American farmer.

What do we do from here? What's the answer? Suppose we could be as successful as the British were in the 1820's and 1830's and get a national crusade going to move toward free trade. What should we do? Many people say that what we should do is to try to engage in reciprocal tariff reductions. True enough, they will say, our tariffs hurt us. But look at what those foreign countries are doing. Japan has tariffs on imports. How can we compete without tariffs, while they restrict trade with tariffs? The answer to that is very straightforward. The Japanese, by imposing tariffs and other restraints on their international trade, hurt themselves; but they also hurt us. No doubt they diminish the efficiency of the international division of labor—they hurt us and themselves. But if we impose tariffs in return we only hurt them and ourselves still further.

It's hard for me to see any justification in harming ourselves in order to harm somebody else. That's not a very sensible policy. Moreover it doesn't work. We have been trying for many years to engage in reciprocal tariff reductions. Every now and then one comes through. But on the whole, it has been a very unsuccessful policy.

I believe that the right policy for us would be to act like the great nation we are, to say we are not going to determine what we do on the basis of what Hong Kong and Korea and Japan do. We are a great nation and we are unilaterally and on our own going to move to remove every barrier to international trade. We are not going to do it overnight. People have made plans on the basis of existing tariffs. Let's take a five-year period, or a ten-year period, that's less important. But let's each year reduce by one-fifth every tariff barrier, eliminate every subsidy to exports by one-fifth, and over a five-year period get to a period at which we have no tariffs and no subsidies to exports. We should do that and we should also completely stay out of the market of foreign exchange. Your government on your behalf has been speculating in the foreign exchange markets for the past seven years and has cost you, up until last year and not counting the speculation of this year, $550 million of losses on those transactions. Money down the drain. Let's stop that.

What is the chance that we shall follow these measures? Candidly, I think the chance is zero and yet hope springs eternal. If we know the ultimate direction we want to go in, then that will improve the chances that the separate steps we take will move in that direction rather than away from it. Moreover I go back to my mentor, Adam Smith. In 1776 when he wrote his great book, *The Wealth of Nations,* he wrote and I quote, "To expect, indeed, that the freedom of trade should ever be entirely restored in Great Britain, is as absurd as to expect that an Oceania or Utopia should ever be established in it. Not only the prejudices of the public, but what is even more unconquerable, the private interests of many individuals, irresistibly oppose it."

He wrote that in 1776, yet seventy years later Britain had complete free trade. What he had said was impossible and absurd had been accomplished. One of the few places in which he was wrong. That move toward complete free trade ushered in the great period of Britain's prosperity and glory. And ever since Britain has departed from free trade she had been declining in prosperity and glory. I don't mean to say that that is the only source of her decline; it certainly is not. But it is not an unimportant source.

In the same way, the U.S. has been a great nation and we have prospered despite the tariffs and despite the restrictions on trade. But we could set a great example to the world and benefit the world as a whole, contribute not only to prosperity but to peace around the world, by moving in the direction of free trade. Because once again, go back to the British experience, the century of free trade was also the century of the greatest international peace. Why? Because if you eliminate government from these matters you enable individuals to deal with one another. If you introduce protection, tariffs, restrictions on trade, they become matters for government-to-government wrangling and they are an enormous source of division. So in the name of both prosperity and world peace there are few steps that we could take which would contribute more than a complete move toward free trade. Thank you.

Charles Collingwood (1917–) is a retired radio and television commentator. After taking his education at Cornell University and Oxford University, he became a war correspondent for United Press International in London. He has covered the United Nations and the White House and has been the chief of the CBS Bureau in London and from 1966 to 1975 was the chief foreign correspondent for CBS. In 1970, he wrote the novel, *The Defector.* He has won numerous awards for his work as a journalist and commentator.

Reflections on Power (and Influence)

Charles Collingwood

When Charles Collingwood spoke in the Landon Series on November 3, 1978, he was able to draw upon nearly four decades of journalistic experience, much of it spent as a foreign correspondent. In many respects, his reflections on power and influence are as pertinent today as when they were expressed. In other respects, however, they seem to have been particularly relevant during that period in the late 1970s when American power and influence appeared to be dwindling on all fronts.

NOVEMBER 3, 1978

I regard it as a signal honor to be invited to deliver some remarks in a series named for and in honor of Governor Alf M. Landon, for he has long been for me an example of those qualities which are most admirable in American life and the American spirit. Moreover, his whole career is a sort of parable of the thesis I will put forward to you today.

Part of my subject is POWER, but you will be glad to know that I am not addressing myself to the energy crisis. Rather, I want to talk about power, and its alternatives, in the context of international affairs. International affairs and foreign policy are things I know occupy Governor Landon very much and are things on which he is very knowledgeable. It also conforms to the bent of my own interests, having been a foreign correspondent and analyst for most of my working life.

"Power" is one of the strongest and in some ways one of the most ambiguous words in our language. We can speak of "solar power" and "occult power." The word can connote both physical force and mystical effects. I want to talk about power in the specialized sphere of international relations—power as a nation's ca-

pacity, usually by military means, to bend other nations to its will
... that capacity which causes some countries to be labeled "super-
powers" or "great powers," and others "minor powers."

And I want to contrast that with something called "influence."

Power and influence are often confused, both in theoretical discourse and common parlance, but there is a difference. As one
whose trade is in words, I make frequent recourse to dictionaries.
Let me quote excerpts from the Oxford English Dictionary. It de-
fines power as, among other things, "The ability to act upon or
affect something strongly ... physical strength, might, vigor, telling
force."

Now of "influence," it says, "The capacity of producing effects
... WITHOUT the employment of physical force or the exercise
of formal authority ... sway, control or authority not formally or
overtly expressed."

It is a crucial difference. The exercise of power in international
affairs is a highly visible, overt act. The exercise of influence often
is unseen. Power depends upon physical strength; influence upon
moral, intellectual, economic, and other forms of persuasion. Quite
often, especially in international terms, a nation's influence also depends upon the possession of power and the possibility that in some
circumstances it might be employed. That is certainly the case with
the United States. The fact of our military power has a great deal
to do with our ability to exercise influence. This is also true of the
Soviet Union. But a nation's influence does not increase in direct
relation to its power.

Thus, if we accept for purposes of argument—and it's an argument I certainly don't want to get in to in this context—that the
United States and the Soviet Union are roughly equivalent in terms
of military power, there is little doubt that the United States has
more influence in the world than the Soviet Union. An instance in
point is the Middle East, where, in spite of our long-standing commitment to Israel, one of the contestants, it is the United States and
not Russia which is influential enough with both sides to act as
mediator.

It can be argued that Russia has great influence in the Third

World, but that influence has proved remarkably transitory and has often depended upon acts of power, such as the introduction of Cuban forces into Angola and Somalia. Incidentally, it is also true that China, which is not in the same league in power terms with Russia and the U.S., also has widespread influence in the Third World—and, of course, so does the United States.

The distinction between power and influence as instruments of foreign policy is becoming increasingly important and is likely to become more important still. The reason for this is straightforward: given the vast nuclear arsenals of the two superpowers, resorts to the exercise of naked power have become increasingly risky for each and such resorts are apt to be much fewer than in the past and on a more limited scale.

If this is so, it follows that the achievement of our foreign policy objectives will depend more on the exercise of our influence to encourage the developments we wish than on intervening with military power to bring them about. The difficulty with this is that much of our doctrine, and the accepted view of our role—indeed, our whole national mind-set—has been based on a willingness to use our military power as a last, or even next to last, resort.

But today, even without the deterring effects of the nuclear balance of terror, we have the profound psychological deterrent of the Vietnam experience. We are now most reluctant to use our military power. So is the Soviet Union, but not as reluctant as we. The Russians will use their power by proxy as we have seen in Africa, or directly, as we saw 10 years ago in Czechoslovakia. Doctrinally, they have by no means ruled out the use of force as completely as we—you can read that in their technical military journals. And how else can you interpret their extraordinary military build-up, across the board, from nuclear weapons to conventional ones? Nevertheless, the Russians are very prudent about exercising their power in ways which might bring them into irrevocable conflict with us involving the likelihood of a nuclear exchange.

So, in the short- and perhaps middle-term, at least, we are entering an era in which the application of influence, backed, of course, by our military and economic strength, will be more important in the day-to-day conduct of diplomacy than the application of force. This inevitably sharply reduces some of our options and greatly increases others.

A case in point: 20 years ago, the delicately-balanced Christian and Moslem government of Lebanon began to come apart at the seams. Civil war threatened. President Eisenhower sent in the Marines and re-established equilibrium. For, say, 15 years thereafter, Lebanon was an oasis of tranquility in the Middle East. But when in 1975, caught in the tensions of the Middle East turmoil, Lebanon began to disintegrate again into the civil war which is still raging, the American option of sending in the Marines no longer existed. It was the Syrians from one end and the Israelis from the other who sent in forces with decidedly mixed results. All the United States could do, and can do yet, is to try to exercise its influence—and the results of that effort have been mixed, too.

I will go further and say that in considerable measure, the difficulties the present administration has encountered in our relations with other countries stems from a failure clearly to understand of what our influence consists and how to bring it to bear in order to further our interests and achieve the ends we seek.

The fact is that the United States influences other nations whether it wants to or not. Influence is inherent in us because of our size, strength, and resources, physical, technological, and of national character. The United States gives off influence the way plutonium gives off radiation. We could not be without influence if we tried. We exert influence when we DON'T do something, as well as when we do. It's in the nature of our whole position in the world. It behooves us then, to understand more clearly how influence works.

Over the centuries, we have learned something about the techniques of the exercise of power. Even when our strategy has been mistaken, our tactics in the application of power have been relatively sophisticated. That is not true of our use of influence, of which we have only a rough and ready comprehension. We have not always used our influence wisely or well.

I am reluctant further to belabor the Central Intelligence Agency, an essential institution whose effectiveness has been much impaired by attacks from both within and without, but the fact is that the CIA has often been a clumsy instrument with which we attempted to exert our influence. Its various "de-stabilizing" programs, of which Chile has been the most publicized, but which also were instituted against governments we thought, rightly or wrongly, to be inimical to our interests elsewhere in Latin America, in Africa, the Middle East and other parts of the world, have not only misled few, but have more often than not resulted in solutions quite at variance with what we wished to achieve.

These were covert uses of INFLUENCE—arms, money, bribery, encouragement—but not military operations. And one result of the failures has been to encourage a feeling of guilt on the part of our leaders and our people which has pretty effectively denied us the option of the clandestine use of influence by the CIA on any considerable scale ... which may be dangerous self-denial, because it is not at all difficult to imagine situations in which the covert use of influence, PROPERLY APPLIED, as it has sometimes been, can be useful.

The open exertion of influence now seems to us somehow nobler and cleaner than covert operations, and perhaps it is, but that does not mean that it is automatically more successful.

A case in point is the administration's emphasis on human rights in other countries. On the face of it, nothing is more laudable or more consistent with the best of our traditions, but as a component of foreign policy it is a very ticklish matter. To use our influence to try to rectify or prevent human rights violations in other countries can involve us in many contradictions and unwanted distractions from other policy goals. The most obvious is that we may appear (and I might say we often have appeared) to be inconsistent and hypocritical if we apply an ideal human rights yardstick more severely toward our antagonists than toward our friends.

Our leaders do not say much about human rights in Iran, for instance, for perfectly understandable reasons—we think the Shah's regime, for all its faults, is a stabilizing influence in the area, also the country has a lot of oil. On the other hand, we talk a great deal about human rights in the Soviet Union and have even toyed with the idea of making our trade arrangements and even the

SALT negotiations contingent upon Soviet acceptance of the kind of human rights standards we approve. This is not just the administration's policy, it is Congress' as well. In 1974, the Jackson-Vanik amendment linked U.S. trade with the Russians to a more lenient Soviet policy toward would-be Jewish immigrants. The immediate result was that the Soviet authorities cut back still further on Jewish immigration.

The fact is that to try to tell other countries how to manage their human rights policies invites, and has frequently produced, confrontation rather than compliance or cooperation. Naturally, this has been recognized by policy makers, and so we have tended to apply our influence in regard to human rights sporadically, selectively, and according to how it affects the realization of other goals in which we are interested. The result is that, as I have suggested, we have unnecessarily laid ourselves wide open to charges of hypocrisy and inconsistency. But the ultimate flexibility was all to the good.

There are other worthy ends to which we have bent our influence. One is to curtail the dangerous international traffic in arms. Yet while deploring it, and antagonizing some countries who sought in vain our weapons, we remain the biggest arms merchant in the world—especially to those countries who, for the moment at least, seem congenial to us, thus producing more charges of hypocrisy.

Again, the Congress is often as much to blame, if that is the word, as the administration. The logic of the Congressional decision to cut off arms supplies to Turkey as punishment for its invasion of Cyprus was based on dubious logic at best, since the same case could have been made against Greece as was made against Turkey. The result was to embitter our relations with Turkey, weaken the southern flank of NATO, push Turkey toward the Russians, and damage the chances for a settlement in Cyprus. I would call it an instance of misapplied influence. The Congress obviously agreed, for it repealed the Turkish arms ban last summer after three years.

There are many other examples which leap to mind, but it is not my purpose to offer a catalog of squandered influence, but rather to underline the importance of influence and the delicacy with which it must be employed to further our purposes.

What is it that gives a country influence? One thing, as I have suggested, is its military strength—the possession of potential coercive power, held in abeyance, perhaps, but there as a last resort. Thus power and influence ARE linked, although they are different.

Who would argue that Israel's military power and its demonstrated willingness to use it, does not contribute greatly to its influence in the Middle East arena? Russia's influence clearly stems in large measure from its military power—much more than from its ideology. The influence of the United States, and particularly vis-a-vis the Soviet Union, also derives to a considerable extent from our military power.

But if power and influence are connected, power is by no means the only component of influence. When Stalin contemptuously asked how many divisions the Pope had, he was talking about power. But not even the Communists would deny the influence which the Catholic Church can bring to bear on a broad array of situations.

Religious influence is also a powerful force in the Islamic world. The most dramatic example is the challenge mounted to the Shah's regime in Iran, led by fundamentalist mullahs. But many another Moslem countries from Mauritania to Malaysia must contend with the growing opposition of orthodox religious leaders—most prominently, Pakistan, Egypt and Turkey.

But next to military power, a nation's influence in the world depends most conspicuously on its economic strength. Much of America's influence derives from our economy with its high technology and huge agricultural surpluses. In many fields of international relations, you can watch our influence wax and wane with the economic statistics, and it is still true that when the American economy coughs, the economies of many other countries develop symptoms of flu.

It is West Germany's economic strength which has made it the dominant influence in Western Europe, and it is Britain's economic decline which has been a major factor in its comparative loss of influence. It is the economic performance of industrious, ingenious, protectionist Japan, a negligible military power, which has raised it into the first rank of nations in terms of influence (which it is often reluctant to employ except in the economic sphere; but it is there). And of course, there is no more obvious example of influence derived from economic strength than that of the oil producing countries—who can hold the whole world at ransom.

Another kind of influence is cultural. The Russians and Chinese are very conscious of this. Denied (or self-denied) many of the continuous contacts with other countries, they make great play with traveling shows of art, archaeology, ballet and so forth expedited to the far corners of the earth as a kind of exertion of influence. Sports is a part of it, as witness the Olympics—and don't forget that it was "ping-pong" diplomacy that paved the way for the Sino-American reconciliation.

The influence of American culture, in the broadest sense, is very pervasive. Our literature, theater, films and graphic and plastic arts, indeed our television programs, are widely disseminated and highly influential in the sense that they, like the dollar, however depreciated, are the contemporary standards by which the currency of other cultures is measured. Indeed, the whole American lifestyle, from fast food chains, to motels, super-markets, popular music, fashions in dress and attitudes is, if not universally admired, at least widely imitated. The contagion of American culture is certainly influential in itself and a symbol of our over-all influence.

The French may be the most successful exploiters of their culture. They have a certainty of their own intellectual superiority not unlike that of the Chinese, and they have convinced a great many people that they are right in this. Partly because of their assiduous cultural promotion, the French enjoy a kind of special standing and influence in all parts of the world out of all proportion to their actual power and size. (Incidentally, it should be said that the French are much less loath than we to use power as well as influence, especially by military intervention in the Francophone countries of Africa.)

A nation's leadership has much to do with its influence. To the extent that the leadership is perceived by others to be wise, strong and stable, it commands respect and often adherence, which is part of what constitutes influence. De Gaulle was an example, as was Churchill, as was Kennedy, even Nixon was always much better thought of abroad than in his own country. When a country's leadership, as has sometimes happened in the present American administration, appears to other people to be unsure, willful, or downright weak, that country's influence suffers.

Not the least of what goes into making a nation influential in a world are the policies it pursues in the international sphere. If those policies are seen to be well-conceived, consistent, generous and in the interests of all rather than one nation alone, then the nation pursuing these policies will inspire confidence on the part of other nations, gain their cooperation and secure their friendship. However, this is true only to the extent that those policies are real and not rhetorical. No amount of high-minded speeches about policy can take the place of policy in action, of the actual pursuit of the goals proclaimed, of doing what we say we want to do. That is another way of saying that a nation's influence depends to an important degree upon its reputation for reliability. A nation, like an individual, must be counted upon to fulfill obligations and see its undertakings through.

As St. Paul said, "If the trumpet give an uncertain sound who shall prepare himself to the battle?"

But a nation's leadership and its ability to execute its policies do not exist in a vacuum. They are surrounded by a sea of public opinion, and that sea is made up of many waves of special interests, special pleadings, special attitudes. For a country to exert influence in foreign affairs, as well as domestic, it must have the understanding, confidence and support of its own people. This nation in particular must inform and convince its public of what it is doing and that what it is doing is right if it is fully to bring its influence to bear.

There are many other factors which contribute to a nation's influence: the general perception of the national character, of its governmental institutions, of its example to the rest of the world. They are, all of them, important for influence is a kind of market basket of all of a nation's strengths—and some of its weaknesses—of its resources, of attributes and governance. It is fundamental to the conduct of our foreign policy.

Influence is as old as power and always has been an associate of it, but through most of history power has had the primacy. I am suggesting that has changed, and that being enjoined at this juncture from a casual use of power, we must accept influence as its substitute—though I pray we will not use our influence casually, because it can be as expendable and unreliable as power itself.

We have heard much of the limitations of power—former Senator Eugene McCarthy wrote a book with that title, although I do not take my theme from him. We must also realize that influence has its limitations as well. The national pride of other countries, their traditions, the stubbornness of their leaders and their public opinion, all conspire to make them resistant to the influence of others. Moreover, by its very definition, since it does not involve the use of overt force or domination, influence implies compromise. Compromise is no easy thing. It involves negotiations, trade-offs, and a sure appreciation of what we want most if we can't have it all. In other words, the influencing nation must often, in turn, allow itself to be influenced by others. It is a two-way street.

This, I may say, has not always been our way in the international sphere. Yet to be influenced by others may not be as great a handicap as the most prideful of us might think. After all, it is the way we have learned to order our lives in our own communities. As individuals we all get along by engaging in a daily series of compromises, doing some things we might prefer not to do in order to be able to do other things we reckon to be more important.

It would seem clear that this is precisely the way we will have to conduct our relations with other states in this period of history if we are to avoid physical conflict which, in the case of nations, is war . . . and it is the avoidance of war which is the ultimate test of diplomacy.

The use of compromise and reliance upon influence rather than power seem to be a relatively straightforward prescription for dealing with international affairs. They are, however, not as easy to put into practice on an international scale as they are in the ordinary lives of individuals. In a world which is both increasingly interdependent and increasingly antagonistic, the range of hard choices which daily present themselves to a decision-maker are enormous. Many of them are inter-connected and rub off one upon another, so that trade-offs are inevitable and as often as not we will have to settle for less than our optimum goals in one area so as not to compromise the achievement of something essential in another.

Thomas Hughes, the president of the Carnegie Endowment for International Peace, has a theory which he has expounded on several occasions. It is that the essence of foreign policy today is the management of contradictions. It is his contention, and I agree with him, that in world affairs in this latter part of the 20th Century, contradictions are inevitable. That is, most situations contain inherently incompatible factors, and the art of diplomacy is to reconcile those without armed conflict. Whether or not that is formally recognized, it is certainly the way this administration and, doubtless the next, and the one after that, will find themselves dealing with problems. The effort to deal with the inescapable contradictions in today's pluralized world politics through influence rather than power is a challenging one.

It involves, as we have seen in the present administration, a number of apparent inconsistencies. It is easy—all too easy—to charge the President with doing something in one situation which he would not do in another at least superficially similar situation. This stems in large part, it seems to me, from our architectonic instinct—our desire to create a model of the world and our role in it which is structured, tidy and internally consistent.

Unfortunately, that is not the way the world is today, if it ever was. But how often have we heard the call for the promulgation of an all-embracing foreign policy, a kind of grand strategy embracing our relations with the Soviet Union, China, Western Europe, the Third World providing automatic answers for dealing with everything from SALT to the Middle East to South Africa, Angola, Zaire, not to mention the oil-producing nations and the complexities of international economics. In our contradictory world, so full of surprises and unforeseen developments, there "ain't no such thing," and cannot and should not be. But we yearn for such a seamless and consistent set of policies. Worse, we often act as though there were such.

My own medium, television, and indeed the daily press as well, contributes heavily to this. We are the great simplifiers, boiling down complexities into easily grasped simplicities. We tend to measure our leaders by how well they measure up to unachievable standards of rigid consistency which the media—I must say with the help of our leaders themselves—have largely created. How many stories have you read or heard of alleged departures from unattainable consistency? The media might do better to explore the complexities of a situation and discuss the true options open to policy makers.

Having said that, let me hasten to add that the present administration has done little to help its own cause in this regard. It sometimes seems that the President and his advisers are as caught up in the mystique of consistency and coherence as the media and the public. When, as is sometimes bound to happen, the administration is apparently caught in an inconsistency, its tendency is not to explain why it acted as it did, but rather to insist until it is blue in the face that there was no inconsistency at all.

I am not trying to elevate inconsistency to a guiding principle of foreign policy, but only to say that some of it is inevitable and that we should recognize it as such and not expect or demand adherence to a spurious coherence in our conduct of foreign affairs. As I have indicated, compromise is essential in the management of affairs in a world in which influence is, on a day-to-day basis, a more important factor than power—and a series of compromises implies a certain degree of at least apparent inconsistency.

The same holds true of other countries, not least the Soviet Union. It is an old habit of ours to hold up our antagonists as exemplars of virtues we fear are wanting in ourselves. Thus, the policy of the Soviet Union is often presented as a model of consistency in contrast to the presumed waywardness of American policy.

I do not think this is true. The Russians blow hot and cold at least as often as we and have, indeed, in many cases, been more willing to abandon unprofitable adventures and seek other avenues than we.

For instance, if we had been as willing to pull out our advisers and cut our investment in Vietnam when the tide was clearly turning against those we supported, as were the Russians to pull their advisers and investment out of Egypt, we would not have had to endure the national ordeal we did. Yet Egypt was at least as important to the Soviet Union as was Vietnam to us. In fact, the Russians have shown themselves adept in many instances to manage short-term contradictions and accept inconsistencies in the pursuit of more distant goals.

As Emerson grandly declaimed, "A foolish consistency is the hobgoblin of little minds, adored by little statesmen, philosophers and divines." The experience of men and nations bears him out.

Let me recall an old and certainly apocryphal story about an alumnus who returned to visit the hallowed halls of his university—it might have been this one. Encountering an acquaintance, he asked how things were and was told not much had changed. He asked whether old professor so-and-so's examinations were still as difficult as ever.

"Oh, yes," was the reply. "He hasn't changed. He still asks the same questions every year."

"Well, I would have thought that would have made his exams pretty easy."

"Oh, no," was the response, "every year he expects different answers."

In a period in which influence is likely to prevail more often than physical power, what is needed is not consistency, or a grand and rigid design, but rather a set of goals and priorities which we should seek to achieve despite disappointments, setbacks, and some sacrifice of pristine consistency . . . new answers to old questions. It is the formulation of those goals and priorities, and the creation of a consensus in support of them, which should be a major preoccupation of our foreign policy and the public discussion of it.

But setting goals is one thing and achieving them is another. If I am correct in my conviction that influence has become a more important tool of foreign policy than power, then it is going to require a great deal of rigorous thinking about what influence is and how it works. We have been so used to thinking in terms of power and the threat of it, that the vastly subtler use of influence has been neglected, if not impugned. Influence, in many connotations, has a pejorative implication. We tend to think of "influence peddling," wire-pulling, under the counter deals, and other unsavory activities. Actually, influence is not—or should not be—that sort of thing at all. It can, and should be, benign.

But it must be said that influence is a much more amorphous concept than power. It is more difficult to define. It resists quantification in terms of megatonnage and predictable accuracy and yield. But it, and not nuclear weaponry alone, is likely to be our principal reliance in resolving the disagreements among nations and in establishing the kind of stable and orderly world we wish to live in.

To use our influence to best advantage will require re-thinking and a change of attitudes from our instinctive and historic addiction to sheer power or the threat of it. The emphasis on influence and the de-emphasis of power will not be automatically popular either among politicians or the public, for influence is not nearly as dramatic as power, and politicians and the public love drama. But the policy makers and technicians will have to learn about influence because it is the major instrument in their hands.

Let me close with an example.

Alf Landon's whole career makes my point. (Although I have been talking about the lives of nations, there are many analogies with the lives of individuals). As far as I know, Alf Landon never commanded much actual power—twice, perhaps in his long career. Once as a lieutenant in the first World War when he had a lieutenant's authority over a small fragment of our military establishment. Again as governor of Kansas when the state police and the national guard were, to some extent, under his command. But it was not these meagre instrumentalities of power which gave him the prestige and authority and capacity to produce useful results which he has had in this state, in this region, in this whole country. It is the influence he has had, based on his accomplishments, the general regard in which he has been held, and above all on his character, his strong convictions, and his willingness to stand up and be counted. Thus, Governor Landon is a living parable for my theory which is that in the wider world, influence can be as significant as power.

Of course, in the long run power is more important than influence. But in the long run, we will all be dead. And that certainly will be the result if the super-powers resort to power rather than influence in settling their disputes. Thus, it is incumbent upon us, while maintaining enough power to defend ourselves and those dependent on us, to understand where our influence lies and to use it where power is unacceptable.

James R. Schlesinger (1929–) is a professor at Georgetown University in the Center for Strategic and International Studies. He received A.B., M.A., and Ph.D. degrees from Harvard and was a professor of economics at the University of Virginia. His public career began in 1969 as Assistant Director, Bureau of the Budget. He later served as Chairman of the Atomic Energy Commission. In 1973, President Nixon appointed him Director of the Central Intelligence Agency. Later in the same year, he became Secretary of Defense. He was an advocate of increased military spending and an opponent of the policy of detente with the Soviet Union. The latter view led to his dismissal by President Ford in 1976. He later served President Carter as the first Secretary of Energy in the new Department of Energy.

American Security and Energy Policy

James R. Schlesinger

Energy policy and American security are recurrent themes in several of the Landon Lectures, especially those delivered during the 1970s. James Schlesinger, as Secretary of Energy, former Defense Secretary, and former CIA Director, was in a unique position when he spoke on April 28, 1980, to discuss the connections between petroleum dependency and American security concerns. Although his theme is closely related to that of Senator J. William Fulbright five years earlier, the two provide very different prescriptions for American policy in the Middle East.

APRIL 28, 1980

It is a special pleasure for me to be here in Manhattan on this glorious spring day to deliver the Landon Lecture. My connection with Kansas State is not solely in the role of a lecturer, for my son studies at this institution—one to which he nostalgically refers as "Silo Tech." (He also refers with some asperity to another institution as "Snob Hill.") He assures me that he is learning calculus, statistics, and money and banking. I do know from direct evidence that he has well learned to distinguish between walleye and the crappie, all about lures, and about the differences between the large- and small-mouthed bass.

Kansas State has grown up with this country, starting before the days of the Morrill Act, and wisely and quickly seizing on that landmark statute to become a land-grant college in 1863. It is a vital part of the American Midwest. The State of Kansas itself represents something of a microcosm of the larger American society. Over time it has reflected all of America's troubles and all of America's strengths from the days of the Kansas-Nebraska Act and of "bleeding Kansas"—reflecting the larger issue: whether this country would be slave or free. Kansas was itself a testing ground and a bloody testing ground of that divisive issue.

In populist days, it was the center of populist controversy reflected in such notable figures as William Allen White and Mary Ellen Lease. It marked the controversies reflecting development of the United States as the major force in world politics, which occurred during the 1930s and 1940s. When Kansas was isolationist, America was isolationist. And when Kansas became internationalist, so did America. Thus, in this way the United States became the greatest power in world affairs. This historical change was reflected, of course, in the public career of Alfred Landon for whom this series is named, and who himself vividly demonstrates the indomitable spirit that is Kansas. When approached some time ago by a reporter, asking whether he still indulged in horseback riding, he replied: "No, I had to give it up because my horse has gotten too old."

These issues of internationalism and isolationism had to be resolved in the 30s and 40s, for the United States had no alternative but to become the great protector of democratic values worldwide. We were reluctant to do it. We would have preferred to have remained wholly disengaged. Later we would have preferred to remain the great arsenal of democracy, rather than becoming directly involved. But there was no true alternative. America thus became the pivot about which international affairs revolved. And, at the same time, Kansas itself changed. Kansas had earlier embodied the history of the Western Movement. More recently, in its role as a microcosm of the American society, it has played its part in the evolution of the western world. And this representative role seems particularly appropriate, for (until the distressing impact of the admission of Alaska and Hawaii) Kansas was the geographic center of the United States.

I allude to this history for a number of reasons. It was Santayana who observed that those who do not study history—will be forced to repeat it. Recently, after breaking my leg, I have had the opportunity to reread Gibbon's study of *The Decline and Fall of the Roman Empire*. Not wholly irrelevant to the present position of the United States, I came upon a most appropriate passage in Gibbon. In the third century A.D., the Romans had, for the first time, begun the practice of paying blackmail to barbarian invaders, and they soon discovered the drawbacks of that technique. As Gibbon says, "And as soon as the apprehensions of war were removed, the infamy of the peace was more deeply and more sensibly felt. . . . But the Romans were irritated to a still higher degree when they discovered they had not even secured their repose though at the expense of their honor. The dangerous secret of the wealth and weakness of the empire had been revealed to the world. New swarms of barbarians encouraged by the success, and not conceiving themselves bound by the obligation of their brethren, spread devastation through the provinces in terror as far as the gates of Rome."

I cite that passage from Gibbon, not as a prophecy, but simply as an admonition. It does suggest the heartaches and the thousand natural shocks to which a great power may be heir whenever it begins to neglect its security.

We are facing a new time of testing for the United States—testing that reflects the interconnection between economics and energy supply on the one hand, and security considerations on the other. Here in the United States, with its boundless resources opened up by the Westward Movement to which I earlier referred, we have not been forced to face the dangers that other great powers have been forced to contemplate. Britain and Germany were able to maintain their status as great powers, but always had to consider the issue of energy supply. It was a dominant motive for what the British called their lifeline to the east: access to Middle Eastern crude.

Until the early 1970s, the United States never was seriously dependent on external sources of energy supply. Therefore, it could, to a large extent, ignore the intimate connection between national security and energy supply. From the close of World War II, under the aegis of American power, the world went through an extraordinary period of economic expansion. That expansion was based upon cheap and abundant energy increasingly exploited at long distances—under the protective umbrella of American strength. Under the umbrella of American power, the world experienced an extraordinary expansion of international trade and investment—

and the growth of living standards, by and large, on a worldwide basis. These favorable developments reflected two preconditions: first, the framework of security provided by the United States; and second, cheap and abundant energy.

Both premises for this extraordinary period of expansion are questionable today. The United States, partly inevitably, and partly through its own neglect, has allowed its international position to erode so that we no longer have the same framework of security. Not entirely disconnected, we today face increasing problems with respect to energy supply, not merely volume and price—but security and access, as well.

Thus, since 1945, the United States has faced two inconsistent trends. First, a growing dependency on foreign sources of supply—indeed, in the ultimate, located in the most volatile region of the world, close to the sources of Soviet power, and subject to interdiction through a variety of mechanisms. And as American dependency gradually rose, our ability to protect our international position gradually shrank—with the decline of our defense posture relative to the Soviet Union.

It is these conflicting trends that I want to examine today.

The pianist, Jose Iturbi, was once asked whether he needed to practice every day. He responded—this is an excellent story in an academic setting—that indeed he had to practice every day. If he failed to do so, on the first day *he* noticed the difference; on the second day the *critics* noticed the difference; and on the third day the *public* noticed the difference. Our problem internationally is that we have failed to practice properly—and have consequently been living on borrowed time. We have reached, as it says in the Good Book, the evening and the morning of the fourth day.

We remain dependent—America and the Free World—upon the resources of the Persian Gulf. There should be no illusion on this question, although there has been. It has been a common illusion in American life that somehow or other, through the waving of some wand, we could alter this condition of dependency quickly and easily. We cannot. The OPEC nations collectively possess 82 percent of the world's proven reserves of oil. And that percentage is tending to *rise* rather than fall, since reserves are being drawn down more rapidly outside OPEC than within OPEC. Down through the Straits of Hormuz each day move some 20 million barrels of oil—60 percent of all the oil flowing in international commerce; 40 percent of all the oil consumed in the free world. And that flow of oil has become increasingly vulnerable for a variety of reasons.

America has tended to assume that it had the luxury of choice with regard to energy supply. I am especially happy to see here today students from the American Nuclear Society, for nuclear power must be a part of the nation's energy mix. Yet, we as a country have regularly assumed that we had the choice whether or not we would use nuclear power, or coal, or liquified natural gas—or whether we were indeed willing to strip mine coal. Dozens of national energy issues have been decided on the basis that we wanted to avoid the cost of doing something. We cannot. We cannot have benefits without costs. We cannot afford to defer the substitutions of alternative sources of energy for the use of oil, which is increasingly in limited supply in the United States, as we increasingly become more dependent upon external sources of supply.

There are no panaceas—neither Project Independence, nor deregulation, nor synthetics. These will all unquestionably be helpful. Synthetic fuel may provide us with some additional supply by the year 1990. But, for the foreseeable future, the United States will remain dependent upon external sources of supply.

From that condition comes a political vulnerability. Yet it is a lesser political vulnerability for the United States in its role as a nation than in its role as leader of the Free World, for, irrespective of our own efforts, Western Europe and Japan will inevitably remain dependent upon the oil resources of the Persian Gulf region. Seventy percent of their oil will come from that region. Consequently, there is now a clear danger of loss of control over the destiny of the Free World. For, if the Soviet Union comes to control the oil tap in the Middle East, that would imply the end of the Free World as we have known it since 1945. Under those conditions, Japan and Western Europe would have no real alternative but to reach accommodation with the Soviet Union—which would then be in a position to control the economic future of both of these industrialized areas. All this quite unmistakably implies that the security of supply in the Persian Gulf cannot be compromised if we are to preserve the general structure of international politics that we have known since 1945.

However, as we observe the developments as they have unfolded during the last three years, there is little basis for complacency. Quite bluntly, the United States and her allies are today in the most perilous position since the darkest days of World War II. Yet, the threat is nothing obvious—or bracing—as was the attack on Pearl Harbor. In the Middle East, on which the Free World depends, the strategic momentum today rests with the Soviet Union. While we welcome it, we should not over-rate the long run significance of the resistance in Afghanistan. At best, that resistance buys us time— time that we can ill afford to squander. For not only has the Soviet Union in recent years possessed the strategic momentum; more importantly, the position of the United States has been deteriorating steadily and continues to deteriorate today. It is this underlying reality that poses for us grave peril.

Let me recall for you some of the major elements in this deterioration. In the spring of 1977, Ethiopian and Cuban forces under Soviet generals established Soviet preponderance in the Horn of Africa. In the spring of 1978, came Taraki's coup d'etat in Afghanistan. Thus, it was in April 1978, not in December 1979, that Afghanistan effectively became a satellite of the Soviet Union. It was at that time that the Soviets developed communications systems in Afghanistan similar to those used in the East European satellites. Indeed, the Afghans then abandoned the green flag of Islam and adopted the red flag as their national symbol. Any Muslim state that suddenly unfurls the red flag is telling us something.

In the summer of 1978 there were simultaneous murders of the two chiefs of state of the two Yemens in the southwestern part of the Arabian peninsula—on the other flank of the conservative states that provide the Free World with much of its oil. The result was the enhancement of the role of South Yemen as a Soviet satellite and a weakened capacity of North Yemen to discourage further adventures.

All through 1978 the Shah teetered on his throne—and ultimately fell in 1979. The Shah was the linchpin of U.S.—and Western—policy in the Middle East. His fall was a cataclysm for American foreign policy. The fall of the Shah represented the final end of the Northern Tier, that belt of nations—Turkey, Iran, Pakistan—first identified in the Baghdad Pact of 1954 and later affirmed by CENTO as the barrier precluding Soviet movement southward into the Persian Gulf.

The establishment of the Northern Tier as a barrier occurred over twenty years prior to the western world's dependency on the Persian Gulf reaching its current precarious heights. But, the Northern Tier has now disintegrated. In 1978, Pakistan decided to shift its premier ambassador from the embassy in Washington to the embassy in Moscow, based on a judgment that Pakistan would have to work its long run destiny with the Soviet Union rather than the United States. Turkey had, of course, been alienated from the United States by the unwise 1975 decision of the U.S. Congress to cut off military assistance as a way of applying pressure in Cyprus. Turkey has also been suffering from grave economic difficulties, largely induced by the rise in oil prices, which has severely strained the Turkish balance of payments. Thus, with the collapse of the Shah, there came the ultimate collapse of the Northern Tier. In itself, that was sufficient disaster. Yet, in the year and a half since the collapse of the Northern Tier, the deterioration has continued and the difficulties have been compounded. The deterioration in the U.S. position has crossed the Gulf into the Arabian Peninsula itself.

Three-fourths of the oil moving down through the Straits of Hormuz each day comes from the western side of the Gulf—notably from Saudi Arabia, that now supplies one-third of all of OPEC's production. Saudi Arabia today is in greater difficulty than heretofore. I want to be very delicate about this problem. Yet we must—though we have not been willing to—candidly face the implications for the United States and the Free World of a collapse in Saudi Arabia. We must be better prepared than in the past to analyze ongoing developments in that Kingdom.

The attack on the Grand Mosque at Mecca, for example, was a most serious development. It went undetected by Saudi intelligence. It took the better part of three weeks for Saudi security forces to eliminate the insurgents. That attack was not simply the action of so-called religious fanatics. It was a well-rehearsed, well-orchestrated action carried out by well-trained men—quite probably drawing their inspiration from South Yemen. We must remember that the Saudi royal family draws much of its legitimacy from its role as Protector of the Holy Places—so that its legitimacy was undermined by its apparent inability to protect the holy sites.

More or less simultaneously, though probably unconnected, there were disorders in the Eastern Province, where the bulk of the oil is produced. Moreover, there is today a heightened sensitivity to the issue of corruption in Saudi Arabia in the wake of Khomeini's rise in Iran—a fact recently acknowledged by Crown Prince Fahd himself.

The troubles continue to grow. There have been press reports that the Saudis are now permitting Soviet overflights of Saudi Arabia to supply South Yemen. Last spring the United States rushed $378 million worth of arms to North Yemen when it was under attack by South Yemen. Yet, this year North Yemen has been moving toward the Soviet orbit and has entered into conversations on prospective union with South Yemen.

Well over a year ago, at the time of the Shah's collapse, the Saudi press began to talk of the Soviet onslaught and of *the passivity of the United States in the face of that onslaught*. The Saudis, as well as the other conservative states of the Arabian Peninsula on which the Free World depends for its oil, believe they are facing encirclement. It is these developments, serious and potentially catastrophic, that make me stress the peril in which this nation is placed today. In contrast to the obvious implications of a Pearl Harbor, the gravity of our position is not fully recognized by the American people. Yet, just as in 1941, it is a crisis that transcends politics. It is an issue of survival.

I submit, therefore, that it is high time for emergency actions to match emergency conditions. I do not now have sufficient time to develop in any detail what, I believe, needs to be done. However, let me briefly run through a number of major elements in a serious national program.

First, we must immediately and seriously address the issue of the balance of power in the Indian Ocean. This nation will not survive on the basis of others' judgments regarding the purity of our motives. Our survival will depend upon the maintenance of a balance of power. And the balance of power in the Indian Ocean has moved adversely to the United States. The Soviet Union today possesses an order of battle, north of the Iranian Border and in Afghanistan, that makes the Soviet Union the militarily dominant power in the region. Such measures as the grain embargo and the boycott of the summer Olympics, taken in response to the invasion of Afghanistan, may make Americans feel a lot better, but they remain strategically marginal. They in no way affect what is critical in the long run—the regional balance of power.

It is therefore incumbent upon us immediately to take steps to redress the balance. In the first place, I believe major components of the American Navy must be permanently deployed into the Indian Ocean, including major deployments of the Marine Corps. Such deployments will require a permanent base structure. A permanent American presence is quite different from the intermittent surging of carrier task forces into the Indian Ocean. It may appear to us that the signal that we are sending to the states of the region is America's capacity to be on the scene. But the signal that is actually gathered by those relatively weak and vulnerable states is the *transiency* of the American commitment—inferred from the American fleet disappearing over the horizon whenever it withdraws. We must be both permanently present and seen to be a permanent presence.

The much advertised Rapid Deployment Force, while most welcome, is insufficient. It will still be insufficient, at that time five or six years from now, when it could actually be deployed rapidly. And, until the mid 1980s, the capability will not exist and will not be available. Thus, the first thing that is required is immediately to redress the current balance of power—at the same time recognizing that we shall ultimately require land-base forces in the region, if we are to have an appropriate deterrent.

Second, we must immediately revitalize the American intelligence community. That should not require a lengthy national debate. Events in the Middle East in recent years have revealed weaknesses in intelligence collection and analysis, but have far more clearly demonstrated the virtual destruction of our capability for special intelligence operations (as well, incidently, as our capability for counterintelligence). The untoward developments in the Middle East might have been far less damaging to our interests or might even not have occurred had we preserved an effective intelligence agency.

One can only observe that the practice of self-flagellation is not confined to Shiite Muslims in the month of Moharram. Here in the United States, we have been recklessly indulging in self-flagellation for at least the last five years, much of it at the expense of our intelligence community. It is now time to end that debate and to revitalize our intelligence arm.

(Let me say in passing that a so-called legislative charter is not the path to revitalization. A legislative charter represents more restrictions, and more restrictions, by any other name, are simply more restrictions.)

Third, we should restore grant military assistance. As the United States reduced its own military forces during this decade, for some unaccountable reason it also phased out grant military assistance supporting friendly forces intended to complement our own forces. As a consequence, this great power is now in the undignified position of begging the oil-rich countries of the Middle East, such as the Saudis, for cash to provide military equipment to friendly states. Alternatively, we can provide a little assistance on a loan basis—at commercial rates of interest. It is hardly appropriate for the United States to be in a position either of begging support from other nations or of lending to impoverished states such as Pakistan at usurious rates of interest which they cannot afford. So we must restore grant military assistance.

These three steps can and should be taken now.

Beyond these immediate measures, however, there are two more fundamental and longer term matters that must be addressed. First, we must honestly and seriously face up to the issue of defense expenditures. We cannot do so by once again indulging in budgetary tricks and manipulations—but only by facing reality. Today, in terms of military expenditures, the United States is being outspent by the Soviet Union by at least 50 percent; in terms of military investment, by almost 100 percent. The latter is the annual acquisition of new military hardware. The ultimate impact of such discrepancies in military investment, cumulatively and year after year, will be to leave the Soviet Union with a force posture twice the size of that of the United States. Sometimes we try to comfort ourselves by saying that we have better and stronger allies than the Soviets, which is true. Nonetheless, the Soviet Union is today outspending all of the Western nations, as well as Japan, on military investment. Inevitably the long-term alteration of the military balance must affect the international balance of power. If the United States is to effectively compete with the Soviet Union in the 1980s and 1990s, it has no alternative but to restore some balance in the pattern of military expenditures.

Finally and indispensably, we need to have a foreign policy which is regarded as firm and steadfast by nations in the Middle East and elsewhere. The United States must be seen as a great power, prepared to support its friends—and one that it is dangerous to oppose—rather than as one that is highly unpredictable.

During the course of the last decade it has become downright perilous to be a Third World ally of the United States. The risks of association with the United States are reflected regrettably, though understandably, in the attitudes of most nations in the Persian Gulf region.

These larger international responsibilities are those imposed upon us by the vast change in America's international role coming out of the 1930s and 1940s—a changing role to which Governor Landon made his contribution.

In terms of the ultimate defense of freedom, there is no substitute for the United States. No other nation can effectively serve as a counterweight to Soviet power. If this nation fails to bear its responsibilities, there is no one else to carry that burden.

What developments in the Middle East tell us, is that time is running out; we must act now before it is too late. History will not forgive us—this nation that bears the burden of defending freedom—if we fail to do so. This is a serious challenge for this generation.

I do recognize that my remarks have been severe, if realistic.

So, in closing, I recount the observation of an American intelligence officer that has some bearing on our current difficulties. As he looked over the wreckage of Pearl Harbor in 1941, he observed: "We are going to win this war; I know that . . . But God bless my soul if I know how." That comment reveals an abiding American optimism and faith in the face of impending difficulties.

I have confidence that we shall meet our responsibilities. We must all recognize that the decade of the 1980s will be a perilous one. We must recognize the need for an American renewal, if we are to protect freedom effectively, not merely here on the North American continent, but elsewhere in the world.

Ronald Reagan (1911–) is the fortieth President of the United States, elected in 1980 and reelected in 1984. From 1967 to 1975 he served as Governor of California. He made a series of tries in 1968 and 1976 to be the Republican candidate for President, narrowly losing to President Ford in 1976. In 1980 he was successful in defeating Jimmy Carter by a wide margin, and in 1984 he defeated Walter Mondale by the widest margin in U.S. history.

Rebuilding America

Ronald Reagan

Ronald Reagan, then Governor of California, was the third speaker in the Landon Lecture Series. That lecture was entitled, "Higher Education: Its Role in Contemporary America." He returned to Ahearn Fieldhouse as United States President almost fifteen years later, on September 9, 1982, to deliver the 58th lecture in the series and to honor Governor Landon on his 95th birthday. He and Senator Mike Mansfield are thus far the only two public figures to have appeared twice in the series.

President Reagan's 1982 speech covered a wide range of the social, economic, and foreign policy issues which have characterized his presidency: cuts in government social spending, banning of abortions, reintroducing school prayer, and others. Senator Edward Kennedy's Landon Lecture seventeen months later, included in this collection, provides a sharp counterpoint to Reagan's speech.

SEPTEMBER 9, 1982

Thank you very much, President Acker, Governor Carlin, Governor Landon, Senators Dole and Kassebaum, members of the Board of Regents, faculty, students, distinguished guests. It is a special pleasure to be with you today, wonderful to be back home on the range. You know, sometimes living in that big white house in Washington can leave you feeling a little fenced in and isolated. But there is a tonic: visit a state where tall wheat and prairie grass reach toward a wide open sky; be with people who are keeping our frontier spirit alive, people who work the soil but still have time to dream beyond the farthest stars; here in the heartland of America lives the hope of the world, and here words like "entrepreneur," "self-reliance," "personal initiative," and, yes, "generosity" describe everyday facts of life.

Right now another fact of life in this heartland is the enormous burden carried by those who produce the food and fiber essential to life itself. And I want with all my heart to see that burden lifted, to see America's farmers receive the reward that they deserve. I agree with your native son, Dwight Eisenhower, who said that without a prosperous agriculture there is no prosperity in America. I feel doubly honored to be with you here in this particular place. Kansas State University epitomizes the leadership that Abraham Lincoln wanted when he established our first land-grant colleges. Schools like Kansas State serve as an entrance to the world, not an escape from it. And you deserve great credit for the rigorous academic program that you offer your students, the research efforts you are making to benefit humanity.

Today is, as has been said, also a homecoming of sorts for me. It was fifteen years ago I participated in this Landon Lecture Series for the first time, so I can see and am aware of the remarkable growth of the University. And as an ex sports announcer I have also been following the Wildcats' victories in basketball. Now it just happens that football was my game and I know that—I know that there have been some trials and shall I say some misfortunes in football. You have tasted the agony of defeat. And I know that taste. And by coincidence when I knew that taste I was wearing a purple jersey at the time. But I happen to be a believer in purple power, so go out there and turn it around. Your state motto says, "Ad astra per aspera"—to the stars through difficulties.

My other honor today is joining you in paying tribute to an outstanding American, a wise, effective and revered leader and a personal friend. And you know, in all my years in Hollywood, I was never a song and dance man. That's how I wound up an after dinner speaker. But I just wonder if we couldn't all sing Happy Birthday to the best darn horseback rider in the State of Kansas— Governor Alf Landon.

I was all set to ask the Governor if he'd like to go riding today and then suddenly I remembered about the Landon legend. He doesn't just ride the horses; he has broken the horses that he rides. And I think I'll save my strength for the Congress.

Governor, if you'd invite me back here to speak five years from now, and if I should happen to be still living in the White House, you could join me on Air Force One and we'd light the candles on your 100th birthday cake in Washington so all of America could join in the celebration.

You know, I'd be remiss if I didn't say that one of the nicest things that Alf Landon ever did for his country was to give us someone as talented and charming as his daughter Nancy—the first woman to be elected Senator from Kansas. And, you know—Nancy—that's a nice name. I like the name Nancy.

Today I want to talk about our challenge to take freedom's next step, and lift mankind another rung on the ladder of human progress. And if you detected a note of optimism in those words, you read me right.

I do not dismiss the dangers of big deficits, nuclear conflict or international terrorism. Each could destroy us if we fail to deal with them decisively. But we can and will prevail if we have the faith and the courage to believe in ourselves and in our ability to perform great deeds as we have throughout our history. Let's reject the nonsense that America is doomed to decline, the world sliding toward disaster no matter what we do.

Like death and taxes, the doom criers will always be with us. And they'll always be wrong about America. Let me, if I could, just jog your memories for a moment. It was just a short time ago when those doom criers were telling us that food and fuel supplies were running out. It was only a question of time before famine and misery would engulf America and the world.

Price increases in America, they predicted, would zoom up at double-digit rates for the rest of this decade. The price of crude oil would race to $100 a barrel. Interest rates would break all the old records and soar to 25 or 30 percent or even higher. Runaway inflation and interest rates would break the back of the free enterprise system, destroy the value of our currency, the savings of our people, and the ability of our country to project power, promote freedom, and defend peace.

Already Americans are proving every one of those predictions wrong. So many so-called "experts" lack faith in the American people. They just don't seem to understand there is no limit to what a proud, free people can achieve. We see it here where the first plow turned the prairie sod and the prairie became a fertile wonder of the world. I'm told that in 1820 a farm worker produced enough food products for himself and three other people. Today he feeds seventy-seven.

We're not running out of food and fuel because we haven't run out of ideas. We're going to feed the world. We're developing new energy resources. Last year we discovered more crude oil than any time in the last 12 years. We've declared war on high interest rates and inflation, and we're winning that war. The American dollar is no longer a condemned currency; it's sought again as a rock of strength and stability. In the last two years, it has risen about 25 percent against other major currencies. And yet I can remember, just a short time ago, a friend returning from a trip abroad very depressed. He told me what a blow it was and how he felt because at that time he was in places abroad where they refused to accept American money. They had lost such confidence in it.

Across the world, Americans are bringing light where there was darkness, heat where there was once only cold, medicines where there was sickness and disease, food where there was hunger, wealth where humanity was living in squalor, and peace where there was only death and bloodshed.

So many delight in downgrading everything American when there is so much in our land to be proud of. We don't occupy any countries. We build no walls to keep our people in. But we provide more food assistance around the globe than all the other nations combined. And no other nation works harder or, I might add, more effectively—than the United States to end bloodshed and suffering and bring about lasting peace in troubled areas like the Middle East.

Yes, we face awesome problems. But we can be proud of the red, white and blue, and believe in her mission. In a world wracked by hatred, economic crisis and political tension, America remains mankind's best hope. The eyes of mankind are on us, counting on us to protect the peace, promote new prosperity, and provide for them a better world. And all this we can do if we remember the great gifts of our revolution: that we are one Nation, under God, believing in liberty and justice for all.

One of America's most valiant, decorated soldiers, Omar Bradley, once said of freedom: "No word was ever spoken that has held out greater hope, demanded greater sacrifice, needed more to be nurtured, blessed more than the giver, damned more its destroyer, or come closer to being God's will on Earth—may America ever be its protector."

Well, let this be our banner. But to be freedom's protector, to be a force for good, we must, above all, be strong. And to be strong, we must offer leadership at all levels of government, in our communities, in our families. We must mobilize every asset we have—spiritual, moral, educational, economic and military—in a crusade for national renewal.

We must restore to their place of honor the bedrock values handed down by families to serve as society's compass. Our time-tested values have never failed us when we've had the courage to live up to them. Speaking here 15 years ago, I was asked, following the speech, a question from the audience—if we weren't—if our young people of that day were not turning away from our traditional values. And I replied that maybe those young people just didn't think we were living up to them. There was a roar of approval from the students present that indicated agreement. They hadn't abandoned those values. They just didn't think that our older generation cared any more. So, it's up to us to make sure they realize we do.

Today I wonder sometimes if we're infecting another generation with negativism. When the tough but necessary decisions to cut back on spending are made, they are described so often in negative terms—how much less government will spend, how many fewer benefits will be given away, how many fewer programs will survive. But cutting back on the runaway growth of government can be a profoundly positive step, like performing necessary surgery on a patient to save his life.

This federal government of ours, by trying to do too much, has undercut the ability of individual people, of communities, churches and businesses to meet the real needs of society—as Americans always have met them in the past.

The time has come to re-think some of the tired old political labels that have blinded our thinking for too long. You know, we Americans have the technological genius to send astronauts to the moon and bring them safely home. But we're having trouble making it safe for a citizen to take a walk in the evening through the park. And sometimes in the world of politics, it seems that our dialogue hasn't gone much beyond "Me Tarzan, you Jane."

For nearly 50 years, those who have taken unto themselves the label "liberal" have argued that government has a duty to help people solve their problems—which it does. Conservatives, on the other hand, have argued that such help can be a threat to individual freedom—which it can. Both sides seem to agree that the two main categories of American society are government and the individual—and never the twain shall meet.

But from our earliest days, there have been other crucial dimensions of our society that transcend these narrow labels. Look around you—there is so much more to America than government on the one hand and individuals with nowhere to turn for help but to government on the other. Between the government and the individual, there are a great number of natural, voluntary organizations which people form for themselves—like the family, the church, the neighborhood and the workplace where people learn, grow, help and prosper. And even individual citizens and institutions like the thing that I have just read—the announcement of the largest federal savings and loan here in Kansas which has reduced the interest rates for home mortgages down to where, once again, maybe something can happen in the home-building industry and people can again live that American dream of owning their own home.

The ultimate and overwhelming positive goal of my administration is to put limits on the power of government, yes, but to do it so that we liberate the powers and the real source of our national genius which will make us great again.

I said that we were a nation under God. I've always believed that this blessed land was set apart in a special way—that some divine plan placed this great continent here between the oceans to be found by people from every corner of the earth who had a special love for freedom and the courage to uproot themselves, leave homeland and friends to come to a strange land and where coming here they have created something new in all the history of mankind—a land where man is not beholden to government; government is beholden to man. Government exists to insure that liberty does not become license to prey on each other. We haven't been perfect in living up to that ideal, but we've come a long way since those first settlers reached those shores asking nothing more than the freedom to worship God. They asked that He would work His will in our daily lives so America would be a land of fairness, morality, justice and compassion.

There was a conviction that standards of right and wrong do exist and must be lived up to. The institutions of family, community and school would play critical roles in the shaping of character, the acquisition of knowledge, and the search for truth. We passed thousands and thousands of laws in our two centuries as a nation—millions maybe—and yet if we simply adhere to the Ten Commandments that Moses brought down from the mountain—and he didn't just bring down ten suggestions—and the admonition of the Man from Galilee, to do unto others as you would have them do unto you, we could solve an awful lot of problems with a lot less government.

Our first President, George Washington, father of our country, shaper of the Constitution, and truly a wise man, believed that religion, morality, and brotherhood were the essential pillars of society, and he said you could not have morality without the basis of religion. And yet today we are told that to protect the First Amendment we must expel God, the very source of our knowledge, from our children's classrooms. One court has recently ruled that in one place in our land children cannot say grace on their own in the school cafeteria before they eat. Now this was done as being in accord with the Constitution, but was the First Amendment written to protect the American people from religion, or was it written to protect religion from government tyranny? No one will ever convince me that a moment of voluntary prayer can harm a child or threaten a school or a state. From the beginning of this administration I have made it clear that I believe that America's children have the right to begin their day the same way that members of the United States Congress do—with prayer.

The time has come for this Congress to give a majority of American families what they want for their children, a constitutional amendment that will make it unequivocally clear that children can hold voluntary prayer in their schools. Now I urge the Congress to work with me in passing an amendment that we can send to the states for ratification.

I know now what I am about to say will be very controversial, but I also believe that God's greatest gift is human life and that we have a sacred duty to protect the innocent human life of an unborn child. Now I realize that this view is not shared by all. But out of all of the debate on this subject has come one undisputed fact, and this has been the uncertainty of when life begins. And I just happen to believe that simple morality dictates that unless and until someone can prove the unborn human is not alive, we must give it the benefit of the doubt and assume it is. Thus it should be entitled to life, liberty and the pursuit of happiness.

As a nation we are struggling to guide ourselves safely through stormy seas. We need all the help we can get. I think the American people are hungry for a spiritual revival. More and more of us are beginning to sense that we cannot have it both ways. We cannot expect God to protect us in a crisis and just leave him over there on the shelf in our day-to-day living. I wonder sometimes if He isn't waiting for us to wake up and if maybe He isn't running out of patience.

Within our families, neighborhoods, schools, and businesses let us continue to reach out, renewing our spirit of friendship, community service and caring for the needy—a spirit that flows like a deep and mighty river through the history of our nation.

But to the lawbreakers and drug peddlers who would harm and prey on innocent citizens, who make our people live in fear, we also have a message: We will demand justice, and justice includes swift and sure punishment for the guilty!

You know, someone once asked, "Which role will you play: Will you be the wrecker who walks your town, content with the labor of tearing down, or will you be the builder who works with care that your town may be better because you've been there?" With the caliber of leadership from people like your president, Duane Acker, KSU's answer is loud and clear. You have every right to be proud.

Let me give you another example of a down-home, private sector initiative that impressed me very much. I mentioned the federal savings and loan here, but just recently 25 Kentucky banks voluntarily reduced their prime lending rate to around 12 percent, so local homeowners would have more investment capital to create jobs and families could afford home mortgages. The banks also challenged other state banks to do the same. Imagine how many jobs could be created if the number of banks in America making that kind of voluntary gesture was not 25, but 50 times 25?

The strengthening of spiritual ties, binding of families and coming together of communities is making America whole again. We are rebuilding. But we've only begun to rebuild.

As we lift our spirits, we must continue to lift the yoke of economic oppression that has penalized hard-working families, weakening our strength, threatening our security. In the last 19 months, a coalition of Republicans and Democrats has begun to rein in a government that is careening out of control, pushing us toward economic collapse, and, quite probably, the end of our way of life. This is no exaggeration. Over a 22-year period, the Federal government has managed to balance the budget only once. It has increased spending more than 600 percent, increased taxes more than 500 percent and mortgaged our future by pushing the national debt over $1 trillion.

Well, the coalition that I mentioned has begun to set things right. Federal spending growth has been cut nearly in half from that suicidal 17 percent-a-year rate that it was running in 1980. Inflation has dropped from 12.4 percent to 5.4 so far this year. And prime interest rates are down from 21.5 percent to 13.5. Leading economic indicators, which forecast future economic activity, have been up for four months in a row now, and that hasn't happened for quite a while.

Yes, recovery has been sighted, but these statistics that I just mentioned are cold comfort to someone who is still out of work. Unfortunately, unemployment is just about the last indicator to turn around after a recession.

The other problem is, unemployment has been gaining on us for years. Since 1976, the unemployment rate in this country has averaged over seven percent, far higher than in earlier post-war years. High inflation and interest rates pushed more and more families to seek a second income. To charge that our administration is trying to reduce inflation on the backs of the unemployed is to stand truth on its head. More than anything else, it was those record interest rates and double-digit inflation that led inevitably to this recession. And it started quite a while ago. And that's what we're trying so hard to turn around. And until we do, we have a responsibility.

Alf Landon reminded us that in a time of trouble, "it is reasonable and nothing less than just that the government exert all its powers to prevent suffering among the less fortunate." This we will do. What does it mean when we say we love America? I think it means we think, before anything else, that we love our countrymen, that we reach out with a helping and healing hand when they cry out or fall behind, and that we tell them, "Don't be afraid. You're not alone."

You may have read the passage in the Psalms which says: "Weeping may endure for a night, but joy cometh in the morning." The American people have endured a long and terrible night, lasting more than a decade and filled with one economic disappointment after another. Today, that long night is ending. We will see a new dawn of hope and opportunities for all our people.

With the help of your senior Senator Bob Dole, we've just passed a tax reform and spending reduction bill, that, along with the budget resolution, can reduce projected deficits by nearly $380 billion over the next three years. And we've done this without cancelling the tax cut passed last year which will save taxpayers $335 billion in those same three years. That means the average family next year will pay $788 less in personal income taxes. But we still have one major hurdle to clear. We must summon the courage to get control of the spending programs which have been the major cause in recent years of budget hemorrhaging, and spiraling deficits and the high interest rates.

I've said before, balancing the budget is a little like protecting your virtue: you just have to learn to say "No." The Congress passed legislation in 1978 requiring the budget to be in balance by fiscal year 1981. But, like Rodney Dangerfield, the legislation "didn't get no respect."

It seems to me that Republicans and Democrats alike want an end to runaway government spending, even if that means pruning some popular programs. The people have something that is often in short supply in government—common sense. They understand that making this government live within its means will ultimately do more to protect their earnings, bring down interest rates and put our unemployed back to work than anything else we could do.

The gist of the message I've been receiving is: "No more ifs, ands, buts or maybes; we want an amendment to the United States Constitution making balanced budgets the law of this land and we want that amendment now."

The Senate has done its job and brought us a step closer to a constitutional amendment. But the House leadership is keeping the bill bottled up in committee. This is no partisan issue. It's the people's will and today we're saying to the House: "Let their voices be heard."

There is one other goal on the horizon that we should all work together to reach. We should go much further in reducing tax rates and make that whole jigsaw puzzle of a tax system more simple and fair for all.

I had someone make out my income tax and when I read it all made out, I couldn't understand it.

Everything we're trying to do from eliminating wasteful spending and regulations to reducing tax rates and returning power and resources to the states and communities and honoring the roles of families, churches and schools boils down to putting you, the American people, back in charge of your country again. We want you to enjoy more opportunities and to have a much greater say in shaping America's future.

Apply that philosophy to agriculture. American farmers were

hurt badly and still have not recovered from the disruption their markets suffered from the grain embargo against the Soviet Union.

We believe that government's proper role is to act as friend, partner and promoter of American farmers and their products around the world. And, as promised, we lifted the embargo. The Soviets have accepted our offer to extend the grain agreement requiring that they purchase at least six to eight million metric tons and we're willing to sell them a lot more.

So far, we've dispatched trade teams to 23 nations in Europe, Africa, Latin America, the Middle East and the Far East. We're committed to opening agricultural markets in all countries. We challenge other countries, particularly our friends in Europe and Japan, to match this commitment.

Again, I want to salute Kansas State University for its invaluable research efforts and the many contributions that it makes with such programs as international grains and the food and feed grain institute.

Looking to the future, big challenges await us in the growing markets of high-valued products and in the development and mastery of electronics in the agricultural field.

We are a peaceful country. We seek a more peaceful world where liberty and enterprise can flourish, bring greater fulfillment to people who are now deprived and oppressed. On my recent trip to Europe, I had the privilege of personally promising His Eminence Pope John Paul II that America will do everything possible for peace and for genuine arms reduction.

But to keep the peace and to keep our freedom, we must stay strong. I have seen in my lifetime, many of you in yours, how despots took the world to the brink because they thought the spark of freedom had died in our hearts.

Sons and daughters of Kansas, as well as the rest of our country—brave war heroes like Bob Dole—proved how wrong those despots were.

To those today who would charge us with being imperialistic or warmongering, let them be reminded of a little history. After World War II, we were the last power undamaged by the war, our industry intact. We occupied Germany and Japan, our erstwhile enemies. We alone had the ultimate weapon, the atom bomb. We could have very easily dominated the world. But that's not what America's all about. We used our power as a force for good, to take freedom's next step and with our Marshall Plan lift mankind another rung. And we applied it to our erstwhile enemies as well as to our friends.

We can do that again and, as you have before, you can help us by leading the way. You have a special gift. I remember how the historian, Carl Becker, wrote about his first visit to your state, to Kansas. He didn't want to come. He missed the green hills of New England. He sat on the train and described the "dreary yards" of Kansas City. But then he noticed a young girl gazing silently out the train window for a long, long time. And finally she turned to her companion and with deep feeling said just three words: "Dear old Kansas." And it was then that Becker said he realized that Kansas is a state, a philosophy, a religion, and a way of life all in one.

You have within you a deep well of goodness, strength, and inner peace that can carry America forward. And I know you will. And to all of the young people who are here today, we not only have faith in you and are going to welcome you out into this society of ours to help with the problems, but there are some of us that hope with all our hearts that we can start making payments on that massive debt so that you and those who come behind you will know that we don't selfishly intend to leave it all to you.

Thank you all very much. God bless you.

Ahmed Zaki Yamani (1930–) is the former minister of Petroleum and Mineral Affairs of Saudi Arabia. He was educated at Cairo University, New York University, and Harvard University. His government service includes legal advisor to the Council of Ministers, Minister of State, and Minister of Petroleum and Mineral Affairs. He has been a director of the Arab-American Oil Company and Secretary-General of the Organization of Oil Exporting Countries.

Control and Decontrol in the Oil Market

Ahmed Zaki Yamani

Sheikh Ahmad Zaki Yamani was not the first foreign official to speak in the Landon Lecture Series, but his lecture was one of the most memorable. As he began to speak from the stage of McCain Auditorium, an eerie jeering howl arose from a dozen or more militant anti-Saudi Muslims who had distributed themselves at various points in the auditorium. When it became obvious that the protesters were unwilling to let Yamani speak without interruption, the auditorium was emptied and the audience then readmitted, minus protesters.

Sheikh Yamani was finally able to speak about 45 minutes later than scheduled. In typically gracious fashion, he asked his listeners not to judge the protesters too harshly. "They are young and so frustrated," he explained.

It is unfortunate that the events surrounding Yamani's Landon Lecture detracted from the content of the lecture itself, a cogent argument in favor of maintaining a controlled oil market and thereby avoiding the devastating price fluctuations characteristic of a free market in that particular commodity. Yamani's comments were reprinted in Vital Speeches *and might profitably be read in comparison with the Landon Lectures of Milton Friedman, Senator Fulbright, and James Schlesinger.*

MARCH 28, 1983

The pattern of economic life which exists today in the world outside centrally planned economies can rarely be described as "a purely free system." I come from a country which staunchly believes in the principles of free trade and the pursuit of private enterprise. These principles are not transplanted into my community, but rather deeply embedded in our Islamic tradition and precepts which regard the human initiative as a fundamental will of God. In the words of the Quran:

> "He hath subordinated land to your labour, so disperse in its wide alleys and eat from what He bestowed upon you."

Similarly, this is a country which is a firm believer in the free system, both for itself and for others. The free system has always functioned with admirable success and efficiency to the benefit of people everywhere.

It is not a coincidence that I come at this moment to speak before this distinguished audience about certain aspects of energy. Our two countries not only share common principles of economic life, but are also among the largest world producers of energy, the utilization of which has been subordinated to certain swift variations with damaging consequences. At times these changes have favored the interests of the oil producers, whereas those of the consumers were damaged. At others, the interests of the producers were damaged while those of the consumers were served. When a supply shortfall existed, prices were pushed to extremely high levels leaving the consumers with a high bill to pay for imported oil. Conversely when demand fell, prices tended to slide downwards, depriving the exporting countries of vital earnings essential for their development plans. In both instances, the price of oil tended to hurt a single party at a time. These oscillations may underscore the contention that the reason for the damage is the absence of a correct judging system under which the price would be set at an equilibrium of supply and demand. The fact that demand has risen and fallen sharply over the last twelve years is evidence enough that, most of the time, the price has overshot the equilibrium level in both directions.

Let us examine some historical events in retrospect and see whether this contention is valid. During the 1950s and 1960s the price of oil was kept at a low level. During this period it remained almost unchanged in nominal terms, which meant that its value depreciated in real terms. This was accomplished only because of the control exercised on production and distribution of this commodity by a group of international oil companies. Such suppression prevented the price of oil from finding its true market level as warranted by the upward movement of all other relevant indicators such as demand, output, energy productivity, prices, labor wages, and incomes.

When the pricing power was restored to the owners of the oil resources, the price, which at one time seemed to have stabilized in the mid-seventies, once again overshot its true value in the early eighties. At that time the indicators, although not readily visible to analysts, were pointing in the opposite direction, namely declining demand, receding output, falling inflation, and stagnant real wages. Nonetheless, the price continued to rise. Market signals failed to reach the price setters, and pressure suddenly mounted to reduce prices massively.

What further complicated the situation is the role played by stock manipulation. It is commonplace now to reiterate the well-known argument that oil stocks management had swerved 360 degrees in the fulfillment of its objectives. Instead of building up stocks when supply was abundant at cheap prices, the managers replenished their stocks to the brim during supply shortfalls and higher prices. Instead of drawing down stocks at periods of high demand and high prices, they are drawing them down when demand and prices have fallen. Should we deduce from those past events then that control was a failure, and that the oil market should be left entirely free for inherent forces to guide the price towards equilibrium for the benefit of the world community? In fact there is a school of thought which advocates this kind of approach. Let us try to investigate this approach and see for ourselves what would be the outcome of its application. In trying to portray a reasonable scenario, our assumptions should also be reasonable and consistent. First it should be remembered that if a purely laissez faire system is assumed for the oil market, such laissez faire must be assumed to apply to other energy sources, international trade, and all other relevant variables. This is essential if a meaningful evaluation is to be made. Under this background let us assume that the oil market is left entirely free from any kind of control, and that its price fell to $15 per barrel. Then the following chain of events may conceivably take place in the short term:

(A) At $15 per barrel for the marker crude, the price of fuel oil could drop to $10 per barrel, undercutting American coal CIF the Atlantic Seaboard by about $5 per barrel. Coal demand and eventually U.S. coal production would fall by about 2 million barrels per day of oil equivalent as end users in the electricity generation industry shift back to fuel oil.

(B) Costly U.S. stripper wells, as well as new production, may drop by another 1 million barrels per day.

(C) North Sea oil production, whose cost is about $15 per barrel on the average, is bound to decline by a further 1 million barrels per day.

(D) Coal imports to West Europe and Japan, whose cost is in the range of $19 per barrel of oil equivalent, may be entirely halted, shifting the resulting energy gap in favor of oil to the tune of 1 million barrels per day of oil equivalent.

In sum, demand for OPEC oil will soon rise by an amount of 5 million barrels per day.

The long-term effects may be summarized as follows:

(A) A pronounced decline in exploration and development of new oil fields.

(B) A pronounced reduction in gas supplies.

(C) A slowdown in the erection of new nuclear plants.

In the financial sector, oil-producing countries, especially those with substantial foreign debts, may withhold their debt repayments or even declare insolvency. Surplus countries now in need of more funds may resort to the withdrawal of their reserves held in Western banks. Those banks and other financial institutions, finding themselves squeezed between massive deposit withdrawals by one group of developing countries and failure in debt repayments by another, are bound to collapse. International trade will also suffer as developing countries' ability to import goods from the industrialized countries is greatly weakened. In fact most of the decline witnessed in international trade during 1982 came as a result of negative growth in oil trade.

Should low prices be sustained for a few years, a new demand for oil will be generated from increased economic activity as a result of the rebound in the world economy which now appears on the horizon. New demand, which may come on top of that which has been shifted from non-OPEC sources, may in a few years gather momentum and bring pressure to bear on the price once again, pulling it to new high levels, and the world may witness the emergence of a new cycle of volatile oil prices. In brief, history will repeat itself. Consequently our scenario for freely determined market prices obviously has not brought about the desired solution. But if previous efforts to control the market have failed, and if a free market mechanism is also bound to fail, then what is it that will not fail? In answering this question, it should be remembered that oil is not an ordinary commodity like tea or coffee. It is a strategic commodity. If it is not guided properly it is bound to create many difficulties of a non-economic nature. This element in itself is reason enough to create a feeling of anxiety that renders its price extremely sensitive to supply security considerations; hence its extreme volatility. In dealing with oil, the market mechanism can provide the best criteria to determine its value provided the element of volatility is catered to. Volatility tends always to obscure the real value of oil as signalled by market forces. This blurring phenomenon explains why control measures in the past 10 years did not bring forth the right pricing decisions. Their failure, however, is not proof that the concept of control itself is inadequate. Nor is it the result of the failure of the free market system itself. Failure lies in the misinterpretation by the controlling body of the proper market signals relevant to the equilibrium price when they occur. The free market is extremely essential as a reference for indicating the true price. The existence of a controlling body is also necessary for setting out the right price as signalled by the market. It must also be assigned with the additional function of moderating volatility and psychological vagaries, which inherently permeate the market, particularly the spot market. Oil is too important a commodity to be left to the vagaries of the spot or futures market, or any other type of speculative endeavor. OPEC, despite its short-comings, is still the best body to assume the role of price setter. Mistakes were committed in the past, but they will serve as a lesson in the future.

When I talk about control, I do not mean cartelization. Control even under the freest of market systems is resorted to frequently as a moderating tool of certain wild market forces. Recent history of economic life abounds in examples of administrative intervention in the market at all levels. High interest rates, that were introduced

more than two years ago, did not come about as a direct consequence of demand and supply of capital funds. They were determined by a governing body as a potent instrument of combatting
inflation. Inflation is an economic malaise which comes to the surface when the rate of price increases surpasses that of goods and
services. If the excess is moderate, it is acceptable, but it turns into
a contagion when the excess is great or runs out of control. Inflation
can occur during stagnation and also after the stage of full employment is reached. Inflation, like oil price volatility, is one of those
things which do not conform to the model of a free-market mechanism. The only means of combatting it lies in control by a public
authority. Unfortunately, in the case of inflation control, the cost to
the community can be enormous, particularly if the trade-off is employment and prosperity. In the energy sector, another form of intervention may be relevant. When demand for oil and energy was
diagnosed in certain communities as excessively high, a misalloca-
tion of resources was spotted by the energy planners. The market
price alone, even at its high levels, was not in itself enough to point
out the long term scarcity of oil resources. Moderating factors designed to reduce demand were therefore introduced outside the
free-market system. Rules and regulations were enacted for setting
out certain standards for energy consuming machines and space
accommodations, in spite of the consumers' choice. The resulting
saving in consumption was a great success, but again the trade-off
was further unemployment and lower production rates. That was
due to the time lags resulting from the slow transition of affected
industries in their restructuring activities designed to accommodate
the new measures. We in Saudi Arabia have suffered a great deal at
periods of high demand as well as at those of low demand in terms
of revenue, while trying to apply policies reasonably based on market realities. Recent developments could perhaps persuade many oil
producers to adopt such policies. OPEC is now seeking price determination policies whose objective is to set the price on an equilibrium course, *that should, of course, be dynamic, and then to protect this
level* in a manner which balances supply and demand, thus further-
ing the cause of stability.

Edward M. Kennedy (1932–) is a U.S. Senator from Massachusetts and the leader of the liberal wing of the Democratic party. He was first elected to the Senate in 1962 at the age of 30 and later became majority whip and, in 1979, chairman of the Senate Judiciary Committee. He was a candidate for the Democratic nomination in the presidential race of 1980, but later withdrew. He was elected to his fifth term in 1982. He chose not be a candidate in the 1984 presidential election.

The Changing Relationship Between Politics and Public Policy

Edward M. Kennedy

Some Landon Lectures are dispassionate and analytical enquiries into a specific issue. The address Senator Edward Kennedy delivered on January 30 1984, was just the opposite—a powerful and passionate critique of a wide range of Reagan administration policies. As such, it should be read in comparison to Reagan's 1982 Landon Lecture as well as to those by other Reagan administration officials, such as Secretary of State George Shultz. On another level, however, Kennedy's comments raised fundamental issues that will remain important long after the Laffer Curve and the MX missile have faded into history. Most importantly, he raised the question of how an opposition party in our political system can articulate its case before the public when a popular president has seemingly succeeded in changing the public agenda.

JANUARY 30, 1984

First of all, I want to thank President Acker for that generous introduction.

And I also want to thank my colleague Nancy Landon Kassebaum for inviting me here. She is a person of strong convictions and an independent voice in the Senate. I intend to be direct and plain in my own remarks today, and she certainly will not agree with everything I have to say. But Senator Kassebaum and I share a common commitment to the civility which holds that friends can differ and still respect one another. And I am proud to call Nancy Kassebaum my friend.

I am honored to come to this campus, for this lecture series, in tribute to that good and decent man—Alfred M. Landon. Actually, I share more with him than our common interest in politics or my

241 "

presence here today. As you may know, we both ran for President—and we both lost. In 1936, he carried Maine and Vermont—and in 1980, I carried the delegations from Maine and Vermont at the Democratic National Convention. It is nice to know that voters in those states can be so persistent in their convictions over so many years.

I am also honored to follow Ronald Reagan in giving this Landon Lecture—which he delivered a year and a half ago. There are some who even suggest that someday I may wish to follow Mr. Reagan in another capacity. But the truth is—I have no present intention of seeking or accepting the endorsement of the Republican Party for President. Of course, I probably have no prospect of getting that endorsement, either.

Actually, I did not choose to run in 1984, because I knew the big spender issue would come up—and I didn't see how I could possibly compete with Mr. Reagan and his 200-billion-dollar deficits.

A generation ago, my friend and the historian Arthur Schlesinger, Jr. came to Kansas to interview Alf Landon for the third volume of his study, *The Age of Roosevelt.* After meeting Governor Landon, he remarked how the reality confounded his assumptions. For the governor was a progressive, not a reactionary; decades after his defeat in 1936, he was looking to the future, not the past. With candor and a quiet good humor, he spoke of his loss, and even of the contributions which Franklin Roosevelt had made to American life. Professor Schlesinger left the prairie with a very different sense from the one he had brought with him. Today, he thinks of Alf Landon as a Kansas Truman.

How fitting it is, then, that these lectures have become your special way to advance his legacy. Here, on the prairie he loves, where he has lived all his years, the leaders of the nation come annually to speak in his honor—and at their best, to question our own preconceptions as a people, and to take a new and truer look at the reality of our national experience.

So it was in 1968, shortly after he announced his presidential candidacy, Robert Kennedy delivered the Landon Lecture, in which he assailed Vietnam as a war which was wrong and which could not be won. That appearance had a special place in his heart—for the cheers he heard on that day were the clearest of signals that young people everywhere were prepared, in a springtime of discontent, to stand and work for peace abroad and for a just and more compassionate America.

I have come here now, many years later—not as a candidate, but with a continuing belief in that same cause. I have come here to discuss the present relationship between our politics and our policymaking—between the tactics of an election year and the directions we will take or not take in the other years of our national life.

Last week, we heard the President's description of the state of the union—which was carefully crafted to fit the coming campaign. In a sense, we all understand this—even the commentators who understated it for the sake of propriety. But I believe it is also time to pause and reflect on the increasing extent to which the momentary demands of our politics now shape the state of our union.

Much of what I say will refer to present events and the present administration; but most of it also applies to past administrations of both parties. And as you will recall, I have not been entirely unwilling on other occasions to criticize presidents of my own party.

But the problem goes deeper than any personality or partisanship. Whether they are Republicans or Democrats, presidents appear more and more tempted to make decisions which will fly until the next election, even if they will falter during the next term or fail the next generation. Choices of policy are keyed to a brief political season and to the claims that may prove to be plausible and persuasive then. Indeed, we no longer even seem to worry about the difference between the rhetoric of the last campaign and the record since then of the successful candidate. We seem to assume that the public has a short and convenient memory.

In 1980, we were told that a supply-side tax cut would generate new savings and new revenue—and that by the end of 1983, we would have a balanced budget. Today the savings rate has dropped and we have the highest federal deficit in history. Measured by that standard, supply-side economics should have been left on the back of the cocktail napkin on which the Laffer curve was originally written in a Washington restaurant ten years ago. Instead, the administration now boasts about a so-called "economic miracle" which is wholly unrelated to any of the claims originally made for their supply-side theory.

They say we have a low inflation rate—and so did Herbert Hoover. In fact, we can always bring inflation down by bringing on a recession—and we have just endured the deepest recession since the great depression of the 1930s.

They point to the steepest decline in unemployment since World War II—which in fact is largely a result of creating the highest unemployment of the post-war era. On election day 1984, the rate of unemployment will still be higher than it was on the same day four years ago—when Ronald Reagan had taken up the cry, "Jobs, jobs, and more jobs."

There is nothing miraculous or mysterious about a temporary election year recovery, wrought by unprecedented deficit spending, on a scale unimagined by the most extravagant advocates of Keynesian economics.

But in fact, the administration simply ignores the other half of the Keynesian prescription—which is that the deficit must be reduced as the economy regains strength. They believe they can make it to the election with a policy that may please the voters, but cannot long continue after the ballots are cast and counted. In fact, there are grim prospects for 1985 and 1986—a renewal of inflation or a new interest rate crunch—or perhaps another, even deeper, recession.

Many economists fear this; many reporters know it—but almost no one writes about it. The press seems fascinated with the flashing headline of the latest statistic. We hear constantly about the silver lining—but hardly at all about the dark clouds looming on the economic horizon.

The President insists that there will be no tax increase to close the deficit, while his advisers wink and hint that of course they will bring him around—in 1985. This may be a winning political tactic; but it jeopardizes economic growth and jobs.

Most of all, what is lost is the confidence of Americans in their own system. Promised one thing, given another, they are increasingly alienated; they register and vote in decreasing percentages.

And so we move from election to election—and the victor is the candidate who can most nimbly manipulate the events of a few months in a single year, to influence the voting of a few hours on a single day.

Obviously, politicians are supposed to play politics—and they always have, from the very beginning of the republic. Events can overtake ideology or issues. The Jefferson who proclaimed limited federal power later purchased the Louisiana Territory with federal dollars. But he did not suspect in advance that he would do the opposite of what he said. Similarly, Franklin Roosevelt pledged in the 1940 campaign, in a legendary example of political phrasing, that he would not take America into "any foreign wars." But at the heights of that campaign, when Britain's survival was at stake, he approved lend lease in the teeth of the isolationist storm. He knew there was a point beyond which the tactic of the moment had no place. Franklin Roosevelt could devise a stratagem, turn a phrase, or reverse his field, but always within bounds—and always with a sure sense that politics could be an honorable profession even if it was not angelic.

How far we have drifted from that standard in the last twenty years. Perhaps the power of television or the changing nature of the press has made the events of the moment matter, at least in many minds, far more than a course of years. And perhaps we have just become accustomed to campaigns as games and to elections as primarily exercises in partisan maneuver.

In 1964, we hardly discussed the most fundamental issue of the next four years—the war in Vietnam. The scant words we heard were irrelevant to the real debate we should have held. A disillusioned student later observed, "I was warned that if I voted for Goldwater we would soon have half a million American troops in Vietnam. I did—and we did."

In 1968, the voters were offered a secret plan for peace—and there were more casualties afterwards in the war than there were before. On the eve of the 1972 election, an administration flourished the announcement that peace was "at hand"—which was followed in December by the fierceness of the Christmas bombing.

Even the most fundamental issue of all time—the threat of nuclear war—has become a hostage of political tactics. In 1976, the Democratic nominee promised a better arms control agreement than the one already negotiated by President Ford. In 1980, the Republican nominee promised a better agreement than the one already negotiated by President Carter. The result so far is no agreement, as each new candidate strives every four years to prove that he can be tougher or more effective with the Russians.

This year again, foreign as well as domestic policy has become a pawn of politics.

Some White House aides talk of the peace issue—as if it were mostly a political problem for Ronald Reagan. Others openly imply that they only need to play for time before launching a wider war in Central America in 1985—which would be a tragic replay of the fateful mistake of two decades ago in Indochina. It would be wrong to pull a Grenada against Nicaragua this year—and it will be equally wrong the year after the election. We must not talk peace in 1984, as a prelude to making war in 1985.

To lessen fears about an administration whose officials have spoken of winnable nuclear conflict, the President says he welcomes nuclear arms control. But what faith can voters have that the President will pursue this professional interest in his second term, when he has been so bellicose in his first?

In the State of the Union message, we were told that America is "safer, stronger, and more secure than ever before." But there is no security in an arms race now spinning out of control; there is no safety in a Latin American policy which has replaced an alliance for progress with a new and dangerous alliance with repression; and there is no strength in a Lebanon policy which has sent our Marines into an indefensible position—to fight and die not for a reason, but for a mistake.

We have all read the reports that political pressures may finally force the administration to modify its course in the Middle East, in Central America, and on arms control. But I am concerned about how this President will choose to face our adversaries after he no longer has to face the voters. Whatever he may say in an election year, Ronald Reagan has spent too much time preparing for war—and not enough time preventing it.

The commentators almost unanimously admire the administration's skill. They agree that the President's strategy is superb politics, even if most of them seldom ask whether it is sound policy. They view the State of the Union message as a path to re-election, not a guide to the American future as it can or ought to be.

In the face of all this, how will the loyal opposition react? How can the Democratic Party advance its own prospects as well as the national purpose?

First, we must challenge ourselves not to accept the conventional terms of the economic debate. We must decline to let the election turn on the last economic report of October when more basic issues are at stake for the longer term.

We can and should do more than brood about the deficits—and with courage, we can and should advocate the tax increases and military cuts necessary to reduce them. We must talk sense to the people, rather than competing with an administration which tells them only what they want to hear.

There are some who suggest that Democrats cannot be trusted to deal with federal deficits, because we have had too many of our own. But the present deficits are the greatest in the history of the nation; they make the most imprudent Democrat look positively parsimonious. The deficit for this year alone would pay for a national health insurance plan five times over. If Franklin Roosevelt had ever hinted at a budget so out of balance, Alf Landon would have carried Maine and Vermont and every other state as well.

When the administration renews its call for a balanced budget constitutional amendment, we must reply: How dare they advance such a proposal again, when they themselves are the biggest deficit spenders in American history? How can they ask the Constitution to balance the budget, when the President cannot do it himself? For three straight years, in his own recommendataions, he himself has sent Congress an unbelievably unbalanced budget.

When the administration demands a line item veto on spending or a commission to cut the deficit, we must ask: What items would they like to veto? Where are their specific budget reductions?

When the President says the problem is domestic spending, we must challenge him: How can that be, when the deficit is now fifty billion dollars larger than all discretionary domestic spending combined? What would he like to slash—child immunization, farm support, student loans, civil rights enforcement?

The President argues that we can reduce the deficit—and I quote—by "reducing the scope of government." But that is a cliche, not a program. Surely, after three years in power, Mr. Reagan can offer real measures, not the generalities of his basic speech. Sometimes, when he condemns government as too big, we have to remind ourselves that he is in office, not in opposition. It is his government, and he must not be permitted to run for re-election by running against himself.

Of course, there are savings which can be made—but here again, there is a fundamental difference. The administration, for example, seeks to reform Medicare by slashing benefits for the elderly; the Democrats want to limit the costs of the program by placing real controls on what doctors and hospitals can charge. A doctor with a $300,000 a year income can afford to charge less; a senior citizen who is sick cannot afford to go without care.

We can reduce the deficit now, and eliminate it by the end of this decade, if we will stand forthrightly for fair tax reform and a fair tax increase, for fair restraints on spending, and for the end of wasteful military projects like the MX missile, the B-1 bomber, Star Wars schemes, and a new generation of nerve gas weapons.

What we hear from the President is a vague plan to overhaul taxes at a later date. He promises to unveil his plan at a very convenient time—December 1984. How do you suppose he chose that date? And who do you think will benefit if this administration has a second term and a second chance to redistribute tax burdens in the wrong direction?

The numbers do not lie. Since 1980, five million more people have fallen below the poverty line. The poverty rate now stands at fifteen percent, the highest level since 1967. And the richest twenty percent of our people now have their largest share of the national income since 1950.

So far, after accounting for inflation and social security taxes, no family earning under $30,000 is better off after the tax cut—but families with incomes of $200,000 have reaped a 15 percent reduction worth over $60,000 each. One more such tax program—and our economy shall be undone.

Instead, we must show in this campaign the truth of Alfred Landon's words long ago: "I believe that a man can be a liberal without being a spendthrift." Actually, before President Reagan came along, we also used to believe that man could be a conservative without being a spendthrift.

A responsible economic policy is also the key to putting profit back into agriculture. Never has the federal government spent more and done less for the farmers of America. Farm exports have gone down by 21 percent under this administration because of over-heated interest rates and overvalued dollars. And federal farm spending has gone up to $21 billion, but family farmers are going down the drain. The Texas Agriculture Commissioner was right when he said: "Ronald Reagan's idea of a good farm program is 'Hee Haw.'"

We must renew the sense of economic hope and opportunity which has moved this country forward at other times. Our people sense that we have fallen behind, that other nations have developed more modern industries with greater efficiency. We can and should shape a new industrial strategy to move America into the 21st century—and we must not be deterred by anti-government slogans. We must not accept a recovery which leaves out the workers of the Northeast, the closed factories of the industrial Midwest, the farms of the prairie, and all those outside the electoral coalition of the Sun Belt. We are one country and one people—and we must never become an economy divided against itself.

Second, and in the same spirit, we must speak for all the Americans who were left out of the President's State of the Union message. We must try to feel and convey the painful despair of the powerless millions for whom these have been the hardest years of their lives.

We must speak for the homeless, the hungry, and the middle-class families driven into deprivation.

Where is the economic recovery for those who are sleeping in the snow and the cold of our streets? Where is the economic recovery for the black teenagers who are out of school and out of work—

and who will never have the opportunity that most of you enjoy? Where is the recovery for the 50,000 farmers who lost their land in 1983 alone, or for the many others on the verge of bankruptcy?

The President says we must break the bonds of dependency. But I do not believe in liberating people to live without shelter, without food, without health, and without hope.

And we must also speak for the civil rights of the minority who are not white—and for ERA and the equal rights of the majority who are women.

Why does this administration exalt government when it builds bombs and missiles, or interferes with fundamental liberties and individual privacy—but scorn government when it vaccinates a child or feeds the poor or helps a young family to own a home?

The loyal opposition must be loyal to an age-old ideal: This will not truly be America until it is the land of justice—not just for some, but for all.

Third and finally, we must reject the standard wisdom that foreign policy is never a decisive issue in a national campaign. For today, foreign policy may decide all the issues before us for all the time to come.

Today we are involved, directly or indirectly, in two hot wars and one cold war—and that is three wars too many.

Rather than their empty calls to endless talks, I call on the administration to negotiate seriously, at once, with the Soviet Union for an immediate, mutual, and verifiable freeze on the production, testing, and deployment of nuclear weapons. I am talking about more than a plank in a party platform; a negotiated halt to the arms race must be the first priority of a new foreign policy and the first priority for the future of our planet.

In the Middle East, our Marines at the airport in Beirut have become the hostages of 1984. They are hunkered down and bunkered in below the ground. They do not patrol; they do not seek out terrorists; they do not man checkpoints in the city. They are entirely preoccupied with barely protecting themselves. That is not a proper mission for any American fighting force, let alone the United States Marines. We sent them there to keep the peace, but there is no peace to be kept.

We give up nothing of any diplomatic value by withdrawing combat troops that have no combat purpose. Our naval presence provides ample military might to preserve our power and prestige while negotiations proceed. And as the last Marine departs, I would advise any terrorist killer, any Druse artillery gunner, any Iranian, any Syrian, any Soviet leader who doubts our commitment—I would tell them to look offshore, and see the battleship U.S.S. New Jersey.

Now is the time to bring the Marines out of Beirut—not because it is right for the election, but because it is right for America, and not another Marine deserves to die.

In 1984, we must also demand that America's role in Central America be stated, debated, and resolved. I oppose the covert war in Nicaragua—and the military escalation in El Salvador. I oppose the policy of scorning human rights in that country, and then putting 5,000 American troops on permanent maneuvers in Honduras. The President may have a different view, but this country has a right to know his vision of our future in that region. Central America must be an issue in this campaign—so that afterwards we will not go to war by the back door, with our people divided and deceived. History has taught us in anguish and retreat the folly of that course.

At stake in 1984 is the very character of our democracy. We cannot afford another election where people vote for promises that will be broken, where the manipulations of the moment disguise deeper realities and different intentions.

After the State of the Union speech, one commentator said that it was "brilliant as a campaign strategy to run on"—that it was brilliant to propose a balanced budget amendment after tripling the deficit because—and I quote—"the public doesn't understand the deficit."

I believe that if the opposition does our part, the public can understand that issue and others. We can insist that words are no substitute for deeds—that we will not accept a secret tax plan and a 1985 tax surprise; that we reject the "eat, drink, and be merry" philosophy of this recovery; that we oppose any diplomacy which speaks of peace but stonewalls arms control; that we resist an administration which talks about protecting the environment but pursues a James Watt policy of protecting the polluters. And the challenge for us is not only to oppose, but to propose—to be bold in standing for our own beliefs and in stating truly democratic alternatives.

I believe that Americans are ready to be realistic, to respond and sacrifice, if we will open the way to change. The President may prefer to debate the past—his own and ours—and to argue about who has done worse.

We must recast the campaign and restate the challenge which has always led to the American future—that we can do better—better for our country and ourselves, better for the weakest among us, and better for the greater cause we all share of freedom and of peace.

Patricia Schroeder (1940–) has represented the First District of Colorado in the U.S. House of Representatives since 1972. Educated at the University of Minnesota and Harvard Law School, she was a practicing attorney before running for Congress. In the House, she serves on the Armed Services Committee, the Post Office and Civil Service Committee, and the Judiciary Committee. She was founder and is now co-chair of the Congressional Women's Caucus. She has been an outspoken advocate of women's rights, of reduced waste in military spending, and for greater efficiency in government agencies.

Great Expectations: From Abigail Adams to the White House

Patricia Schroeder

It is an unfortunate commentary on the role of women in American public life that only four of the seventy-three Landon Lectures delivered in the first two decades of the series were given by women. Anne Armstrong, Shirley Temple Black, and Lesley Stahl addressed topics not unlike those addressed by male speakers in the series. Congresswoman Pat Schroeder, however, dealt specifically with the issue of women in America. Her comments place the issue in both historical and personal context and display some of the optimism of the activist politician that the cause will triumph despite temporary setbacks.

Representative Schroeder's opening comments, concerning skiing in Kansas, are explained by the fact that she arrived at Kansas State University on Sunday, March 18, 1984, in the midst of a massive ice storm. By the time of her lecture the next morning, an unseasonably heavy snowfall had deposited several inches of snow on the campus and on Manhattan city streets. Although the unexpected bad weather cut into the size of the audience, it failed to dampen the enthusiasm of either the speaker or the audience.

Pat Schroeder's Landon Lecture was reprinted in Vital Speeches.

MARCH 19, 1984

Thank you all very much. Let me tell you I came to Kansas State University to ski. Don't tell people that in Colorado; I'll get in great trouble. I have seen some posters that say "Ski Kansas." I never took them seriously until today, but now I think they are right.

I was trying to figure out exactly how to handle all of this today and what kind of context to put it into. I was thinking that had we been raised with different *sayings* we wouldn't even have to have this speech today. If we had grown up hearing such things as "render unto Cleopatra those things that are Cleopatra's" or "no woman is an island" or "I never met a woman I didn't like," we wouldn't have to be here talking about Abigail Adams' first struggle to get equality for women and the continuing struggles ever since then.

Abigail Adams was really the Thomas Paine of the colonial women's movement. She was there and she was writing to her husband—as he was writing all those documents with his friends for this new country—saying "please include women." You remember her plea, "Remember the ladies," and she kept saying it over and over and over again. She said:

> "If particular care and attention are not paid to the ladies, we are
> determined to foment a revolution and will not hold ourselves
> bound to obey any laws in which we have no voice or representation."

Well, they didn't give her any voice and they didn't give her any representation. Women didn't have the right to vote and women didn't get to participate at that time. The revolution finally came, but it took a lot longer than Abigail Adams had thought to get moving. Nevertheless, when you look at the whole history of women in America you realize that they really have been participating since they first put their foot on the shore. I keep reminding people that we do not know enough about women's history and we ought to do everything that we can to reinstate it.

As much as we all agree with the men who wrote that Declaration of Independence, and as important as it was, I remind you that *writing* the Declaration was not a crime. George III could not have cared less what one wrote. *Printing* it was a crime, because then you could send it out to the colonies and everybody else might get the idea that they ought to revolt, too. So after they got it written, as you well know, they went around and tried to find someone to print it. All the printers that they found in Philadelphia said, "I love the document," "terrific," "great idea," "wish you all the best, but I really like my head right where it is and I have a family and I certainly wouldn't want to run the risk of being held for treason." They finally found a woman who had inherited her husband's printing press. Her name was Mary Goddard, and she said, "Lovely document. I understand it is treasonous. I want George III to know full well what I am doing." She is the one who printed it and she wrote her name on the bottom of the Declaration of Independence so George III would know that she knew full well what she was doing.

So, yes indeed, there is the name of a woman on there and, yes indeed, she did gamble a lot and many women gambled a lot to see that this country got started. Abigail Adams tried to tell them and they didn't listen. Nevertheless, what they did do was make Mary Goddard the Postmaster General of Baltimore—she was the highest paid federal woman employee, for, I think, 150 years—and forgot all the rest of them. But women went on to continue to contribute in this country in all sorts of ways and in all sorts of forms and I could give a whole lecture on just the history of women—*minutewomen* as I like to call them—and how we ought to bring them all back and talk about them more, but that is not quite our purpose here today.

The Abigail Adams rebellion has been some time fomenting. Her plea went unheeded and the Constitution ignored "the ladies." Women did not issue their declaration of independence until almost 75 years later, at the famed Seneca Falls convention in 1848.

No one at that convention lived to see women get the right to vote because that didn't happen nationwide until 1920. So it was a long, drawn-out situation. I am always amazed at the number of people who say to me, "Why do you re-introduce the ERA? You had your one chance." I answer that if they had done that with the right to vote, we would have never made it. You had your one chance and it was over in '48—1848 as a matter of fact—so it would have never transpired. But women worked very hard and men worked with them, finally, to get the right to vote and to participate.

In the interim they did all sorts of other things. Harvard Medical School has been coming out with several new books about how women have a different left brain-right brain weight from men. You've been reading all of that. And maybe that's why we haven't looked at what women have done in the past as being as valuable as what men have done. One of the things that they talk about as they are doing this whole new area of discovery of women's brains versus men's brains, is that it is very difficult for anybody to identify with the victim of anything unless he is a victim himself. It is very hard to imagine what it is like to be a victim of civil rights discrimination or any kind of persecution unless it really happens to you, and then we tend to get all activated. The interesting thing that women have been doing with this different-weighted brain is that it has been easier for them to make that connection with victims without being the victim themselves.

We all know and we all remember women's contributions in the past to people in mental health institutions. It was very courageous women who turned around how we dealt with the mentally ill. It was women who said, "Wait a minute. The way we are dealing with prisoners is wrong," and it wasn't very popular to feel sorry for prisoners and look at prison reform, but they were there.

When you look at the abolition of slavery, women were making that connection so that the rest of society could start to identify with what was going on. Let me give you an example. In the South you had Harriet Tubman. Harriet Tubman was running the underground railroad. She knew that if she wrote down the code for the railroad somebody would be apt to find it and break it. So instead, they wrote all those spirituals that the white folks thought were just nice little songs; but they were all codes for the underground railroad. If you memorized the code and sang the songs you knew how to get out. Thousands of people were able to escape through the underground railroad by knowing that code.

In the North there was another Harriet: Harriet Beecher Stowe, wanting desperately to help end the slavery conflict, thinking that it was one of the greatest social injustices in this country. But being very frustrated because people didn't understand how the victims felt, she wrote the book, as you all know, *Uncle Tom's Cabin*. So for the first time white America was able to make that leap and start identifying with the victim, and it was very helpful in dealing with abolition.

We know that women worked very hard in the child labor restrictions. Women have been active in all sorts of areas that our society hasn't always felt was important—software problems, people problems, victim problems, outcast problems, equality problems, education problems, and so forth. And again I could give you all sorts of incidents of women as innovators in these areas that follow on the new Harvard School theory of left brain-right brain.

We keep moving, we keep moving through this whole historical perspective. What we saw happening then was this giant head of steam coming to fruition in 1920 when the women did get the right to vote. People hoped that it was going to make a big difference in how electoral politics turned out. It did for a while—whole women's slates were run in some states and won. Many states then suddenly had co-chairs of their parties, men and women. There were a couple of states that had women on the Supreme Court.

All sorts of things started to happen in 1920. New laws got through in the Congress that really were very beneficial to women. People forget that in World War I, if a 10th generation American, as a woman, married a foreign national, she lost her citizenship. And in World War I many women in that situation who were married to Germans had all their property taken from them because they instantly lost their citizenship with marriage. That was changed. It was decided that women should be able to retain their citizenship just as men did, that women were not chattel to be traded.

Then the other thing that they found out was that during World War I more women in this country died in childbirth than we had troops dying in the war. And they found that the Congress was spending more money for vaccinating hogs than they were for looking at the problems of women and the maternity problems in getting live babies here and keeping the mother alive, too. In Colorado you can really see that. You can go through a lot of the old graveyards and look at the number of tombstones that say, "Died in childbirth." It is really quite shocking and you really realize what a revolution we have had in health care.

Those are some of the very major things that women voting in the '20s were able to get through, because they organized in Washington and they said, "These are our priorities."

But the movement ran out of *political* steam. Many women thought the battle was won and their interests turned elsewhere. The Depression hit, followed by World War II, the Cold War, and the Korean War. Women never quite got back to getting everything going and to changing the world the way they had hoped to be able to do it when they were asking for the right to vote.

In the 1950s, women ended up being portrayed as people who should be terribly happy if they had their floors waxed. And a lot of women started to ask, "Isn't there a little more to life than this?"

In 1960, *Redbook* magazine featured an article, "Why Do Young Mothers Feel Trapped," and asked their readers to write in with their stories. Over 24,000 mothers did. All was not well.

Betty Friedan's book, *The Feminine Mystique,* came out in 1963 and sold two million copies over the next 20 years. The mystique was "the problem that had no name"—the problems that had prompted 24,000 letters from *Redbook* readers.

Friedan focused attention on the identity crisis many women experience, the lack of fulfillment, the mystery that being a women was enough, and she gave it a name.

I think many of us who lived through that period understand how polarized we were. I often get into an awful lot of trouble with the women's movement by talking about this but I always tell them I was not raised in a stereotypical way. I went to Harvard Law School. My parents allowed me to fly airplanes. I studied Chinese. I did all sorts of things. I worked. But when I ran for Congress, if I had ever thought I was going to win, I wouldn't have run. Now that makes people very upset when they hear that, but I must say that even though I did all of those things, and even now, I come from a family where my mother worked—she was a teacher—and I didn't think of that as extraordinary. The whole concept of having a two year old and six year old and being a Congresswoman—in my head I said I could do it, down here in my stomach I said, "No way! What have I done to my life? What have I done to my family? Have I ever messed up! Tell me I didn't win." My husband kept saying, "You can't have a press conference and say, 'I was kidding.'" And I could sit there and say, "You know it really doesn't make any difference to my children whether I sort their socks or someone else does, or whether I do the grocery shopping or someone else does." But still down in your stomach, your cultural thing says, "What are you trying to do? You are trying to have it all, and maybe you can't." I was right in that shifting-sand area.

When I applied to Harvard Law School I remember my counselor saying, "That is terrible. Do your parents know you are doing this? They will probably never be grandparents because who in the world would marry someone who went to Harvard Law School." I remind you that that was not that long ago.

So at each step, I kept wondering if I really was doing the right thing. Because everyone wanted to remind me that I had sold out on femininity, that I couldn't be a mother, that my mother wouldn't have grandchildren, that my father wouldn't have grandchildren. "Isn't this awful? How can you deny them that privilege?" And I kept saying, "Don't you think they will be proud of me because I went to Harvard Law School?" My counselor said, "No." And he even said, "What is this going to do to your brother?" It was all very befuddling.

I think many women in my generation went through that era of trying to sort out who they were and what they were. We were allowed to go to college. We were allowed to get degrees. But when we came out of college, we weren't quite sure what we were supposed to do with the degree. At Harvard, when I was ready to graduate, I went into the personnel office and they said, "Look, you know nobody wants to hire young women. First of all, you're married. You will probably have babies and they just aren't going to be interested. We only try to put our students out that we feel really have some chance." And I said, "I have been paying you guys for this degree for three years. What am I supposed to do with it— hang it over the sink?" They kind of laughed and said, "I guess so." This sort of thing was going on in many young women's lives. Trying to figure out how that all happened. And these changing patterns just really left us all looking for our identity crisis. I think that's what Betty Friedan and many of the people in the women's movement captured in the early '70s as they started to talk about these issues. And yet we were a long way from being there.

In 1972 when I ran for office, the women's caucus in the Democratic Party, which I had helped found, endorsed my opponent because it was too early for a woman to run. So even those who were professed feminists weren't quite sure what we were supposed to be doing or where we were going.

We now see that we have sorted through more and more of this, and have become much more comfortable with it, and have a much better idea of what has really transpired. Basically what's transpired is that you have got more and more women in the work force and, let's face it, they are going to stay there outside the home and inside the home. Let's face it, all mothers are working mothers, outside the home and inside the home and they've got all sorts of balls to juggle in the air. The question is, what do we do with a society that really hasn't changed its laws or pretends that family life in this country hasn't changed since 1932? They would like to see all family life as a 1932 Norman Rockwell painting. Now, 17 percent of America's families look like that and the other 83 percent are different. You see man and wife both working, children in school, everybody is struggling to keep up with everything else and they really need different kinds of support.

You see the massive movement in the feminization of poverty. Two out of every three adults in poverty are women and the census bureau tells us it will be three out of three by the year 2000 if the trend continues. Now, who are the women moving into poverty? They are older women who suddenly find out that there was no pension to vest, or they didn't have survivor's benefits, or that they were treated under the inheritance laws like they have been lying around eating bon-bons, and anything they got from their husbands was a windfall, and they have to pay taxes on it rather than an economic partner. All that kind of discrimination has put older women in many instances below the poverty line for the first time in their life, and that's very cruel and very hard to adjust to. At the age of 43 I find it more and more difficult to be flexible, but suddenly to wake up and find that you are below the poverty line when you are 70 must really make it hard to be flexible and figure out what you are doing.

So you have the elderly woman and you have the younger woman of two different types. You have the single-parent-family woman, many of whom got married at a very young age, had children right away, don't have the job skills because they were told they didn't need them if they had a husband. They suddenly find themselves divorced with young children and they are 25 years old and have their whole life in front of them and they haven't been able to find the jobs that they can do that will support them, so that is very critical for them and it is very critical for their children.

Today we have five million more women and children living in poverty than we had just three years ago. For this society that is a very, very sobering factor. What we have been trying to do in the Congress is transcend what happened to the women's movement in the '70s. In the '70s I think it is most unfortunate that the women's movement got portrayed as a sporting event, and I think you know what I mean. The great thing was to get two fighting cats on television—you know, one going rah-rah and the other going rah-rah, and after you get all that done you didn't learn a thing. Look at how the media treated women's issues. George Washington University has done a very thorough analysis of the press in the '70s on six major women's issues. Domestic relations was one of the issues they looked at. Rather than looking at the lack of child support enforcement, rather than looking at the trend in courts not to give alimony or not to allow alimony to be collected, the whole focus concerning domestic relations was how hard Charlotte Ford was hitting up Henry Ford in their divorce suit. It makes great press and it's fun to read about.

The '80s haven't changed much; now we read about the Carsons. But the real families are not having that kind of problem because you are not talking about divvying up megabucks. You are trying to figure out how they survive if they come apart. And those real kinds of things are still not being addressed.

On the Equal Rights Amendment in the '70s, they looked at 2,200 newspaper stories. They found that fewer than 50 of those 2,200 newspaper stories quoted anyone that could be said to be an expert. Everybody else was putting out the same old garbage and misinformation on the Equal Rights Amendment—you know, unisex toilets and combat boots. People were saying that we couldn't have the Equal Rights Amendment because it would make us all the same. Now if anyone in this room can figure out how you can legislate to make everyone the same—you just can't do it. It reminds me when I first came to Congress and the beef shortage was on, and a Congressman from New York introduced a bill to shorten the gestation period of a cow. That probably would have helped the shortage, but you can't do that. Again, the Equal Rights Amendment doesn't bring unisex and it doesn't make everyone the same. It makes people *equal* in rights for pension, social security, for legal things that are out there. That is what it does. It is that simple. But again this document shows how people cannot understand that because the stories written about it were different. Of all those 2,200 stories written about the Equal Rights Amendment only 30 percent even copied the 24 words correctly. So people didn't even know what the amendment really said.

How do we transcend the polarization between women and women and between women and men, to achieve the new human wholeness that is the promise of feminism, and get on with solving the concrete, practical, everyday problems of living, working and loving as equal persons? That is the challenge of the '80s.

What were the changes in society that moved us this far, and where are we headed? Over the past several generations, while political feminism rose and fell, there were major social and economic changes going on in America. Some, like the migration of Americans from rural to urban areas, are well known. Others are less known, or are seen as recent trends. In fact, however, they have been building for decades. For example, female participation in the salaried work force has been steadily increasing *for the past century*. It is not just a post-World War II phenomenon. In 1890, only five percent of married women and 20 percent of all women were in the salaried work force. By 1910, ten percent of the married and 25 percent of all women held jobs outside the home. The rates dropped during the 1920s, and began to climb again during the Depression and war years. More significantly, the work participation difference between married and unmarried woman all but disappeared. *By 1980, half of all women in America were in the work force.* "My wife doesn't work," the former boast of many American men, was wrong on two counts. She either worked at home, in an unsalaried job, or she worked outside the home in a salaried job. In many cases, she did both.

Look at education over the past century, the number of undergraduate degrees awarded to women climbed slowly but inexorably.

In 1870, 15 percent went to women; by 1930 the number had risen to 40 percent. The G.I. Bill era reversed that trend, but only temporarily. By 1970, the gap was narrowing again. In 1980, women received 49 percent of all undergraduate degrees.

Female students were now majoring in traditionally male fields such as engineering—up 830 percent between 1972 and 1982; agriculture—up 429 percent; business—up 247 percent; architecture—up 130 percent; and computer sciences—up 123 percent.

Similar changes were occurring in the professions: between 1972 and 1982, women receiving degrees in law quadrupled from 7 percent to 30 percent; medicine more than doubled from 9 percent to 23 percent, dentistry went up sharply, from 1 percent to 14 percent; and veterinary science almost quadrupled, from 9 percent to 33 percent. The percentage of doctorate degrees awarded to women in the last ten years had almost doubled—from 16 percent to 30 percent.

These rather remarkable educational advances contrast with the Supreme Court's recent decision to restrict equal opportunity in education—the Grove City College case. Schools that receive federal financial assistance are now allowed more freedom to discriminate.

I always thought that if you paid equal taxes you ought to get equal services. That was an issue in 1776, and now it's an issue again.

Likewise, the federal government has recently moved to weaken the Women's Educational Equity Act, which had been a leader in funding programs to open math, science, technology, and vocational ed courses and careers to women. The current "budget zero" funds the program—that's Washington talk for eliminating the program.

Meanwhile, paradoxically, as women have made great strides in education, their economic fortunes stagnated. Because of job segregation and pay inequities, the wage gap between men and women has widened. Contrary to what one might expect, the wage gap is about the same regardless of educational level. Women—high school drop-outs or college graduates—receive less than 60 cents for every dollar earned by equally educated man. In my opinion, the single most important women's issue in the 1980s will be comparable worth—equal pay for jobs of comparable value.

A history lesson. Just over twenty years ago, in 1963, Congress passed the Equal Pay Act requiring businesses to pay equal wages for equal work. If you think that was a simple move, you're wrong. The fight to pass that law went on for years. Employer organizations argued it would cost them too much money and was improper government interference.

The equal pay fight was just the beginning. The simple fact remains that occupations filled with women—nursing, teaching, and secretarial—are generally low paying. Comparable worth does not mean pay men less, nor does it mean pay women more. It means pay *people* what they are worth. In many cases it will mean paying women more—I'm sure we can live with that.

Now the naysayers argue that there are no standards—no one can determine what a job is worth. If you will permit me a farm term, that's hogwash. Every business, company, union, and government agency has standards to set wages and salaries. Large corporations even have rules to decide the size of your office, the carpet on the floor, and the size desk you get. No, the problem is not lack of standards. *The problem is that there are standards and the standards are wrong.* When a nurse or a high school math teacher with a college education is paid less than a liquor store clerk with a high school education, there is something wrong with our wage standards, not to mention our values.

One of the naysayers, Phyllis Schlafly, was in Colorado recently. She said that liquor store clerks should be paid more than nurses because they lift heavy boxes; and tree timmers should be paid more than teachers because they work outdoors. Fine, let's pay nurses the same as surgeons, because they both work indoors. And secretaries the same as lawyers because neither lifts heavy boxes. Furthermore, the kids who deliver our newspapers should be paid six figure salaries because they drag around heavy bundles *and* brave the elements.

The real cause of the wage disparity is that most women's jobs—80 percent of all women are in 25 job categories like nursing, teaching, service, and office jobs—are not highly valued. Can someone explain to me why cutting a lawn is more valuable to society than teaching kindergarten?

In the first successful, major comparable worth lawsuit in the U.S., the federal case decided in Seattle last month, the judge found that there were standards, and the state of Washington violated them. There was a 20 percent wage disparity between jobs held largely by women and jobs held largely by men.

Paradoxically, as we see more women in the work force and more women getting more education, we are also seeing the feminization of poverty. The startling rise in the number of female heads of household and poor elderly women has feminized poverty. Divorce is a pivotal factor. Although there are indications that the divorce rate may have plateaued in recent years, between 1920 and 1980 it more than tripled. And if it has leveled off, it's a rather high plateau—more than 50 percent of marriages contracted today will end in divorce, separation, or desertion. The economic effect of divorce on women, especially those with children, is nothing short of disastrous.

Less than half the women who retain custody of the children receive their full, court-ordered child support. Almost one-quarter receive nothing. A California study of 3,000 divorced couples found that one year after divorce, the woman's income dropped 73 percent while the man's had increased 43 percent! It is little wonder, if present trends continue, that by the year 2000, the poor in America will be almost entirely women and children.

The anti-ERA lobby talks a lot about women needing to be "protected." But that's exactly the point of the ERA: inequality is no protection. Whatever the standard—wages, pensions, child support, survivors' benefits—women come up short. It is no wonder that the ERA has become an economic issue. The gender gap, the difference between how men and women tend to vote, is largely based on economic issues. Inequality is an economic issue.

Most public opinion polls show that men and women agree on what are called "women's issues" like ERA, day care, etcetera. The disagreements are on economic and peace issues. The margin in the gender gap polls ranges from five percent to 15 percent—a large margin considering that women make up 53 percent of the voters.

These trends are reshaping American politics because our political system accommodates itself to shifting currents. Women have adjusted to the new interest by male politicians in women's issues, and men have adjusted to the increased role of women and women's concerns in politics.

When I first came to the Congress there was no women's caucus, and that's because we had some members who said, "I'm not just a woman and I didn't come here and . . ." Finally we got everybody together, but only on the basis that we did nothing unless we had unanimous consent and the dues could never be more than $50 a year. Trying to get unanimous consent out of anything is hard, and $50 a year does limit your ability to do much more than have tea parties. When I took over the caucus I decided that the time had come to end that nonsense. I raised the dues to $2,000 a year and dropped the unanimous consent rule. We're big enough that we can disagree on some things and agree on some things, but we can't tie the hands of the caucus. It is important that we have a voice and it's important that we spend the money to have the research and data behind us. Obviously some of the women dropped out, but we decided that there were several men in the Congress who had a 100 percent voting record on women's issues and that we would invite those that had good voting records to join us.

The Congresswomen's Caucus changed its name to the Congressional Caucus for Women's Issues. Over 100 men joined and the total membership is now 129, making it one of the largest caucuses in the Congress. Senator Nancy Kassebaum is on our executive committee and Congressman Jim Slattery is a caucus member.

We decided that what the thing really was is not the women wanting to walk in front of men and it's not women walking behind men—we want to walk alongside. We want to do our part. We want to carry our load and we want to do whatever it is; but we would be much more effective if the men joined us. The men have joined us and we are now the biggest caucus on the Hill. I think that that is really the model—it is now men and women working for very major issues that used to just be called women's issues, and when people said that they would snarl. Women's issues basically are family issues. They're aging issues. They are human issues. What we have done in the caucus is put together a whole list of legislation that we are trying to move. Democrats and Republicans alike, liberals and conservatives, have been pushing bills of interest to women. Suddenly, IRA expansion, pension reform, Social Security changes, child support, Title IX, are hot tickets in the Congress. The Economic Equity Act—a package of tax, retirement, insurance, alimony and child support, day care, and regulatory reforms to improve the economic security of women—now has 131 cosponsors in the House and 32 in the Senate.

We are dealing with child support enforcement which we got out of the House with a very, very wide margin. It is now in Senator Dole's committee and we hope it gets out of the Senate very soon. What it says is, we really should not force families to go on welfare to get child support enforcement. We need to have child support enforcement because it is the children that are suffering. It shouldn't be male versus female—it's "remember the kids." Most states do better at car payment enforcement, which is not saying very much.

We have all sorts of pension packages so that women don't find some day that they never had any survivor's benefits, and it's always too late when they are the survivor. So that we find out more about the vesting and women have a much better crack at knowing when they are vesting and the portability of pensions. There is a whole variety of things dealing with federal pensions, state pensions, private pensions. I promise I won't go into that on this snowy day. I just tell you it is a very important part of this package that's moving.

We allow women who choose to, to form an IRA. They should be able to put money away for an IRA. Then we say that there should be tax provisions for any kind of dependent day care. It shouldn't be just children. Many families have elderly parents that need dependent day care. They have handicapped individuals. They have people who are sick. All of those are a business cost and they should be treated as such. It is outrageous that you can write off a three martini lunch but you can't write off taking care of another human being who is in desperate need of it. In fact, we got this through the inheritance provision that I mentioned before and that was that if a man and wife worked on the farm all their life and the man dies, the wife was treated as if it was a windfall, but she had to sell it to pay the taxes. That is outrageous. You shouldn't tax intragenerational transfers such as that—and we did get that through the federal level.

Then, we deal with the whole package around the economic area, work, part-time, flexi-time, short-time. Trying to find new ways in the work place so it is not quite so oppressive on parents. Also, dealing with the latch-key day care issue, for $15 million over the next five years you could almost solve all latch-key day care in America. You do it on a model that came out of Denver. What does it do? It says that there all these schools qualified under all state laws. The taxpayers paid for them so it gives a little seed money for non-profit groups to put together after-school programs for kids whose parents are working. And it makes sense, because what is happening to our children today with their parents working is they stay home and watch soap operas. They are not getting the music lessons, the ballet lessons, the computer lessons, the games, all the things that they used to get. So for a very small amount, that model could go all over America. The infrastructure is there. You don't need to buy one brick. It's just the start-up to get everybody together to find out who wants to do it and how to move forward with that.

We have the whole area of redoing Title IV, which says that if you get federal money, then you provide equal education for young women if they want to take a course; that the school shouldn't say, "Why do you want to take that? You can't take that—your chromosomes are wrong." If they are qualified, they can take it. That is half the reason that I went to the University of Minnesota as an undergraduate—because I wanted to take aerodynamics engineering and most universities said that I couldn't. And I really didn't think that was quite fair. Well, this says that you can't do that if you are getting federal money, and we are trying to reinstate that whole thing after the Supreme Court knocked it out. We are trying to reinstate the Women's Economic and Equal Education Act, which has also been gutted. There has been a whole lot of gutting that has been done and we are trying very, very hard to transcend the competition between men and women and make them understand that family life is going to be a whole lot better—everything will be a whole lot better, the whole country will be a whole lot better—if you use your software, i.e., your people, to allow people to get educated to whatever level they want to go. Then you provide a way that they can continue to use it other than put it on ice, i.e., hang your Harvard diploma over the sink and look at it. There is nothing wrong with doing the sink work, but there is also nothing wrong with using the Harvard diploma. Otherwise, you just wasted all that money educating and there is a way to put it together.

Now, we have done some other very interesting things that many people may not approve of, but it's been very exciting. We decided that when you really look at these issues, they are children's issues, too. Children get forgotten in the private sector because they don't have money to buy things, and they get forgotten in the public sector because they don't vote. So we formed the Committee on Children, Youth and Family. Actually, almost everything that is a woman's issue can just move right into the children, youth and family area—part-time, flexi-time, latch-key day care—all of that.

We had some fascinating hearings on fatherhood, because part of what I keep saying is that we are not going to get changes on a lot of this until we have the men working with us as vigorously as the women. Harvard, once again, has done some phenomenal studies on fatherhood. You know, they have movies showing that a baby identifies with the father as much as the mother at birth. Absolutely astounding movies! What happens is the father then goes into a work setting where he never sees the child. He leaves when the child is in bed, he comes back when the child is in bed. What they articulate so well is that you have a society where you set up the mother as the gate keeper of the child. Now I can even think about that in my own day. My husband would come in and he couldn't understand the children and what they were saying. I was the translator: "They said they want a cookie." That's got to be very difficult. So we started all of that dialogue trying to get the federal government and trying to get everybody else looking at this a bit to find out how we keep fathers very much involved. They used to be. People forget that before World War II almost everything was a ma-and-pa operation. They lived over the store, they lived on the farm, the children saw the father as much as the mother and it really has been the creation of all the separation—the father goes away, the mother stays home—all that. Where you really polarize it and the whole emphasis on fatherhood and the fatherhood projects going on in some of the major cities, is a very important component of it. So making fatherhood okay again, getting all these things coming forward where we can talk about the needs of children rather as the needs of children than a male versus female issue. That's what we should be doing as a society, and that's how we are moving as much as we can.

I see it all the time in the military. I've been sitting on the Armed Services Committee for 12 years. Time after time a general comes to me and says, "The biggest problem I have is day care." I keep saying, "Terrific, but don't tell me, tell the men on the committee. I'm not surprised that your biggest problem is day care. For a long time my biggest problem was day care." My biggest fear was losing my housekeeper. I can deal with anything but that. So I'm not surprised at all. So I would say, "Tell the men on the Committee that." And they would say, "No, no, no, I can't." I would ask, "Why?" "Because they will think I have lace on my shorts. You just don't do that, you know." You are supposed to talk about tanks or guns, but you don't go talking about day care if you are a general. Well, what I would say to them is unfortunately they are going to get a whole lot more response if they tell them than if I tell them. Because if I, Pat Schroeder, say, "Okay, the biggest problem in the military is the day care," the men on the Committee say, "There she goes again! Can you believe this one—you plug her in and all she talks about is day care." I'm saying the generals are going to get much more response if they say it to them, rather than if I say it to them, because I say it a lot. I understand it, but it is stronger coming from a general.

Finally, that is starting to happen. We are seeng a real change in military families, and they are coming forward and talking about some of the needs and how they've been overlooked because it is just much "cooler" to look at hardware problems.

It is the same in the private sector. It is very "cool" in the private sector to talk about how you need a physical fitness track and a steam bath, but it is not real "cool" to say you need to do something about day care unless you're a woman and everybody says, "Obviously she is saying that because she is a woman." We've all got to say it together. We've all got to look at education together. We've all got to look at all of these things. After all, women have been paying equal taxes, and to ask for equal benefits and equal treatment is not too much, especially when you really see it as coming to the child. When the woman is asking for equal pay, she is talking about the prices she pays for her children's clothes are the same as the men who get more on the same job. So she is really having to short-change her children if she doesn't get that. So we will be working on pay comparability, education, all of these issues, and moving them forward. We have a whole package called the Economic Equity Act. We are making a major focus on the day care with the men alongside, which makes a big difference, and I think that is very exciting.

I hope that as we see women now voting in stronger numbers than men and we see the gender gap standing up, what it finally means is that women are not afraid to have their needs addressed. For so long we felt guilty about saying anything about our needs. We just were trained that that was wrong and pushy and we shouldn't do it. As a consequence, we often got pushed to the bottom of the priority list. We're learning how to lobby. You lobby just like Exxon does; you not only ask what their position is, you ask what priority it is.

The second thing that they don't like anymore is that for so long a member would send his wife to address women's groups on their issues and the member never even learned about the issues. Now, can you imagine what would happen if I sent my husband to talk to men's groups? I'd be in real trouble. That's starting to come around. Women are starting to focus on that and saying that it is delightful that your spouse came, but we want to make sure that the husband understands that we want him on this legislation and we want it moving because it is not just for us, it is for everybody. So many of us are getting around to saying we are very tired of a lot of thugs dressed in pink out redefining women's issues. It's wrong. Women really just want equality and nothing more—the ability to walk alongside.

The sudden burst of talk about a female vice president may very well make possible what no one thought probable as recently as one year ago. There is a "Why not?" spirit to the question. And why not a woman as president?

More importantly, the new feminist awareness in politics makes it more likely that the presidential and vice-presidential nominees, male or female, will be committed to social, political, and economic quality for women.

That commitment, by the way, is nothing more than the Webster's Dictionary definition of "feminism." I always chuckle when I hear someone say, "I'm for equal rights, but I'm not a feminist"— as if being a feminist was a misdemeanor. It's like saying "I'm for the free market, but I'm not a capitalist."

The real immediate impact of the gender gap, however, is that women have the power, in numbers, to provide the margin of victory for the next president. If you find that hard to believe, ask the governors of New York, Texas, and Michigan, who were all elected in 1982 with the women's vote.

The number of female elected officials has been slowly increasing, especially at the local and county levels, which serve as farm teams for higher office. At the congressional level, however, the increase has been glacial. Successful female congressional candidates averaged about nine during the 1940s; 14 during the 1950s; 12 in the 1960s; 16 in the 1970s; and is running about 20 in the 1980s. At these increments, women will have reached parity in the House— half the seats—in about 400 years!

Since 1971, when the National Women's Political Caucus began keeping tabs, the number of women mayors has increased from seven to 76, state legislators from 362 to 992, and members of Congress from 15 to 24. With both parties now scurrying to find female candidates for the House and the Senate, we might see a sharp increase in women elected to Congress next year—but don't count on it. If women want to increase their numbers in Congress, don't wait to be asked, run! Politics is a game of inches and angles.

Women are putting a 5 percent to 15 percent edge on issues of interest to them, increasing their numbers among elected officials, and becoming a leading political indicator, drawing men to their standard.

The legislative agenda that can be moved forward is long overdue. Abigail Adams has been waiting since 1776. I think we are getting much closer to getting it done, and I think it is a very exciting thing to see that the biggest caucus on the Hill is now addressing itself to those issues.

Jose Napoleon Duarte (1925–) was elected President of El Salvador in May, 1984. He was educated at Notre Dame University as a civil engineer. He practiced engineering and has been a professor of mathematics and engineering in El Salvador and in Venezuela. He served three terms as mayor of San Salvador and has been a leading figure in the Christian Democratic Party. After winning a national election for President in 1972, he was exiled from El Salvador from 1972 to 1979 by a succession of military governments. In 1980 he was named a member of the Revolutionary Junta. In 1984 a new constitution of El Salvador was approved in popular election and Duarte was elected President.

The Democratic Process in El Salvador: The Meeting at La Palma

Jose Napoleon Duarte

*This lecture was given only two weeks after a historic meeting—in a church
in the little town of La Palma, El Salvador—between President Duarte and
representatives of the Faribundo Marti Front for National Liberation
(FMLN) and the Democratic Revolutionary Front (FDR), two guerrilla
groups waging civil war in El Salvador. President Duarte set aside his
prepared text, asked for a blackboard, and gave an hour long classroom style
lecture on how he saw the political situation in El Salvador and what he told
the guerrilla leaders he had met in La Palma. The "round things" he refers to
are circles on the blackboard: two at the top representing "ideology"—in
particular the communist ideology—and "reality"—in particular the reality
of 50 years of right-wing dictatorships in El Salvador. The third circle,
representing "revolutionary democracy," was below the other two circles, and
midway between them, forming a triangle with the apex at the bottom.
Duarte's lecture was focused on the issue of how to create a democratic
government and economic system in El Salvador which would avoid
the ideologies of both left and right and the violence both sides had
chosen to employ.
President Duarte's lecture was made even more dramatic by the simultaneous
presence on the Kansas State University campus of Arnoldo Ramos, one of
five delegates in the United States representing the FDR and FMLN.*

NOVEMBER 2, 1984

I had prepared for this morning a written speech which expresses
the sentiments that I have concerning democracy and concerning
the process of my country. But, on my way down I started to think
over, and I said, I cannot waste this beautiful opportunity to be back
in the University, to remember my Notre Dame student time and

"

to remember my life in the school conditions, to try to explain to the people of the University what happened in La Palma.

I think that what we made in La Palma explained what is happening in the whole country. It gives an idea of the process of confrontation of ideologies, and in a forum like this, you have to excuse my lack of knowledge of the political science theories, but this is the way I feel, and this is the way I see it. Therefore, let me forget for a moment this written speech, and I will try to explain what I think is my concept of what happened in my country, and what is the concept, in my opinion, of the left and the revolutionary people, and what are the controversies between these two concepts. And then you will see why I have asked for this La Palma meeting, and you will also see why I made this offer of peace to my country. For that, I'll go back to school and I will use the blackboard, and I thank you for this opportunity. So let's see what I can do with this blackboard.

I want to say another remark. This is the first time that I'm going to try to present this, so I might make mistakes on the presentation, and especially on the language, but you have to excuse me.

All right. Now, here we go. This round thing is supposed to be the ideology, any ideology of any force. And this is the reality, any reality. Any force, political force or ideological force, always strives to change the realities into what they think is the ideal. And for that they establish a strategy in which they want to move this reality into their ideology. This is for everybody.

So the communists, in 1970, started to analyze the reality and tried to present a strategy to move this reality to the way they thought. They established, then, the system of violence, the popular prolonged war strategy. They used the violence in order to destabilize this reality which was, at that moment, inserted into the capitalistic . . . and here I'm going to use an academic word . . . a liberal capitalistic structure. By liberal I don't mean your American concept of liberal, but I mean the European concept of liberal, which is conservative.

So, the conservative groups had a real control of all the reality of El Salvador. In 1970, the communists decided to confront this situation. Obviously, there were other ideologies which wanted also to change this reality. But for many years, the people who controlled the reality, the rightist groups, decided to eliminate all of them. They established an hegemony of power. This hegemony of power was based on a political party—the official party—the government, the absolute control of the government, the absolute control of the economy, the absolute control of the army, the military people, and the support of the international forces. This is why many, many years ago I said that the United States was leading in democracy, but it was exporting dictatorship, because they were supporting a dictator.

So these forces were the only available and possible forces in the country. They tried to eliminate everybody else. And they established a dictatorship for 50 years. So this is a very strong force, and the reality was absolutely controlled by these forces. This is the reason why, since there were no other means, the communists thought that this was the moment to confront this reality. So they established the method, the strategy to obtain a goal, and their goal was the violent revolution.

This is how it started, the whole process of political violence. But when this scheme had already started, there was a group of military people who analyzed the situation and thought that they had to dismantle this hegemony of power. And by dismantling it, they would start changing the structure. So they created another concept, the democratic revolution. And they established a new strategy, democracy. So they started to dismantle this and made a coup d'etat in October 1979 and they eliminated the official party. They eliminated the concentration of power in the government. They started changing the army, and at the same moment, because of the conditions of the policies of the United States, there was also a change in the international situation. So, there was a change here, too. The only thing left was the economic power.

So this is the reason why this democratic revolution and this strategy meant the reforms—the agrarian reform, the bank reform—in order to reduce the power of these forces, the political power, not taking away their money, but taking away their power. So the strategy of the concentration of the rightist force was diminished. That made it possible for the reality to start moving away from this concept. Of course, the extreme left, according to their strategy and according to their violent concepts, started to move a little better in that direction. But also, the reforms started to move.

What happened was that the reality moved. Instead of moving in the direction of the communist ideology, it came up to a new point in the direction of the democratic reality because the right started to hold back. So they reorganized this structure by creating a political party of the extreme right which is called ARENA. They created a provisional government in which they had a very important control of the national assembly. They strengthened their economic control, and they created the death squads to replace the actions of repression in the country. They even came to the States to obtain international support. So, the right created this structure in order to act against the communists, and also against the democratic solution because they were against the reforms.

At the same time, the communists attacked the rightist groups. But they didn't like the idea of having a democratic solution, so they also attacked the democratic solution. So you see, this is a triangle, and in the middle was the reality, and it started to move, and it moved in the direction of democracy. This is important to understand.

So according to my theory, I believe that at this moment there is a definite move, a definite change between the old reality and the new reality.

But the communists did not change their strategy. They still think that the violent revolution and the strategy of violence in the popular prolonged war is the solution. So they wrote a new document in 1980 and another in 1983, and all are based on two things: the antioligarchy and the anti-imperialism. There is a difference in these three documents, but the three are based on this concept: they are not changing their methods, and they are not changing their instruments; they are only changing their presentation. But the reality has changed.

So, in the United Nations, I presented my offer of peace by saying that the people who have lived outside of El Salvador, the groups of the left who are moving around the world, have forgotten that this has happened in the last years. And therefore, the only one who knows this is the commander of the guerrillas who lives in the mountains. And when they come down to the town, they expect to be received as heroes, but they are not, because the reality is different. Because the people have made a different decision, a decision that the representatives of the FMLN/FDR outside of the country don't even know. But they don't even want to recognize it. But this is the reality.

So I said to them, "You are antihistorical because now what you have to do is to establish a new strategy concerning the new reality against your ideology." And I said to the right that they also are antihistorical, because they are not considering that the only possibility of solving the problem is not to hold around their own concept, but to lead away a little, so that they could try to establish against the new reality, establish a new policy. This is the reason why I say I am offering to change the concept of hate for the concept of tolerance. This is the reason why I say, let's try to find a way in which we all understand each other, so that part of these people could move closer, so that we could form a very important shell to attract the reality closer to democracy. This is my presentation of the La Palma idea.

What did the left say? They started by saying that nothing has changed, absolutely nothing. And they say the reality—the reality that they see—is the same that it was in 1970. There are five points, they say. There are five points that they believe are the basic points in which the reality has not changed.

So they spent just about two and a half hours talking, trying to explain to us—which we let them do—why they believe this reality has not changed. They say the reforms and the economic situation are still under the control of the oligarchy, and therefore nothing has changed at this moment. The reforms, they say, have not changed anything. The economy will need 16 years to rebuild, and is absolutely destroyed. They say, concerning the political situation, "We don't believe in the elections, we don't accept the results of the elections, and we don't accept your presidency because we were not in the election process. And since we were not there, we don't believe in the pluralistic concept." And internationally they say, "You are absolutely dependent on the United States. You are not nationalistic; you are not free. And therefore, we believe that you are under the control of the policies of the United States, and the United States directs your doings, and you, Duarte, are only a puppet of the United States." Everything was based, then, on the imperialistic concept.

But finally they came up on the war analysis, and here they say that what happened is that there is an insurgent concept, which is the product of the strategy of not changing the realities. The only solution is to change it by the violent revolution; and therefore, the actions of the insurgency are absolutely moral. Against this insurgency, the army has presented a contra-insurgency. So the war is nothing else but an escalation between the insurgency and the contra-insurgency.

This is what they presented to us, their theory. "Therefore," they say, "your theory is not correct because nothing has changed. The absolute control of the society is under the hands of the right, the extreme right, and the reality is the same. So our concept, our ideology, and our strategy are correct."

Our answer to that? We say the reforms. Up to this moment, 30 percent of the land of the country is in the hands of the campesinos. Before, there were somewhere around 300 people who owned one-third of the most productive land of our country. Now, there is at least somewhere around 200,000 campesinos who own that land.

So, you are forgetting that now the banks, which were in the hands of the 14 families, are now in the hands of the government, and that the credits that before were given to friends around the 14 families, now are given to the campesinos and the cooperatives. Just to give you an example, before, somewhere around 300 million [colonas] were given as credits, agricultural credits, to a group of somewhere around 500 people. Now this same amount, 300 million, is handled by 300 cooperatives. This is a change. There's no question about it, and everybody knows it. There's no question that at this moment the power of the economic forces has diminished, and that even though they're still strong, they have not the influences that they had before.

Politically, we say that there is a big change, a change in creating parties, a change in making elections. And they say that the elections were not valid because they did not participate. And I say, "You did participate, when you said that you were opposed to the elections, when you decided to get your guns out to stop the people that went in to vote, when you shot and the people went down to the floor because you didn't want them to vote; you were participating. You were participating in the negative system." But at the end, the people stood up, stayed in line, and went to vote. And there are 1,000 newspaper people as witnesses from all over the world. And there were 250 representatives of people from all the countries who went there to see this election. And there was not only one election; there were three elections in a row with the same concept and the same magnitude. So the legitimacy of the political result isn't debatable.

Now, they said, "Concerning your concept of pluralism, we believe that it cannot be pluralism without us." But they also say in order to have a real pluralism, it has to be a popular pluralism without the right. So I said, "So you want a pluralism with one side out, and replace the extreme right by the extreme left. That is not pluralism. Pluralism is to include all, and to give all the right to be there, the right and the left, and the center, and all the parties, and all the factors. So you are absolutely wrong on this concept.

"Internationally, there is a change. Before, everybody knew that the government was responsible for all the factors of violence in the country. And now, the whole world is conscious that the government is making its effort in order to change the reality. And, of course, there is no question that we are, at this moment, dependent on the help of the political and economic and military aid of the United States. There is no question about it: we know it. But that dependency is not only on one side. You, commanders, are also dependent on the aid of Russia, Nicaragua, and Cuba.

"So both sides are in the dependency condition. This is not an argument. And the third is the word which has something to do with dependency. If you insist that there is no change in the reality, and that by not changing the reality, the insurgency is valid, then the contra-insurgency is a very natural thing. But, the problem is that this insurgency has escalated into warfare. And this escalation made the contra-insurgency escalate." So this thing kept on going higher and higher.

So they said, "We believe that before, the army was a national army, and that it has passed from the national army to a contra-insurgency army. And now, it is moving into a puppet army, puppet of the United States. The United States tells them what to do and how to do things." This is their argument.

And I said, "But you're doing the same. Cuba tells you what to do. Cuba plans whatever you have to have, and the arms that you have to have. So you see, the war problem and the contra-insurgency and the insurgency, is nothing else but the result of your concept of violence, and your concept of understanding that there is no change of the reality."

So they say, "The solution is simple. Eliminate the contra-insurgency, and then immediately the insurgency will disappear."

I say, "Another mistake, a historical mistake. Because you started by saying that the insurgency was a product of the reality. And now you say that the insurgency is a product of the contra-insurgency. This is not true. So," I said to them, "you started the escalation of armed forces. In the beginning the army had arms which were bought somewhere around 1950, 1960. They had rifles (G-3 mark) and ammunition 20 years old. But you started obtaining new rifles and machine guns that made it obligatory for the army to have more arms to control this unbalanced situation.

"But then you came up and had more sophisticated arms. The Russians and Cubans gave you special grenades which were used with rifles. Then, they gave you special Chinese rockets. And finally, they have given you these recoilless guns that the army of El Salvador never had before." And today, we're suspicious that they have special rockets, earth to air, that they might use to destroy the air force.

So the escalation has come from the insurgency area, and this is the reason why we need the help to obtain the arms capable of controlling this. But, what is more important, neither the insurgency groups nor the government groups have the capacity to buy these arms and to buy those ammunitions. These are billions, millions, millions of dollars. And neither the commanders and the guerrillas, nor the army has the capacity, the economic capacity, to have it.

So this makes this war a definite dependency on the international foreign forces. And this takes the problem away from El Salvador. This is the reason why I presented a nationalistic proposition—a proposition in which the problem has to be understood.

It has two dimensions: the national dimension which has roots in this structure that I have already explained to you, and the international dimension of dependency, over which we do not have any control. So, actually, this is the reason why I have presented the guerrillas with this offer of peace.

This is the reason why I made this strategy of going all through the world talking to the Congress in the United States, talking to the government of the United States, talking to the countries in Europe, talking to the countries in Latin America, because I needed a shell to protect this reality against actions that might try to destroy internationally these efforts of reality. And if I can get them to understand that there are two extreme positions, polarized positions between the revolutionary violence and the actions of the death squads, and that I need protection against this, too. And for that I need an army to understand that it has to protect this reality against the death squads and against the violent actions of the extreme left.

This is the reason why I did not start a dialogue immediately after taking office. I had to work before in order to get this scheme, and to get the people back in the idea of trying to solve the problem in the democratic way.

When I did that, and when I thought that I had everything ready, then I made the offer of peace at the United Nations. And the offer of peace then, is to try to get the new strategy of the left to move to an area closer to the democratic revolution so that the democratic revolution is strengthened with the concept of your so-called effort of the social justice of the people. And I also called on the right for a dialogue, to come up here and strengthen the concept of the private inititive and the economic, because between the three, we can form the forces capable of stabilizing the democratic process.

They tried then to say, "No, we don't believe in this. We believe that what you are trying to do is to take time." And here is the main thing they say: "We believe that there is only one way, a global solution." A global solution which means to obtain everything, to have negotiations in which they will be able to have their revolution, absolutely on their changing everything immediately. I say, "All right, now what you want is paradise, paradise today, and that is impossible in any society."

What we are presenting is a process. So the actual difference between the concept of the guerrillas, the ideological concept, is that they want a global solution which means, "Let's negotiate—let me, the violent revolution, participate in the government, have a control in the government, have a control in the army, destroy all the factors"—the five factors that I mentioned—"try to make the country free from the control of the United States. Let's have negotiations and relations with friends like Russia and all. By having that, we will have complete control on the conditions in order to have the changes of the structure."

This is the global solution they presented. And I said that is impossible. What we need is a process. And for that, we need to understand the changes of a structure. And they say, "We believe that there is no change of the structure, we believe that your theory of the process is only—how would you call that in English—makeup. It is only a cosmetic solution, and therefore, there is no real proof." And I said, "The best proof is that you have entered into the country, have gone through the whole country, have gone to La Palma, and you are now sitting down here in front of the president. This is a reality, and this is a change. You could not have done this five months ago. You can only do it because there is a new concept, a new idea, and a new reality." This is the moment in which I said, "We cannot come out of this room without something to tell our people who are outside waiting. We cannot discourage our people. We have to give them faith that there is still an opportunity for peace."

So they accepted and we signed this communication that we presented to the world, in which it says that we will form a central committee to study all these offers and to try to look for a solution, and second, that we will try to humanize the concepts of war. This is what happened in La Palma.

All right. I think that with this information you have now clear my points of view concerning the two basic confrontations—ideological confrontations—in which there is not a polarization between the extreme right and the extreme left in our country, but three polarizations. There are three forces trying to change the reality: the extreme right, trying to maintain it; the extreme left, trying to make the violent revolution; and us, and when I mean us, I mean everybody who believes in democracy and is working in the democratic line. That includes other parties, too, who are working with different points of view on the democratic revolution.

When they ask me who's winning the war, I always said I know that who is losing the war are those who want violence, and who is winning the war are those who want democracy and who want peace. This, I think, gives you an idea.

And now, I will put myself into your hands for any questions concerning my country.

Thank you.

Bob Dole (1923–) is senior Senator from Kansas and Senate Minority Leader. He has been in the Senate since 1968. Prior to that he served in the U.S. House of Representatives for four terms. He has been Republican National Chairman and, in 1976, President Ford selected him as his running mate. In 1980 he ran for President. Although that bid was unsuccessful, his Senate reelection that same year was historic—he won in every county in the state of Kansas. From 1984–86, he was Senate Majority Leader.

The Dream of America

Bob Dole

During the spring of 1985, the two most powerful leaders in the Congress, Senate Majority Leader Robert Dole and House Speaker Tip O'Neill, both appeared in the Landon Lecture Series. Their presentations should be read together for both reflected on the dreams and the changes they had experienced in public life. Despite their differing political party affiliations and constituencies, their lectures display some interesting continuities. Senator Dole's lecture was special in another way. It was the first to be given by a Kansan since Governor Landon initiated the series in 1966. An unwritten rule had precluded inviting Kansas political leaders to be Landon Lecturers. Were it not for such a tradition, Senator Dole might have appeared much earlier in the Landon Lecture Series.

MARCH 25, 1985

Thank you very much, President Acker. I'm not used to a big crowd like this, so if I'm a little nervous, that will explain why.

I am very proud to be here. I've been to many Landon Lectures where presidents have spoken, governors, and I think even one Arab sheikh, and I know it's a very prestigious platform. I'm particularly honored to be here since I understand that not since Governor Landon inaugurated this program 19 years ago has a Kansan been asked to speak. So I appreciate that very much, and for that I'm very honored.

I'm also pleased that Governor Carlin is here. A lot of people think that because one may be Republican and one may be a Democrat that there is no communication. Let me suggest that if the Soviets and the Americans could communicate as well as I do with Governor Carlin, we would have had an arms agreement a long time ago. I say that because Governor Carlin also has a prestigious position in this country today as chairman of the National Governors' Association. And he has the same commitment, the same sincere hope as I do and as I think most everyone in this audience has that we finally will come to grips with this massive federal deficit that's going to have an adverse impact on everyone in this audience if we don't deal with it. So I want to publicly thank Governor Carlin for his support, for his willingness to listen, for his many trips to Washington to talk to all of us, Republicans and Democrats, on what we consider to be public enemy number one, the federal deficit. So Governor, I appreciate very much your being here. As I said, if anybody starts throwing anything, maybe you can catch some of it for me.

I think about a lot of things when I stand before a group where I see many of my friends and some people I don't know. I think about Russell, Kansas, or somewhere else in Kansas. But I also take inspiration from another man. That man is Governor Landon, a man who held my party's banner aloft in those bleak days and bleak years when many questioned its future. I think he and I had more in common than our Kansas underpinnings. We have both run for high national office, with rather conspicuous lack of success. Back in 1936, when Alf opposed Franklin D. Roosevelt, Republican strategists decided to make the Kansas sunflower the emblem of their campaign. Of course, the Democrats promptly issued bumper stickers proclaiming that "sunflowers die in November."

That may be so, but there are principles which outlast any growing season. And, Alf Landon's principles are tireless. They are the Kansas virtues of self-reliance and a tender conscience. They combine common sense and uncommon sensitivity. He was a man of courage who denounced the Ku Klux Klan when other politicians were willing to tolerate its presence—a man of vision who proposed recognition of the People's Republic of China a generation before an American president set foot in Peking. All his life, Governor Landon was willing to do the unpopular thing if he judged it to be the right thing.

Someone other than the governor once labeled his race against FDR as a contest between Harvard—Roosevelt's alma mater—and the rest of the United States. Personally, I've always thought Landon closer to the unabashed spirit of the man who presided over Harvard in those days. His name was James Bryant Conant, and on the wall of his office he kept a cartoon with the caption, "Behold the turtle. He only makes progress by sticking his neck out."

Universities are built by and for the long-necked people. They exist not merely to fill our minds, but more importantly to stroke our imaginations. Above all, they nurture our dreams. "The republic is a dream," proclaimed prairie poet Carl Sandburg. "Nothing happens unless first a dream." A nation's dreams are the rich harvest of individual ones by the millions. They are implanted early in most of us, in the family living room or public classroom, in church pews and on athletic fields. My generation grew up believing a future that promised everything hard work and strong faith could achieve. From Main Street in Russell, Kansas I looked forward to a world that would yield up its secrets and mend its sometimes murderous ways.

In many ways, my dreams have come true—thanks in no small measure to the men and women on campuses like this. Contrast the world of Alf Landon's boyhood or my own with this era of instant communication and awesome technology. Today we can reach into the heavens for perspective on this small, shimmering planet. We can take food from the ocean depths. We can grow crops resistant to insects and indifferent to rain. Since I was a boy, we have virtually wiped out the crippling scourge of polio. We have revolutionized life itself through human or mechanical organ transplants. We have diminished distances between peoples. No longer are national boundaries equated with natural barriers to commerce and culture. Problems of hunger and poverty—though they still exist—and disease, problems as old as the human race, seem closer to solution than at any time in the long struggle of man to fulfill his potential.

In the same period, I have seen one roadblock after another cleared from the paths of women and minorities. When Alf Landon ran for president back in 1936, only a handful of women exercised influence in the political life of the nation. By 1988, another Landon, my distinguished Senate colleague Nancy, may well find herself on a national ticket. Come to think of it, you'd better not quote me on that. Elizabeth might find out, and a man can survive just so long on frozen dinners, so I might have to be a little careful of that.

By any measure, the twentieth century has witnessed a remarkable flowering of human achievement. Yet some things will elude us. The dreams of a world at peace with itself, a world where no one drags a chain and no one wields a sword—well, this world seems as remote as sunlight from shadow. Nor have we lived up to Carl Sandburg's dream of a republic without walls, in which economic plenty extends to every home in the land.

Instead, such visions are held hostage to an unbridled nuclear arms race and our own seemingly uncontrollable urge toward national bankruptcy. If my generation can address these dangers now, then your generation will know a world whose dreams are no longer haunted by the mushroom cloud of Armageddon, and a country where no one is condemned to live on the outskirts of economic hope.

Barely ten days ago, I returned from a trip to Geneva. There were ten senators—five Republicans and five Democrats. I designated five and the minority leader Senator Byrd designated five. We went to Geneva to observe the opening round of the U.S.-Soviet arms control or arms reduction talks. We made the journey amidst the advent of a new leadership in Moscow. It was a time of anticipation and, for some, expectation. But let me correct some early media profiles of the new Soviet boss, or correct them as I see it. The new Soviet leader is a young man, 54 years of age; he's going to be around for awhile. In the first four and a half years of Ronald Reagan, we saw a change of four leaders. But I would point out that notwithstanding his age and his charisma, whatever that is, that he is no choirboy. He is a communist hardliner who will demand tough bargaining at the negotiating session. The faces may change behind the imposing walls of the Kremlin, but the philosophies remain the same. Peace is priceless—but not peace at any price. It was our own resolve that brought the Soviets back to Geneva. And it will be future resolve that leads to viable, verifiable arms control.

In my view, when two nations as profoundly different as the United States and the Soviet Union sit across from one another, the only way to narrow the potential for misunderstanding is to speak candidly of our differences and our own determination. Until the last few years, this country spoke with an uncertain voice. We permitted our defenses to go stiff in the joints, and our foreign policies to confuse the world that was with the one we wished for. Yet, in the modern world, the appearance of weakness invites the exploitation of weakness. And the 1970s will be remembered as a dismal age when the Soviets ventured almost at will into Afghanistan and Angola, Cambodia and Ethiopia.

Then came 1980, and a new administration pledged to rebuild our defenses and restore a coherent sense of direction to U.S. foreign policy.

Promptly, we set out to modernize both our conventional and strategic forces—a process that continues with last week's senate vote to authorize 21 MX missiles, far more than a simple bargaining chip. I must say, in our conversations with Max Kampelman, who happens to be a protege of Hubert Humphrey, a Democrat, the chief negotiator, and with John Tower, a former colleague, a conservative Republican senator, and with Ambassador Mike Glickman who worked for Paul Nitze and probably the scholar of the three as far as arms control and the weapons systems are concerned, I believe the reason the senate approved the MX missile by a 55 to 45 vote—I'm not certain what will happen in the house on the morrow—but I believe the underlying reason was that it would seem to many of us that if the Congress shot down the MX missile at the same time we were in our first two weeks of negotiating with the Soviet Union, it would take away not just a bargaining chip, but a lot of leverage. I think we made the right decision.

I think also we find today the Western alliance is more united than ever before. It is that unity which has helped lure the Soviets back to negotiations. They walked out a year ago and said they weren't going to come back unless we did not deploy Pershing missiles.

But they are back at the table. I had the opportunity just this past weekend—on Friday night and Saturday night—in Miami, Florida, to sit down with 15 members of the Soviet delegation, headed by Vladimer Schuschev, the deputy trade minister, to talk about some of our problems. As I have indicated earlier, we can't solve our problems if we don't have a dialogue. We talked about agriculture. We talked about the Soviet Union. We talked about the problems in our country. We talked about the fact that they're not buying as much grain as many of us believe they should. I'm not suggesting we solved anything, but at least we understand each other a bit better. We may recognize each other if I should visit Moscow or Mr. Schuschev should visit Washington. He also has very close ties to Mr. Gorbachev, the new Soviet leader. I have a very strong feeling, as I hope I've always had in public life, that you have to discuss the problem if you seek to find the answer.

But we have the unity. NATO is united. And now we're talking. I think it's important that the Congress prepare itself to advise and consent on a possible arms control tready. I can't think of anything that I would rather do while I'm the majority leader of the United States Senate than to bring before the United States Senate for ratification a verifiable, sound, good—not arms control treaty—but arms reduction treaty that would mean a great deal to this generation, future generations, not only in security and safety, but also in less spending of American dollars and the same for the Russians.

But I think one thing we must caution, and that is patience. We Americans are very impatient people. We have the best technology in the world. We don't like to wait to solve a problem. We want it done yesterday. The Russians have a different system. They don't have to check with Congress. Ronald Reagan or Jimmy Carter—whoever the president might be—has to negotiate first with the Congress and then with the Soviets. The Soviets come to the table without any of those problems. They live in a closed society. There's nobody commenting on the evening news. They make the best deal they can. Whatever deal that is, it's accepted. They get their instructions from someone up here.

Ours is a better system. Ours is an open system. Ours is a democratic system. But I say, above all, the thing the negotiators try to tell senators like myself and Senator Kennedy and Senator Byrd and Senator Nickles and others who were in Geneva, be patient.

The first SALT treaty required nearly a decade to negotiate, the second one close to seven years. So, if we're looking for a quick fix, it's probably not going to happen. Sooner or later, maybe some-time this year, when Mr. Gorbachev comes to address the United Nations, there will be an opportunity for President Reagan and Mr. Gorbachev to sit down and talk about some of these things. To me, I think that would be very helpful.

At any rate, my point is that the ice has been broken. Perhaps one day, before too much longer, both countries can come in from the cold.

So we must wait for lasting peace. But we cannot afford to wait for lasting prosperity. Winston Churchill liked to say that the in-herent vice of capitalism was an unequal sharing of blessings, while the inherent virtue of socialism was an equal apportionment of mis-ery. Thanks to the economic policies pursued by the Reagan admin-istration, the blessings are more plentiful indeed. More people are working than ever before. Taxes have been reduced and may yet be significantly reformed as well—if not this year, next year.

As a young man in Russell, I hope I learned that most anyone could climb the economic ladder, and I certainly learned that every-one should be given the chance to try. And what's more, I learned that once you scrambled up from the bottom, you reached down to lend a hand to others making the ascent on their own. So, for a long time in this country we behaved as if only government had the com-passion or the competence to extend such a helping hand. In the process, we siphoned off hundreds of billions of dollars to Washing-ton which might have been more profitably invested in new ideas, basic and applied research, at state, local, and community levels—the breakthroughs which carry a society from one age to the next. This has changed, and we are all the better for it. But the process is far from complete. What we're trying to do now is shift back some of these responsibilities to states and local governments.

One of the advantages that I've detected over the years of living on the great plains is that you can see a long way in all directions. Sometimes you can even see into the future. You don't have to look far these days to see a black cloud called the federal deficit. A cloud that even now some of my colleagues in Congress would like to seed with more federal programs and higher federal taxes. A cloud that others ignore altogether. Unfortunately, whoever takes credit for the sunshine must be prepared to shoulder blame when it rains. That's sort of where we are now in the so-called budget process.

I don't want to bore anybody with statistics, but I want to cite just a few because I have a feeling if everybody in America or everybody in this audience really focused on where we're headed in this country unless we take immediate action—as Governor Carlin will tell you and I will tell you quickly—we want some action.

I was very encouraged today to meet with a young group of students from Fort Hays and Kansas State to talk about the student loan program and have them submit to me some positive ideas for change that would save money, because they're concerned about the deficit. It's one thing to have a student loan, but if you can't get a job when you get out of college because of inflation or the federal deficit or high unemployment, that may be a factor. I was also highly pleased and encouraged to meet with a number of my friends who say they're senior citizens. They're about my age group, so I was very pleased to meet with them. They tell me that their biggest problem is not the COLAs, it is medicare. They thought maybe I ought to check into some of the medicare problems.

But the point is that wherever you go, whether it's the American farmer or the American worker, the senior citizen, the student, and in many cases the federal employee, I find almost a unanimous view that we have to do something. Let's make it clear at the outset, it's always easy for someone to advocate doing something to you if it doesn't touch me. A lot of people will send you a lot of programs to cut, and then they'll say, "I get a little help in this program, but we can justify ours." I don't quarrel with that. That's the way it should be. You have a right to state your case.

But then you look at the federal debt. When I was chairman of the finance committee we had to pass out bills every so often just so the government could pay its bills. Right now, the federal debt is $1.8 trillion. That's a lot of money, I'm told. It's money we owe. If that figure is too mind-boggling, the interest on that debt on an annual basis now is about $145 billion in interest payments. It's headed for $200 billion a year in interest payments by the end of this decade, which is more than the entire federal budget for the entire government as recently as 1970. Paying the interest doesn't help anyone. It doesn't help agriculture, it doesn't help a university, it doesn't help anyone who might be handicapped or out of work or receiving food stamps or the WIK Program or medicaid. It's interest on the debt.

We had four economists come before the Senate Finance Committee about three months ago—a Democrat, a Republican, a liberal, and a conservative. They all had different ideas on how to make it happen, but they all agreed in the questioning period that followed that if, in fact, the Congress and the president would make meaningful reduction cuts of somewhere between $200 and $275 billion over the next three years in spending, that real interest rates could drop as much as two or three points, and that we would see a moderation of the strength of the dollar that might mean that some of the things we raise on Kansas farms could be exported.

So, I don't know of any higher priority that we have than reducing the federal deficit. It's going to touch a lot of nerves and a lot of people are going to be unhappy. It's going to mean maybe losing revenue sharing in a couple of years. It's going to mean losing Amtrak—I hear about that at home. Elizabeth's public view is that she wants to eliminate it, but at night she wakes up yelling, "Amtrak, Amtrak." I think her private view is to save it. But all these programs that the federal government ventured into—Small Business Administration, 5,000 employees, last year made 14,000 loans and there are millions of loans made in this country in the private sector. And it's not because anybody is hostile to any of these groups. I think if you were trying to sell one of those programs today in Washington, whether the Amtrak or small business or mass transit, whatever it might be, you wouldn't even bring it up because we're faced with this big deficit.

And don't let me overlook the Pentagon. I think it's been said many, many times by the press that you have to treat defense spending a bit differently from any other program. After all, we are dealing with another super power and we do have some responsibilities, particularly to the student body at Kansas State University and others across the country who don't want us to do anything that might indicate weakness. But that doesn't mean that, with a budget the size of the Pentagon, they can't show some restraint— and they have shown some restraint. In a luncheon meeting with the president on Friday I got an indication that they may be willing to show more restraint.

So, there are things we can do on defense spending that will help. I must say from the defense secretary's standpoint, about every time he thinks he's got it going, somebody comes up with another horror story. Yesterday, it was $700 pliers from Boeing, a little Kansas company. Two weeks ago it was a $600 toilet seat. I hasten to say I didn't take a position on that one. But in any event, you've got all these horror stories coming out of the woodwork. About the time you think you've got the lid on one, something else crops up. I didn't mean it quite that way.

I must say that I enjoy my job as majority leader. The last majority leader in Kansas was Carl Curtis, 60 years ago. In fact, I was elected 60 years to the day after he was elected majority leader. He became Herbert Hoover's vice president. I ran with Jerry Ford and I'm still working. I must say, it's sort of like the Truman thing— "If you can't take the heat, get out of the kitchen."

I've got to believe that many of our problems are going to be solved if there is a total understanding of what the problem is. I must add that even though we do all of this deficit reduction, don't get any ideas that we're going to balance the budget. We hope by 1988 we can get the deficit down to $100 billion a year. Right now it's running $215, maybe $220 billion a year. And you've got to pay interest on that new debt you create every year. You just figure out the rate and multiply it by how much new debt you're adding and you've got new interest payments. So I believe the time has come for the Congress to have some help.

I'm reminded of what Alf Landon said again in his acceptance speech in 1936, and this is a quote. He said, "Crushing debts and taxes are usually incurred, as they're being incurred today, under the guise of helping people—the same people who must finally pay them. They invariably retard prosperity and they sometimes lead to situations in which the rights of people are destroyed. This is the lesson of history. . . ." This was Alf Landon nearly 50 years ago.

I'm reading a book by Stephen Ambrose about Eisenhower's

second term. And the thing that's striking in the book—it's a very good book about Eisenhower—but the striking part about it as far as I'm concerned, because we're now wrestling with the same problem, the two biggest frustrations Eisenhower had in his second term were that he had a $2 billion deficit and he couldn't get the generals at the Pentagon to stop spending money. Well, nothing's changed, except that they've got more generals and more debt. And so it's been going on and on and on. I hope we're making progress.

I think it's a painful lesson that we've learned. And I don't want to see it repeated. That's why I believe that it's time that we amend the federal Constitution to limit our ability to incur debt year after year. I'm talking about a balanced budget amendment. And again, with John Carlin's help, the National Governor's Association went on record in support of a balanced budget amendment at the federal level. We can't go in debt in Kansas, we can't go in debt in many states, but we can sure go in debt in the federal government. As I said, it's about $1.8 trillion. We need it. We need the discipline. I think most members of Congress—Democrats, Republicans, men and women—are well-intentioned people. And they're all compassionate and sensitive and sometimes it's hard to say no. Sometimes you shouldn't say no. But we've gotten to the point now where I think we need a little help.

A lot of people think that it's an extreme idea to amend the U.S. Constitution. But I would remind you of Dr. Conant's turtle who only makes progress by sticking its neck out. The tools we have now are plainly inadequate to the task. Certainly, Congress has to be responsive to the demands of constituents—that's what we're there for, that's how our representative system works. But this response to outside pressures makes it all the more essential that we build in some kind of internal restraint into the system.

We passed a constitutional amendment in 1982 in the Senate. It didn't pass the House. We're going to try again this year. There's an old saying that when you're through changing, you're through. I would say that throughout our history we have not hesitated to reform the Constitution when the existing document fell short of our needs. The Civil War amendments that barred slavery and mandated equal protection of the laws; the 16th amendment authorizing the federal income tax; the 25th amendment providing an order to succession to the presidency in times of presidential disability or death: each of these arose out of necessity, fiscal or structural problems that had to be dealt with. Each was demanded to correct abuses unchecked by the legislative process alone. I hope that we can do that.

I would like to see the president of the United States have what 43 governors have—a line-item veto. The president of the United States, when somebody sends him down a great big appropriations bill with a lot of pork barrel stuff in it, he doesn't veto the entire bill, he just line items—he vetoes this item and that item and that item. It gives the president, whether he's a Republican or a Democrat, more leverage with the Congress. Let's fact it, it's not always the president who wants to spend more money. Sometimes it's the Congress. Sometimes they're Republicans and sometimes they're Democrats, and sometimes they all get together. So, we need that discipline.

I would just conclude by saying, back where I started from, I wish we had the balanced budget amendment today. Then if some group came to us and said they've got a real problem, or they've got a great idea and all they need is $100 million or $500 million or $1 billion, we would simply say we can't do it. We've taken in so much money, we've spent so much money, and we've reached the limit. Now, that doesn't mean we shouldn't reorder priorities in government—go back and look at old programs and kick out some of the programs that aren't very efficient from the tax standpoint, or from a taxpayer's standpoint.

I hope we can put together this so-called budget package that we've been working on with the president. I hope it can be bipartisan. I have a friend, Senator Boren, a Democrat from Oklahoma, who feels just as strongly about the deficit as I do. He's working with Democratic senators and I'm working with Republican senators. I'm working with the president to see if we can't find some agreement.

I believe the president has a reservoir of strength in this country. When you carry 49 states to one, you've got a lot of strength. You lose the one by 3,000 votes. It means you've got a pretty good mandate. There's got to be something out there for the president to carry all those states.

If we can get together on a deficit-reduction package, and the president would get on television two or three times, I've got to believe that members of Congress will respond and make the hard decisions.

So I say shrink the size of government, but only so individual dreams can grow and prosper. Especially the American dream which flashes across the face of a prairie farmer or a ghetto mother, and which economic growth alone can accommodate. Who can doubt our capacity to realize such a dream? Certainly no one in my generation, who witnessed our parents cope with crippling hardships, who went off to combat the scourge of Hitler and Tojo, who launched the nuclear age and have maintained ever since our precarious hold on the window ledge of coexistence.

Whatever we may have accomplished, I want something better for young people today. I want to make certain we hand your generation a torch, instead of a hot poker. I want your dreams to exceed my own. And I want this dream of a republic, in Carl Sandburg's words, to live up to the promises on which it was founded. For we have not journeyed all this way, across the centuries, across the continents, across the seas and boundless frontiers of space, because we were limited in our ambitions. To the stars through difficulties, we Kansans like to proclaim. But always—to the stars.

Thank you very much.

Thomas P. 'Tip' O'Neill (1912–) was elected Speaker of the House in 1977. He won his first public office, to the Massachusetts House of Representatives, shortly after graduating from Boston College in 1936, serving as Speaker of the State House of Representatives from 1949 to 1952. O'Neill replaced John Kennedy when he gave up his House seat to run for the Senate in 1952. He was a strong supporter of New Deal liberalism, civil rights, antipoverty programs, and federally funded health care programs. He retired from the House of Representatives at the end of the 99th Congress, October 1986.

Half a Century of American Achievement

Thomas P. "Tip" O'Neill, Jr.

Speaker Tip O'Neill's Landon Lecture was delivered on April 22, 1985, in his last term as Congressman and as Speaker of the United States House of Representatives. He took the opportunity to reflect on the changes he had seen during his half-century of public life. It was not an occasion for nostalgia, however, but rather for reminding his audience of how far America had come through the collective efforts of public and private enterprise during that period. In many respects, then, his message was much the same as that of earlier Landon Lectures by Hubert Humphrey, Edward Kennedy, and others—an appeal not to abandon the positive power which government could provide to bring about beneficial social change.

April 22, 1985

President Acker, Governor Carlin, my good friend Congressman Jim Slattery, members of the Board of Regents, faculty, students, and friends.

Forty-nine years ago, the name of Governor Alf Landon appeared on the ballot as the Republican candidate for the presidency of the United States. In the Commonwealth of Massachusetts, there appeared on some of the same ballots the name of a young Democratic candidate running for state legislature—Tip O'Neill.

It was my first successful campaign for public office. And I appreciate the opportunity to come out here today, to the home state of Alf Landon, to honor the man who headed the other political team back in 1936.

I am glad to be here for another reason. As you know, President Reagan often invokes the words of Franklin Delano Roosevelt. I think it is only fair that if a conservative Republican president can bring himself to honor a great liberal, Democratic president, Franklin Roosevelt, the least I can do is come out here and honor the Republican who ran against him.

I would like to take this opportunity to say something complimentary about our president. When President Reagan was first elected, I, like many others, made the mistake of underestimating his unique abilities. When I first met him I kidded him by saying, "Welcome to the big leagues, Mr. President."

After five years of dealing in close combat with the President, I can now attest to the fact that when it comes to communicating with the American people, when it comes to stating his philosophy clearly and plainly, when it comes to making the strongest possible case for what he believes in, Ronald Reagan, our president, is in a league by himself, and an all-star, as a matter of fact, a hall-of-famer.

In the few minutes I have this morning, I want to offer you my *own* views of our country's history, my own philosophy of our American democracy and of our American government. I want to put today's headlines in perspective, to review what our country has achieved in the past, what challenges it faces today, and what role it can play tomorrow.

First, I want to report to you on two matters that have been very much in the headlines: my recent visit to Russia and tomorrow's vote in the Congress on Nicaragua.

A week ago today, I returned from an important and dramatic visit to Moscow and Leningrad. Our delegation was bipartisan (Robert Michel, a Republican leader, was with me as a cochairman) and I carried with me a letter from the President to Mr. Gorbachev, the new general secretary of the Communist party.

I have returned with a strong determination that relations between our countries be improved. It is clear to me that the new Soviet chairman is tough, vigorous, and shrewd with a charisma, a Madison Avenue approach, a style you have never seen in the Communist and Russian leaders before. He proved to us in a meeting lasting almost four hours that he is a skilled advocate of his government's positions and will be a tough negotiator.

The key question for the United States is whether this change in leadership will lead to a change in relations between our two countries. Beginning with the Soviet invasion of Afghanistan in 1979, Soviet-American relations have declined steadily. We are experiencing what one historian has called a "period of peril" in our relations, similar to the one that happened just after World War II.

These periods of high tensions between the United States and the Soviet Union are a cause of enormous concern. Our two nations are nuclear superpowers. We have the capability of destroying not only each other, but all of civilization.

For 40 years, we have been locked in an economic, ideological, technological, and strategic competition with the Soviet Union, a competition that has spanned every corner of the globe. The invasion of Afghanistan, the suppression of Solidarity in Poland and suppression of human rights in their own country, the shooting down of a Korean airliner, and the recent shooting of an American military officer, Major Arthur Nicholson, in Germany have worsened our view of Soviet policies and intentions.

Yet, fortunately for the world, the intense feelings between our two countries have not led to a direct military conflict. One of the reasons is that our two governments have maintained full diplomatic relations, consulted regularly, and concluded several important arms control treaties.

I have returned from my trip to Russia convinced that, at the very least, we need to maintain these vital lines of communication.

I have come to appreciate something even more—

Too often in the past, we have reacted to Soviet behavior with sanctions, such as a grain embargo, that have hurt us almost as much as they have hurt the Soviets. We have to be tough in our dealings with them, but we haven't played it smart through the years and we should play it smart.

Recent Soviet behavior in Afghanistan, Poland, and internally has created major obstacles on the road to normal relations between our two countries. The road to smoother relations is a long, tough, and difficult one, but this much is clear: the farther we advance down that road the easier it will be to avoid war and to guard the peace.

My visit to the Soviet Union reminded me of the difference between the democratic and Communist countries. Here in the

United States we have the oppportunity to freely discuss our differences. We have the right to speak openly, to question national policy, and to propose alternatives.

Let me say a word about an area of national policy that is the source of major controversy at the present time. I refer, of course, to the administration's policy with regard to Central America.

In Congress, as you know, we have voted to give massive amounts of military and economic aid to the government of El Salvador. The purpose of this aid is to help that country build a united, democratic nation that is secure against aggression.

It is one thing to help a country like El Salvador that we support. It is another to aid in the overthrow of a government like Nicaragua that we do not support. Too many times in this century, the United States has tried to solve Latin American problems with the use of force. So-called "gunboat diplomacy" has gotten us nowhere; it has only earned us enemies in the Central American region.

Instead of acting to overthrow governments, we should be working with Latin nations attempting to build peace in the region. Our best bet in Central America is not gunboat diplomacy but smart diplomacy. We need to ally ourselves with the process that began at Contadora and base our policy on a firm foundation of regional cooperation.

The Contadora, of course, are the nations of Venezuela, Colombia, Panama, and Mexico. I have talked, within the last month, to the various leaders of nations. About eighty days ago I was in Spain. I met Gonzalez, the prime minister of Spain, there. Spain is a socialist monarchy. They have a parliament just like Canada and England. While they call themselves a socialist government, actually they are a democracy. Gonzalez is one of the young leaders of the world. In his conversation with us, he said the policy of the United States government is wrong. The United States, instead of militarily funding the Contras, should be working for a compromise, and they should be working through the Contadora.

The president of Argentina recently addressed the Congress of the United States. In my private conversation with him he said, "You should beef up the Contadora. You shouldn't be thwarting their will. You should give them the money to be able to organize. With their expertise, their culture, their language, their knowledge of the area, they can solve this problem for you. Argentina, Brazil, Peru, and Spain would stand there as overseers to see if they can help in the prospect."

I have talked with Moi, the president of Kenya, and to the Taoiseach [Prime Minister] of Ireland. Whatever leaders of the nations that I talked to, they all tell us that the policy of the United States government is wrong. And I believe that we should go the Contadora route. If it fails, then it's time to look at some other matter. But first, we should try them.

I came here today to discuss a broader, philosophical debate on our country's future. It deals with the role of the government in American life, what we can and *should* do together to improve the chances of every American for "life, liberty, and the pursuit of happiness."

I want to begin by doing what President Reagan does so often, quoting Franklin Roosevelt.

The year was 1942, in the dark early days of World War II. The Nazis controlled almost all of Europe. In Asia, the Japanese empire was at its zenith. Our country, having just entered the war, faced the terrible challenge of mobilizing a peacetime economy, still staggering from the Great Depression, into a war machine capable of stopping and beating the worst menace to mankind in history. Franklin Roosevelt never doubted what a united American people could accomplish.

"The most significant fact in recent American history," he said, "is the ability of American people to face a tough situation and to take orderly and united action in their own behalf—and in behalf of the things in which they believe."

Those are not merely the stirring words of a great leader. I testify, as an eye-witness, to what our American democracy can accomplish. I know, because I have witnessed it myself, in my own half century of public life. I have seen for myself, in my own lifetime, what America can achieve.

There are those who come to young people today and preach to them gloom and doom. They tell everything that is wrong with our political system and with our government. They tell you how great things were *way back when,* and how bad things are today.

Please don't believe that message. People who talk about the "good old days" have either forgotten about the past or never lived through it in the first place.

Let me take a moment to describe a country to you—

This country is a desperate place. Half the people live in poverty. Twenty-five percent of the work force is unemployed. Life is little better for those who are working. The policeman works 12 hours a day—84 hours a week. The fireman is on duty even longer—108 hours a week. The postman delivers mail six days a week, even on Christmas Day. For most, the work week is six days long. The only time workers have for themselves and their families is on Sunday. If you become sick, your world collapses. For most people, health insurance is out of the question.

Life for the elderly is filled with uncertainty, dependency, and horror. When you get old, you are without income, without hope. Only the lucky few, about ten percent of the nation, have pensions. Social security does not exist, and only three percent have health insurance.

In the country I describe there is only the very rich at the top and millions of poor at the bottom—with huge and terrible distance between. There is a handful in the middle class. Only a small elite, just three percent, go to college, if you were lucky enough to have been to high school.

This land I describe is not some third-world nation in Africa. It is the United States of America, the America of the 1930s, the America I knew when I first entered public life.

When I look at the problems we face today, I never forget how far we have come in a half century. By the 1970s, we had cut poverty in this country from 50 percent, where it was in the 1930s, to just 11 percent in 1979.

The America of the 1980s is no longer a nation with a small upper class and giant lower class. In America today there is a broad middle class. Sixty-five percent of our young men and women are able to go on to college. Ninety-nine percent of our workers have some form of health insurance. Social security has made it possible for people to retire with a minimal, steady income, not to have to live in fear and dependency. Without such protection, half of those people now living on social security would be living in poverty.

This massive improvement in American life did not come about by accident. It happened because, in F. D. R.'s words, our people faced up to a tough situation and took united action in behalf of the things they believed in. It resulted from national policies that stimulated the development in energy, housing, transportation, and every other sector of the economy. Economic growth came about, most of all, because government at every level was willing to invest in the most vital of all national resources, the individual human mind.

We did these things . . . the Congress of the United States, the presidents along the line . . . because in a democracy, you respond to the will and the wishes of the majority of the people.

These achievements in economic and social progress were not the work of just one political party alone.

America survived the dust bowl of the 1930s because of the grace of God and because the American farmer developed the know-how to take agriculture to the level of a science in this country.

Our agriculture is the wonder and salvation of the world because of universities like Kansas State, established more than a century ago through the inspiration of the greatest of all Republican presidents, Abraham Lincoln.

It was Franklin Roosevelt who saw the calamity that old age could be and founded social security. It was FDR again who sent a group to study those who were overseas fighting. They came back saying that the greatest desire was an education. The Congress passed the GI Bill of Rights that gave so many of your parents and grandparents the chance to go to college and that helped create the great American middle class we have today. Education has been the greatest asset that this nation has.

It was President Dwight Eisenhower of Abilene, Kansas who oversaw construction of our great interstate highway system that has helped to open up the heartland of American to economic progress and development. It was this same Republican president who signed the National Defense Education Act, which offered so many deserving young Americans the opportunity to go to college and which established education as a vital element in our nation's strength and security.

The social progress of the past 50 years has improved working conditions, provided health protection through Medicare, and provided secure retirements through social security. At the same time, our society has accepted a strong role in caring for those who cannot care for themselves: the sick, the handicapped, the elderly. We have provided a safety net for those who need protection, who cannot, for whatever reason, fend for themselves.

Such achievements are rarely recognized today. Whenever I meet with a group of successful business people, someone always stands up and says we would be much better off *without* government. For such persons, I have a very simple question: Who paid for *your* college education? Was it a state government that helped pay for a state university? Was it a community college or a city university? Or was it the GI bill that financed your education—or was it a government-sponsored loan?

Then, I have another question for them: If they, the "success stories" of this country, needed a helping hand up the ladder of success, why should we not try and give the same help to those young people who are trying to get ahead today? If government could offer opportunities to young people back in the 1950s and 1960s, why should we deny that same help to young people in the 1980s?

I believe it is wrong for someone who has found his way up the economic and social ladder to pull that ladder up behind him, to deny those who are at the bottom the chance to pull themselves up. No society can exist on a public philosophy of I GOT MINE; FORGET THE OTHERS.

We Americans believe in fair play. As citizens of this country we accept the duties as well as the privileges of a democratic society. Just as parents must take care of their children when the childre are young, so must children ensure the livelihood of their parents when they grow old. That is the basis of modern society and of civilization itself.

Too often we hear politicians and journalists *demean* the role of government enterprise and tell us what we cannot accomplish. But those who argue that government cannot perform valuable services go against the history and against the grain of this great nation of ours.

America has worked, America has progressed, because we have combined our enterprise, both public and private, for the good of all. That is how we pulled our nation out of the Great Depression, won the second World War, released the power of the atom, and put Americans on the moon. That is how we built the fairest, freeest, most progressive society in the history of the world.

Much of our progress has been based not on the work of one party acting alone but through the building of a *consensus* between our two great political parties.

In the days after World War II, President Harry Truman launched the Marshall Plan which saved Europe and laid the foundation for the Western Alliance. He could not have done so without the aid of such Republicans as Senator Arthur Vandenberg of Michigan and Congressman Christian Herter of Massachusetts.

In the 1950s, President Eisenhower did not dismantle the New Deal, but accepted such advances as social security.

President Lyndon Johnson could never have signed the Civil Rights legislation of the 1960s without the bipartisan support of Republican leader Senator Everett Dirksen of Illinois.

Many times in our history, one party has managed to learn from the other party.

For years, Democrats argued we should end the isolation of China and open up ties with the People's Republic. When a Republican president finally took this historic step, we Democrats applauded him.

For years, we Democrats have argued for a tax reform, that the system is wrong, for the need to make the system fairer. If President Reagan presents such a measure, we Democrats will be there to help.

For years, Republicans argued against the evils of big deficits. They convinced many Americans, including many Democrats, of the need for greater fiscal responsibility. Unfortunately for the country, some Republicans seem to have forgotten their own lesson along the way for the deficits keep growing.

Today, we face serious challenges.

Despite the economic recovery of the past two years, there are serious pockets of economic despair.

The poverty rate, which had declined dramatically by the 1970s, has risen since 1979 from 11 percent to 15 percent of our population. It is particularly high among younger Americans. A disturbing 25 percent of our children of preschool age are living below the poverty line.

Across much of America's industrial belt there is a rust bowl to rival the dust bowl of the 1930s. We need to rebuild American industry and to establish fair trade laws that give our industry a fair chance to compete in world markets.

Hundreds of thousands of American farm families face a terrible dilemma. They are caught in a tightening vice of high interest rates that drive up the cost of doing business and a high-priced dollar that cuts their markets both here and abroad. While the administration remains opposed to our legislation to extend farm credits, I am hopeful that it will take some steps to cut interest rates and restore a reasonable price for the dollar.

Most of our problems relate to the budget. Our national debt has doubled since 1981. It will triple again by the end of this administration unless we take the tough steps that are needed. If President Reagan accepts tough reductions in Pentagon waste, we will be ready and prepared to find savings on the domestic side. Just as we reached agreement on revenue policy in 1982, and social security reform in 1983, we can achieve an agreement on budget and tax reform in 1985, and I predict that we will.

I cite these challenges not because they are insurmountable but because they can and will be overcome.

I began my public life in 1936 on a slogan of "work and wages." I remain convinced that our greatest goal is to give the average family the opportunity to earn an income, to own a home, to educate their children, to take care of the family in questions of health, to have time for recreation with them, and to have some security in their later years. That is still the American dream and it is still worth fighting for.

Today, there are those who argue that the way to achieve this dream is to go it alone, to forget about those less fortunate. This new morality says that the young should forget about the old, the healthy should ignore the sick, and the wealthy should forget the

In America that is an alien philosophy; our country has never stood for that. We Americans believe in hard work, in getting ahead, but we also believe in looking out for the other fellow. That has been the tradition of America, from the early days when settlers got together for barn-raisers. It continues today, as Americans, down to the youngest school child, chip in to help the starving in Africa. How pleased we are. That is the American way of life. Thanks to the know-how of the American farmer and the generosity of our country itself, you here in the bread-basket of America are pursuing the work not only of man, but of God.

I have just come from a country, the Soviet Union, that recognizes neither the existence of God nor the rights of man. I have returned to a nation that has insisted from its earliest beginnings that the individual human being is of fundamental value; that the humblest, meekest person has the right to be treated with dignity and respect.

Our whole history has been a 200-year struggle to strengthen and enlarge the benefits of democratic freedom; to include women and minorities and young people into our electoral process to protect the individual rights and welfare of all our citizens, to build social and economic opportunity for everyone. Looking back at a half century of public life, I have seen the greatness of this struggle and I have seen truth in the optimism of my friend Jack Kennedy—

"Our problems are manmade—therefore, they can be solved by man. Man's reason and spirit have often solved the seemingly unsolvable and believe they can do it again."

With American ingenuity and American generosity, this, our nation under God, will not only survive our current challenges; it will prevail, it will flourish.

These are the views of man who, in the twilight of his career, as he steps out of public life and pulls down the shade, truly looks at America.

Thank you.

George P. Shultz (1920–) has been Secretary of State since 1982. He was educated in economics and has been on the faculty of MIT, the University of Chicago, and Stanford University. He was a member of the Council of Economic Advisors under President Eisenhower. Later, he served as Secretary of Labor, followed by Director, Office of Management and the Budget, and then Secretary of the Treasury under President Nixon. In 1974 he joined the Bechtel Company in San Francisco and became its president the next year. In 1981, President Reagan recalled him to Washington to chair the Economic Advisory Board. In June, 1982, he was named Secretary of State.

Moral Principles and Strategic Interests: The Worldwide Movement Toward Democracy

George P. Shultz

Secretary of State George Shultz delivered his Landon Lecture on April 14, 1986. His presentation was a strong argument for a forceful American presence abroad in support of democratic regimes and in pursuit of democratic principles. It was a speech which would not have seemed out of place during the 1960s but would have appeared quite anachronistic in the post-Vietnam era of the 1970s. Among the Landon Lectures reproduced in this volume, the best statement of the opposing point of view is probably that of Robert Kennedy, delivered some eighteen years earlier.
During the question period following the Secretary of State's address, most of the audience's attention focused on Nicaragua and Central America. Only later did news reach the American public that American planes had bombed Libya that day.

APRIL 14, 1986

Thank you very much. Thank you, President Acker. Thank you. We were talking away there while we were waiting to come in about all of this academic background that was mentioned in the introduction, and I was reminded of those good old saws like "Old Deans Never Die, They Just Lose Their Faculties." Actually, I'm now a member of the faculty of Stanford University on leave. It's the only connection with civilian life, so to speak, I was allowed to keep when I entered this job. And not long ago, for reasons that escaped me, Stanford decided to award me a named Chair. And it is quite an honor as all of us who are part of the university world know. I said to them I felt honored and privileged, but when I left the job that I'm now in, I wouldn't be able to use a chair—I needed a couch, but they didn't have any couch to offer me.

It's, of course, an honor and a privilege to take part in an event that is named after Governor, as he's known throughout the country, Alf Landon. It has the symbolism of dignity, of intelligence, of commitment, and of humor. And I might say those virtues are embodied in Washington in Senator Nancy Kassebaum, with whom it is my pleasure to work, particularly since she is a member of the Foreign Relations Committee, the committee that I report to. And, of course, we have Senator Bob Dole who is giving us leadership in the Senate and other members of the Kansas delegation.

Someone once said that "Alf Landon, like every typical Kansan, is an honest believer in self-government and civil liberties." So the Landon Lecture Series is an appropriate forum for some basic questions about self-government and civil liberties. Today I would like to talk about democracy—although not inside the United States, but abroad.

A struggle is spreading around the world for democracy. Kansas itself is a symbol of our own national struggle for this ideal. Kansas—"BLEEDING KANSAS"—was once an infamous battleground. In the middle of the nineteenth century, this state—and this country—were bitterly divided by an institution that denied human beings their most fundamental rights. The destruction of slavery was slow and agonizing, requiring the bloodiest war this nation has ever known. But by redeeming its democratic promise, America was able to survive its wounds and, ultimately, to prosper.

The Movement Toward Democracy

Today, an extraordinary movement toward democracy is unfolding in diverse corners of the globe. Only a few days ago, the Roman Catholic Church published an *Instruction on Christian Freedom and Liberation,* which observes that: "[O]ne of the major phenomena of our time ... is the awakening of the consciousness of people who, bent beneath the weight of an age-old poverty, aspire to a life of dignity and justice and are prepared to fight for their freedom."

The evidence of this movement is striking, particularly in the developing world. The most dramatic example is the growth of the democratic center and the decline of social oligarchies in Latin America and the Caribbean. Today 90 percent of the people of this neighboring region enjoy democratic government, compared to only one-third a decade ago. Examples in other areas include the return to democracy in the past dozen years in Spain, Portugal, Greece, and Turkey; a new government in the Philippines; and the movement toward democracy in Pakistan, Thailand, and Haiti.

We should also note the prosperity and stability under free institutions, of the Association of South East Asian Nations, so-called ASEAN, and other Asian countries. The movement toward more open governmental and economic arrangements there and elsewhere has been aided by a growing recognition—in states as diverse as China and several in Africa—that socialist economics does not spur development, that free markets are the surer path to economic growth.

The best evidence for the growing power of this movement comes from people struggling against tyranny—particularly Communist tyranny. The Soviet Union and its satellites, once thought immune to popular pressures, are now being challenged around the world: most notably by resistance movements in Afghanistan, Angola, Cambodia, Ethiopia, and Nicaragua.

Nations have undergone different types of transitions to freedom and self-government. It is a complex process, which can move slowly and imperceptively, or explode in violent convulsion. Indigenous factors are central, and what is crucial in one place may not be in another. Nonetheless, there are certain overlapping factors common to most democratic transitions.

The first is the *ruling order's loss of legitimacy*. Economic decline, war, corruption, the death of a long-time leader—each factor alone, or with others, signals the failure of the ruling order and creates pressures for a new one to take its place.

A second consideration is the *temper of the people and of the nation's elites*. They have to "want" democracy. Elites favoring democracy, or who at least accept it as a practical necessity, are essential to providing the leadership necessary for the transition. Connected to this is the *quality of leadership*. Mrs. Aquino is proving an able leader in the Phillipines, and King Juan Carlos has proven a model constitutional monarch in Spain. But poor leadership was a factor in the failed democracies of Latin America in the 1960s and early 70s, and in many of the states that became newly independent in the 1950s and 60s.

The third factor is *Western political and economic support.* Democratic transitions take place through the efforts of the people themselves, but support from the United States and other Western countries can be crucial. In El Salvador, the United States' involvement has been decisive; and it has been important in Ecuador, Uruguay, and elsewhere in Latin America. Such support played a helpful role in the return of Spain and Portugal to democracy, and in Turkey as well.

A fourth factor has been *local reconciliation and amnesty.* Without an effort to "bind up its wounds," a nation in transition cannot build the tolerance and compromise that are essential to democracy.

A fifth factor in transition to democracy is the *role of independent power centers,* such as the military, and in Roman Catholic countries, the Church. The military is usually a crucial player: It may help to throw out the autocrat, as in Portugal and the Philippines. It may be a positive force for stability and encouragement of movement toward democracy, as in Brazil. Or it may acquiesce in the transition, as in Argentina and Uruguay. In recent years the Roman Catholic Church has played a key role in countries like Spain and, again, the Philippines. There are other factors shaping the complex process of democracy, such as the degree of literacy, the size of the middle class, the condition of the economy, and the strength of the democratic center against extremes of left and right. My point is simply that democratic transitions are complex; they are fragile; and they require careful nurturing to succeed. Just because we played a successful role in the Philippines doesn't mean we will always succeed. Some people fear the risks in such transitions, recalling developments of the 1970s in Iran and Nicaragua. But the many successful transitions to democracy that I've noted should give us confidence. And if we use our power wisely, become engaged where we can help, and understand the local forces at work, we can advance the ideals we hold so dear.

The Democratic Movement and U.S. Foreign Policy

This democratic movement is out there; it's happening. The United States, as the strongest free nation in the world, is in a position to influence it. How should we respond? Our position is unambiguous. The Reagan administration supports human rights and opposes tyranny in every form, of the right as well as the left. Our policy is unequivocally on the side of democracy and freedom [applause]. I'm glad to hear there's support for democracy and freedom in Kansas.

But not everyone thinks we should respond. A leading argument against an activist U.S. policy comes from the "realist" school of critics. It accepts the fact of American power in the world, but argues that we must exercise that power through a cool, if not cold, a detached, if not amoral, assessment of our interests. Our interests must predominate. In this view, the promotion of democracy abroad is a naive crusade, a narcissistic promotion of the American way of life that will lead to overextension and ill-advised interventionism. Moral considerations, we are told, should not have important weight in our foreign policy.

There are two problems, in my view, with this argument. The first is that the American people believe in our nation's ideals, and they want our foreign policy to reflect them. That is the reason why our recent actions in Haiti and the Philippines evoke such widespread support at home. The second is that the basis for this argument—the old dichotomy between realism and morality—is one whose meaning has changed sharply in today's world.

The realist critique ignores the crucial fact that our principles and interests are converging as never before. The reason is that in the modern world, which is shrinking to intimate size through new technologies, the growth of democratic forces advances our strategic interests in practical, concrete ways. What happens in southern Africa or East Asia matters to us economically, politically, and socially; and television and jet planes won't let us ignore once-distant realities.

I find this convergence of principles and interests one of the most promising developments of this decade, because it gives us an opportunity to rebuild the once great bipartisan consensus on foreign policy, the consensus that fragmented over Vietnam.

Just how does active U.S. support for democracy serve our interests?

First, on the most fundamental level, we are aligning ourselves with the desires of growing numbers of peoples throughout the world. But there is more. We believe that when governments must base policy on the consent of the governed, when citizens are free to make their views known to leaders, then there is the greatest prospect of real and lasting peace. Just as people within a democracy live together in a spirit of tolerance and mutual respect, so democratic states can—and do—live together the same way. The European Community and other inter-European bodies, for example, are models of international cooperation.

The second reason is that democratic nations are the best foundation of a vital world economy. Despite our current trade problems, international commerce is central to our own economic well-being. Twenty percent of our Gross National Product is connected to trade today, compared with only ten percent in 1950. People overseas have to be able to afford our goods; and nations that permit open economies, that give free rein to the individual and minimize government interference, tend to be the most prosperous. Not all such nations are democratic, but most are. They have confidence in their citizens and encourage them to act in ways that stimulate, rather than hamper, economic growth. Democracies also provide the political stability needed for economic development. Further, nations that experience rising living standards through peaceful trade do not want to risk their prosperity in war.

President Reagan put it simply to the U.N. General Assembly last October: "Free people blessed by economic opportunity and protected by laws that respect the dignity of the individual," he said, "are not driven toward the domination of others."

Third, the movement toward democracy gives us a new opportunity to advance American interest with only a modest commitment of our resources. In the past, it was thought that we could advance our interests, particularly in the developing world, only with a massive commitment of our political, economic, and sometimes military power. Today the reality is very different: We have partners out there eager for our help to advance common interests.

America's friends and allies are all the more important today given the limits of our own resources, the steady growth in our adversaries' power, and the understandable concern of the American people that our friends carry their fair share of the burden. In Central America, Southeast Asia, Turkey, the Philippines, and elsewhere, the success of democracy furthers our own strategic interests.

Fourth, I believe that prudent U.S. support for democratic and nationalist forces has a direct bearing on our relations with the Soviet Union. The more stable these countries, the fewer the opportunities for Soviet interference in the developing world. Remember that it was Soviet intervention in Angola and Ethiopia, and especially in Afghanistan, that helped to undermine confidence in Soviet-American relations in the late 1970s. Success by freedom fighters, with our aid, should deter the Soviets from other interventions. A less expansionistic Soviet foreign policy would, in turn, serve to reduce tensions between East and West.

In an imperfect and insecure world, of course, we have to cooperate and sometimes assist those who do not share our principles, or who do so only nominally. We cannot create democratic or independence movements where none exist, or make them strong where they are weak. But there is no mistaking which side we are on. And when there are opportunities to support responsible change for the better, we will be there.

Prudent Activism

Our national interest in promoting democratic forces requires us to take a long, hard look at the means available to us. Despite recent successes, we have to be sober about what we can achieve; and we should anticipate setbacks. As I said earlier, political transitions are fraught with complexity. The United States possesses a wide range of instruments for promoting our interests abroad. Decisions about which to use, and in what combination, will vary from case to case. Congress has to give us the necessary flexibility. Excessive restraints and micromanagement only complicate our efforts.

One factor is a fundamental aspect of every situation: *our own military and economic strength.* Diplomatic efforts and economic assistance cannot succeed if the United States is seen as unable or unwilling to defend its ideals, its interests, and its friends. That's why President Reagan's achievements in rebuilding our military and restoring our economic prosperity have done so much to enhance our position in the world. Congress ought to keep this in mind when it votes shortly on proposals that would sharply cut back on defense preparedness.

Let me now turn to the more specific instruments used to implement our policy. The first is *economic assistance.* Sound economic development is conducive to democratic political development and stability. Openness to fair trade on our part contributes powerfully to this objective, and benefits us as well. And this objective also explains why economic assistance has constituted the overwhelming percentage of our direct help to other governments. Under the Reagan administration, three-quarters of our aid to the countries of Central America has been economic, rather than military, assistance. Worldwide, in the past five years, almost two-thirds of our assistance has been economic; only one-third military. And the Administration's Caribbean Basin Initiative, as an example, opened special trading opportunities to small neighboring economies.

American economic aid can be a powerful tool for democratic development. In Haiti, for example, we exerted the influence of our economic aid at a key moment to facilitate a peaceful transition to a new era, bringing the promise of democracy to a country long ruled by dictatorship. And we are now doing all we can to support the parties trying to establish democratic government there.

The second instrument is *security assistance* to friends, which often complements our economic help. Security assistance serves a number of purposes: it helps allies and friendly countries to defend themselves and to deter threats of outside interference; it gives us influence to help mediate conflicts; it helps sustain our access to valuable bases and strategic areas; and it gives us the opportunity to promote the importance of respecting civilian government and human rights. Security assistance also enables allies and friends to accept defense responsibilities that we might otherwise have to assume ourselves—at much greater costs in funds and manpower. Dollar for dollar, it's the most cost-effective security money can buy.

El Salvador is the most recent example of how our military and economic assistance work together to enhance our security even as they strengthen indigenous democratic institutions. Five years ago the communist guerillas in El Salvador had launched their so-called "final offensive." Right-wing death squads seemed out of control. And to many, the prospects for democracy seemed hopeless. Our critics—many of whom also oppose aid to the Nicaraguan democratic resistance today—opposed our aid program as a waste of money, as support for an oppressive regime. How wrong they were!

After considerable debate, a majority in Congress came to support our program. The results are something all Americans can be proud of. Today, strengthened by our military aid and stabilized by our economic assistance, El Salvador is writing an extraordinary chapter in the history of democracy. In the midst of a guerilla war, four fair elections were held in three years; a constituent assembly drafted a constitution; and a president, national legislature, and local officials have been elected according to the constitution's rules. Our assistance gave the long-suffering people of that country the chance to speak out and choose democracy as the road to a better life.

And they are carrying on the fight themselves. Contrary to the critics, we have not been drawn into any quagmire in El Salvador.

The third instrument of U.S. policy in promoting democratic reform is *diplomatic engagement.* In the Philippines our influence helped to bring about an election that enabled the Filipino people to make their views known, an election that ultimately led to a new government. Throughout that crisis, we put our prestige firmly behind the principles of democratic choice and nonviolence. The jubilant faces of the crowds in Manila in the days following Mrs. Aquino's ascension to the presidency demonstrated for all the world to see just what America's ideals really mean.

Our diplomatic efforts directly advanced our strategic interests as well. A new, friendly government whose legitimacy is firmly based on the will of the people offers far better prospects for our future base rights in the country. Imagine the enmity we would have earned—and deservedly so—had we tried to block the will of the people and encouraged the use of military force to suppress them. What would have been the future prospect of our bases then?

We are also active in trying to help resolve a number of regional conflicts, believing that in each case a lasting solution depends on the choice of the people involved: in Afghanistan, Cambodia, Ethiopia, southern Africa, and Central America. To facilitate such solutions, last October President Reagan proposed at the United Nations a plan designed to persuade the Soviet Union and the warring parties to work for peace, rather than continue to pursue a military solution in each of these areas. We're still waiting for a positive response from Moscow.

We have broad agreement in this country on the use of these foreign policy instruments—U.S. military and economic strength, economic assistance, security assistance, and diplomatic engagement—to promote our goal of democratic development.

The last of our policy instruments, one which evokes some controversy, is *U.S. military power.* It includes a variety of options: weapons sales, the use of military advisors, training, and as a last resort, direct U.S. military action—as in Grenada.

Political support and modest U.S. military assistance to those resisting Soviet-supported or Soviet-imposed regimes are certainly a prudent exercise of U.S. power. In most cases, the resources involved are small. One hundred million dollars for the Nicaraguan democratic resistance, for example, is a modest investment in a region so critical to our security.

In such a case, the power developed through our assistance may be the only force capable of bringing Communist rulers to the negotiating table. But if the adversary won't negotiate, we must be prepared to offer the material assistance needed for victory. We do not favor open-ended escalation, nor a cynical policy of using the struggles of courageous people to "bleed," in Mr. Gorbachev's phrase, the Soviet empire. But we *will* help these people be effective in the fight that *they* have chosen to make for themselves.

Sometimes our aid needs to be covert. Friendly countries who would funnel our aid may fear open involvement. The local group we are helping may have legitimate reasons not to have us identified as its ally. Covert U.S. aid may give us more room for political maneuver, and our adversary more room for compromise. There are other factors as well.

We can never succeed in promoting our ideals or our interests if we ignore one central truth: *Strength and diplomacy go hand-in-hand.*

No matter how often this is demonstrated by history, some people simply cannot—or will not—grasp it. Over and over again we hear the refrain, "Forget strength, let's negotiate." No chips; no cards; no hand to play—just negotiate. Unfortunately, it's an objection based on an illusion.

As we work to support the trend toward democracy in the world, we must also remember an important lesson: formulas abound for transitions from traditional authoritarian rule, and recent history shows that such transitions *do* occur. But there are *no* successful, *peaceful* models for getting rid of Marxist-Leninist totalitarian regimes.

That is why our aid to the Nicaraguan resistance is so crucial. The tools we are working with—diplomatic and economic—will not prove effective without a sustained program of military assistance to the democratic resistannce. If America is stripped of this tool, we inevitably will face the unwelcome choice between helplessness and starker action. Negotiations are a euphemism for capitulation if the shadow of power is not cast across the bargaining table. How many times must we learn this simple truth?

Critics who would deny us that tool refuse to face the fact that power is the language the Nicaraguan Communists understand.

These critics favor moral ends—the human rights that have always comprised the idealistic element in U.S. foreign policy—but they ignore the fact that power is necessary as a guarantor of these noble ends. They advocate utopian, legalistic means, like outside mediation, the United Nations, and the World Court, while ignoring the power element of the equation—even when faced with a Communist regime whose essence is a monopoly of power and the forcible repression of all opposition.

Such an approach is riddled with contradictions. It applauds our support for freedom in the Philippines, Haiti, and South Africa. Some of its advocates even endorse our support for freedom fighters in far-off Afghanistan and Cambodia. But it opposes active efforts to bring freedom to nearby Nicaragua, where democrats on our very doorstep are fighting to save their country from Communism.

This schizophrenic approach is not a policy; it's an evasion. It would doom the very ideals and hopes for negotiated solutions it advocates, and would make the United States impotent where we are needed most.

Terrorism and Democracy

My topic today has been the significant trend toward democracy in diverse areas of the world, and the consequences for the United States. Events—and U.S. policy—have been fostering a world of greater openness and tolerance. But democracy faces many enemies, brutal leaders who feel threatened by tolerance, by freedom, by peace and international cooperation. These enemies will stop at nothing in trying to destroy democracy: deception, propaganda, terrorist violence against innocent men, women, and babies. No tactic is too gruesome in their destructive manipulations. They are at war with democracy, and their means make all too clear their hostility to our way of life.

The terrorists—and the other states that aid and abet them— serve as grim reminders that democracy is fragile and needs to be guarded with vigilance. These opponents of our principles and our way of life think they can vanquish democracy by exploiting free peoples' love of peace and respect for human life, and by instilling fear in ordinary citizens to demoralize them and undermine their faith in democracy. The most challenging test for the global movement toward democracy—the sternest test for all free nations—is to summon the will to eradicate this terrorist plague. Because terrorism is a war against ordinary citizens, each and every one of us most show a soldier's courage. If the terrorists cannot instill fear in us, they are beaten. If free peoples demonstrate what Israel's Ambassador to the UN calls "civic valor," and if we do not hesitate to defend ourselves, democracy will prevail.

A Rebuilt National Consensus

We live in a dynamic era. In the 1950s and 60s Marxist-Leninist revolutions and socialist economics seemed the wave of the future in the developing world. But today those models have proved bankrupt—morally, politically, and economically. Democracy and freedom are the wave of the future.

This trend is opening up new opportunities for U.S. foreign policy. We helped to create this trend, and we continue to help it along with prudent policies that support other peoples as they strive to realize their own aspirations. In so doing, we advance both our moral ideals and our national interests.

This notable convergence of ideals and interests is the reason I am optimistic about the future. As the world's first constitutional democracy, we Americans have always felt a profound stake in the ideal of democracy and its future in the world. As citizens of a nation founded on ideals, the American people want their foreign policy to promote their highest values. I am confident the American people can support the goals I have enunciated here today.

I am also confident that we have broad public support for the basic policy instruments I have outlined. When we reach a broader understanding of the inescapable role of military power—our friends' power as well as our own—as one of these instruments, we will have completed the rebuilding of the once great bipartisan foreign policy consensus. And the United States will be an immeasurably stronger force for peace and freedom in the world.

Thank you.

ALF M. LANDON

Reminiscences of the
Landon Chairmen

William W. Boyer, Chairman from December, 1966 to May, 1969

I arrived at Kansas State University in August 1965 as the first head of its department of political science. During that first academic year, I was invited to have lunch on campus with Governor (I never called him "Alf") Landon and others, including KSU president Jim McCain. The Governor and I hit it off from the first, so I sent him a copy of my recently published book, *Bureaucracy on Trial.* I recall that he wrote a complimentary acknowledgment and invited me to visit him at his home in Topeka, which I was to do almost monthly thereafter over the next three years.

My visits to his home in Topeka became almost routine. Typically, I would drive the 50 miles from Manhattan and arrive around ten in the morning, just after the Governor returned from riding his horse. Sitting in his book-lined study, we did nothing but talk politics all day, breaking only for lunch with his wife, Theo. We would discuss such subjects as Communist China (he was among the first to advocate U.S. recognition), Vietnam (he was critical of our intervention), presidential politics, and Topeka's latest statehouse issues.

My initial estimate of Governor Landon was that he was Kansas' greatest natural resource—a towering national political figure, but one long since forgotten and relegated to the scrap heap of history by Kansas and the nation. I was struck by the disparity between the historic image of Governor Landon (as the man Roosevelt defeated by a landslide in 1936), and the image of him I was experiencing as a vital common-sense statesman.

I found him to be a vibrant near-octogenerian and a voracious and sagacious analyst of public affairs. International affairs were of as much interest to him as were domestic politics. And the present and future surpassed his interest in the past. I was surprised about how well informed he appeared to be on all developments stretching from Topeka to Washington and the remotest corners of the earth.

Here, too, was truly a "100-percent political animal"—the first and last I have ever known. Politics was his all-consuming passion; I never recall his talking about anything else. Of course, as a political scientist all these qualities delighted me, and during my four years in Kansas he truly became—despite the nearly 40 years between us—my closest friend, and I dare say (from what others told me) that he regarded me as his closest friend also.

During one of these early visits, I broached the idea of a public affairs lecture series. We discussed the University of Chicago's lecture series, named in honor of E. L. Godkin, former editor of *The Nation.* Why not a lecture series named after Governor Landon?

KSU's president, Jim McCain, did not need prodding; he readily agreed, and so was born The Alfred M. Landon Lectures on Public Issues at Kansas State University. Jim asked me to be in charge of the series, and he, the Governor and I set about to select the speakers.

It was agreed that Governor Landon, of course, would launch the series, and this he did at the auditorium of KSU's student union on December 13, 1966 with a lecture entitled "New Challenges in International Relations." As I recall, this first lecture comprised many ideas we had discussed during my Topeka visits.

Ralph McGill, publisher of *The Atlanta Constitution,* became the second Landon lecturer in May, 1967. Meanwhile, I was also coordinator of the University's Convocation Lectures, and I found that the early success of the Landon Lectures made it easier to attract outstanding speakers for the former series such as Norman Cousins, Senator Fulbright, Dr. Martin Luther King, Muhammad Ali, and Edgar Snow.

The Landon Lectures became major national media events in the fall of 1967 when two aspiring presidential candidates appeared—first, Governor Ronald Reagan of California in October, followed by Governor George Romney of Michigan in December. Reagan's appearance forced us to move the lectures to the Field House where an estimated 15,000 people showed up, one of the largest indoor crowds in the history of the state.

This turnout of 15,000 was matched with the appearance in March 1968 by Senator Robert F. Kennedy of New York. I had visited Kennedy's Washington office in November and suggested to his press secretary, Frank Mankiewicz, that the Senator's forthcoming lecture be on Vietnam. I knew Kennedy was against the war and that for him to speak on that subject would mean an open break with President Johnson, a fact acknowledged by Mankiewicz who suggested "The Crisis in Our Cities" as the title instead. Although we had advertised that topic, Kennedy announced for the presidency two days prior to his appearance and chose to speak against our involvement in Vietnam after all. Indeed, Robert Kennedy launched his presidential campaign at Kansas State University with his Landon Lecture.

Preceding Kennedy's appearance was that of Dr. Martin Luther King as our Convocation speaker two months earlier. They were the only speakers about whom I had received threatening hate letters beforehand, so I called in the FBI to strengthen our security. Both spoke out against our Vietnam involvement which dominated public discussion in those days. Their assassinations that Spring devastated me, and some of my zeal in managing KSU's major lecture series dissipated. I simply no longer could put my heart in it.

The Kennedy lecture also marked the beginning of the Patrons of the Landon Lecture Series whose donations paid for the printing of Landon Lectures plus other incidental expenses. We had no budget for the Landon Lectures, and we never gave any remuneration to any of the Landon lecturers, at least until I left KSU in June 1969. They came to Manhattan, Kansas in honor of Governor Landon.

When I moved from Kansas, I left behind a friend—Governor Landon. My life has been greatly enriched by our friendship, and I am proud to have had a part in establishing the Landon Lecture Series—an enduring tribute to a great American.

Joseph Hajda, Chairman from September, 1969 to May, 1976

President James A. McCain asked me to become Bill Boyer's successor as Landon Lectures coordinator shortly before Bill left Kansas State University in 1969. The President and I had become well acquainted during the previous twelve years: I taught political science classes at KSU, participated in public affairs at the local, state, and national levels, served on the White House staff as a specialist in international trade policy, and assisted President McCain's efforts after he appointed me as KSU director of international activities, chairman of all university convocations, and coordinator of lectures on controversial issues.

I had met Governor Alf Landon on several occasions before 1969. As a result, I knew firsthand about his political orientation and perspective, and about the breadth and depth of his political knowledge. Soon after my appointment as Landon Lectures coordinator, Bill and I visited the Governor at his Topeka house. It was a memorable session. We explored an array of national and international policy issues and options, and we examined several ideas regarding the selection of speakers.

This first visit gave me a real foretaste of the many spirited and stimulating discussions I had with the Governor at his home the next seven years. The periodic conversations with him were closely linked with my frequent and candid deliberations with President McCain. On the basis of my close acquaintance and observation, I came to regard both of them as spokesmen of unusual spirit and dedication on public issues. They really enjoyed their very active involvement in selecting the speakers and in every aspect of the program. They were always ready to devote as much time and energy to the Landon Lectures as necessary. And, in fact, they always had the final say about the speakers.

I found the task of coordinating the Landon Lectures interesting, enjoyable, and fairly demanding. We insisted on high standards. Inviting leading public figures with the highest qualifications in terms of experience and savvy was our prime criterion. Equally important was the understanding that they would present their lectures as a tribute to Governor Landon: the lecture series was designed to honor him as a most distinguished Kansan and elder statesman.

We made no attempt to hide our expectation that the speaker would make a substantial contribution to reinforcing the vital role of KSU as a free market of ideas. We asked them to address vital issues of our time and share their wisdom and insights not only with our university community but also the public at large.

On balance, I thought that most of the 24 Landon lecturers who appeared at KSU between October 1969 and April 1976 lived up to these expectations. My judgment was substantiated by the many favorable comments from KSU students (inclulding a contingent of international students), faculty, staff, alumni, and friends. Most of the lectures generated feelings of vitality and enthusiasm. As it became a major KSU drawing card, the program attracted new patrons and campus visitors. Colleagues from other universities lauded the lecture series, as did the press and other media. According to some of the media commentary, the Landon Lecture Series became known as the best and, at the same time, the least expensive lecture program on public issues in the country. Seasoned observers credited the lecture series with improving the image of KSU, not only locally, but statewide and nationally. One of them said that the list of our speakers began to sound like a veritable Who's Who in America. It was not unusual to hear the comment that KSU gained much luster by entertaining such a parade of topflight public figures.

Our university community welcomed the heavy media exposure because it generated special recognition of KSU. President McCain, along with the staff people responsible for public relations, made sure that all persons covering Landon Lectures for local, statewide, and national media were always given a warm welcome. And Governor Landon used every opportunity to display his public relations skills. The combined effort of the whole team won my professional respect.

The President, Governor Landon, and I greatly appreciated the interest and support of the patrons, whose number grew under the able chairmanship of J. Robert Wilson, a leading citizen of Manhattan. We also highly valued the interest and assistance of several distinguished Kansans, such as Senators James Pearson and Bob Dole, and Governor Robert Docking.

As the fame of Landon Lectures spread to different regions of the country, I received phone calls and letters asking, "How do you do it?" Several universities solicited my advice and counsel with the hope that the prestigious Landon Lectures could serve as a model for developing similar lecture series at their own campuses. It was gratifying to see that our privately-supported program sparked the starting of lecture series elsewhere.

By far most of the comments and messages about Landon Lectures were on the bright side, but there were also occasional complaints. Some of the local commentary bluntly expressed the opinion that the Landon Lectures slates were stacked in a direction leaning predominantly to the conservative side of the political spectrum. I felt great concern over this problem. In my consultations with President McCain, Governor Landon, other members of our university community, and outside observers, I always spoke in favor of a tendency toward prudence in selecting the speakers, so as to achieve a satisfactory balance between Republicans and Democrats and between different currents of political thought. At times my efforts produced the desired results, but at other times they were not enough to achieve this goal. Nor was I always successful when I expressed my reservations about inviting some public figures. However, I preferred to deal with nuances and differences through quiet diplomacy behind closed doors.

The sharpest criticism was voiced by a vocal group of KSU students and faculty before, during, and after President Richard M. Nixon delivered his Landon Lecture on September 16, 1970. His speech was the first before a university audience after he ordered the invasion of Cambodia. His action intensified the poisonous atmosphere of mistrust, constitutional crisis, and foreign policy disaster. After the lecture, the protesting students and faculty demanded an opportunity to present their views. President McCain knew where I stood and told me that it was my job to meet this problem. In fact, we found a peaceful solution.

We received numerous complaints about scheduling William F.

Buckley's lecture on November 2, 1973, in the auditorium (now called McCain Auditorium) rather than in the fieldhouse. I supported the idea of holding the lectures in the fieldhouse to allow for larger crowds (up to 15,000), but starting in May 1971 most of the lectures were held in the auditorium: it was better for both TV and audience acoustics, it was more comfortable, and it was less than one-tenth the cost—but space was limited to the 1,800 seating capacity.

We were also criticized for restricting access to the fieldhouse on March 4, 1974, when the great evangelist Billy Graham delivered his Landon Lecture. I argued against limiting access to KSU students, faculty and staff, but my view did not prevail. The decision to restrict access drew fire from persons outside our university community who wanted to attend the lecture and who pointed out that the audience was several thousands below original expectations.

We had to cope with another dilemma on March 19, 1975—due to circumstances beyond our control—when the capacity audience in the auditorium had to leave without hearing the scheduled speaker. Secretary of the Treasury William E. Simon arrived at the Manhattan airport somewhat circuitously and more than an hour late for his lecture. Because of marginal weather conditions, his jet had to land in Salina. After his helicopter ride from Salina, I greeted him at the airport and informed him that we had to move his lecture to the much smaller banquet rooms of the K-State Union, with only the patrons of Landon Lectures and special guests as his audience.

But the program flourished, notwithstanding the occasional complaints and dilemmas. The prevailing opinion was that the special recognition accorded the program was fully justified. I thought that thanks to the efforts of President McCain, Governor Landon, and other persons associated with the program, the Landon Lectures earned this special recognition and acclaim. As pointed out in a local commentary, the lecture series' hallmark was a singular distinction of tone and message. I was especially pleased with the clear, wise, direct messages of the former Vice President Hubert H. Humphrey, the two religious leaders Rev. Billy Graham and Archbishop Fulton J. Sheen, Chief Justice Earl Warren, the two leading economists J. Kenneth Galbraith and Walter H. Heller, and Ambassador Daniel Patrick Moynihan.

It was a great privilege to be part of the prestigious Landon Lectures for seven years, to get to know so many public figures with the highest qualifications, and, above all, to be a close associate of President McCain and Governor Landon in their efforts to contribute to the quality of the discussion of public issues. When President McCain retired from his office in 1975, I agreed to coordinate the Landon Lectures another year, with the understanding that I would terminate all my administrative responsibilities and move to teaching and research on a full-time basis.

Looking back from my present perspective, the Landon Lectures on Public Issues—at least the ones with a singular distinction of tone and message—contributed something productive and worthwhile to the public discussion of the old myths and the new realities of our time.

Barry L. Flinchbaugh, Chairman from September, 1976 to February, 1981

Serving as chairman of the most prestigious lecture series in the nation's colleges and universities is indeed a privilege but an experience most difficult to relay to those interested in what goes on "behind the scenes."

There are many reflections that simply cannot be relayed because the subjects are still alive. It wouldn't be fair to them to make public "happenings" that they thought would remain private.

Working with Alf in and of itself is indeed a privilege, but also at times a difficult experience. Since he is of Pennsylvania extraction perhaps when he and I were debating who should be invited it was two stubborn strong-willed "Deutschman" having the time of their lives. He thoroughly enjoyed a good argument and loved to have me challenge him, especially over lunch at his favorite Topeka restaurant—Tommy's. Contrary to his reputation, he always paid the bill. Of course, I supplied the cigarettes. I don't believe he has purchased any cigarettes since the '36 campaign. Mrs. Landon drove the Governor to the lectures and is a most gracious lady. Mrs. Flinchbaugh thoroughly enjoyed her. Once when we sent her flowers for her birthday, she remarked that we should only remember the birthday of the important member of the family. She is, in my judgment, the unsung hero among the Landons.

I had only limited involvement with Senator Kassebaum in my years as chairman. Alf was still representing the Landon family, although his granddaughter Linda was a KSU student at the time and most gracious to work with and to involve in the series in a limited way.

Mark Edelman, student body President and I, drove Senator Mathias of Maryland and Alf from Topeka to Manhattan. Senator Mathias's father was Landon's state chairman in Maryland in 1936. They regaled each other with stories that were just delightful. For example, Alf recalled how Governor Allen of Kansas was offered the vice-presidential seat on the Harding ticket but declined. As Alf put it, if he hadn't have been so damn stubborn, he would have been President instead of Coolidge.

Another part of the experience that is very satisfying is my relationship with the patrons' chairman, the late J. Robert Wilson. J. Robert had a keen intellect, was fiercely conservative but liked to bring the liberals to campus so that he could debate them politely and, as he frequently told me, help him discover what makes those of the liberal philosophy "tick." He staunchly supported whatever I did as chairman and we developed a mutual respect of which I am most proud.

What goes on "behind the scenes" involves hours of hard work on the part of many people and weeks of preparation. I had the services of two excellent secretaries, Carolyn Reich and Lavon Wells, who filled in for the lack of my "detail attention." Recently I asked Carolyn which lecturer paid the most attention to her. Her answer, which shows the character of the man, was Gerald Ford. She also recalled Senator Percy "chewing her out" because there was no phone in the dressing room in McCain. The cooperation of the Union Food Service folks and the KSU Police will remain in my mind as a very pleasant part of the series. I particularly remember several "cowboy patrons" being unhappy with us for serving chicken at the Ford luncheon and Detective Tubach getting kicked in the shins during a demonstration against a controversial lecturer.

The real "eye-opener" is the police work and Secret Service procedures which go into protecting lecturers. I recall the debate over landing Mondale's helicopter in front of Anderson and walking him to McCain versus the football stadium and driving him to McCain. The Anderson lawn won, but he was heavily shielded by Secret Service agents and sharp-shooters on the roofs of Anderson, Fairchild, and McCain during the short walk. At the time, I was serving as assistant to the President and I clearly remember the Vice-President's remark to me that we did whatever the President didn't want to do. So then we compared Jimmy and Duane and what we exchanged will forever remain between us.

Before I place a label on each lecture I chaired, allow me to make a few observations which will humanize the great lecturers that appeared in the series, but shouldn't be attached to names. First, an admission on my part that I was so involved in the preparation and the excitement of the day that it is difficult for me to remember lecture content. I had a tendency to think they were all great and then I became angry when the *Manhattan Mercury* editorial, for example, was less than favorable.

One lecturer, when asked, "What can I do for you?" asked for a can of beer and so I dispatched a student to Aggieville and served beer in the President's office in Anderson Hall. Another chain-smoked and was extremely high-strung. Smoking in President Acker's office was taboo, but we found an ashtray and kept the boss quiet. Another rather nervous lecturer downed a pint of vodka which he had in his briefcase prior to going on stage and then proceeded to sweat it out under the lights.

The wife of one of the lecturers asked me for the check before the lecture. I refused and said I would deliver it to the lecturer after the fact. Another arrived in his private Lear jet and never charged the series one cent. One of our most controversial speakers left his speech in his suitcase and, you guessed it, the airline lost his suitcase. He spoke without any notes and was most elegant.

Perhaps the most fascinating private story related to me as I sat next to the lecturer in the back seat of the automobile transporting us to the airport was how the speaker was completely broke as a young man and was on his way to drop out of college when he found a $20 bill among bus transfer slips on the floor of the depot. Instead of dropping out, he enrolled for another semester. His comment to me that day, "If I wouldn't have found that $20, I would have likely ended up a pimp in _________ city.

We took one lecturer to our house for a reception. I remember clearly, he was smoking a pipe and chewing tobacco and when asked what his pleasure was for a drink, ordered a double shot of scotch straight and proceeded to down it with one gulp. He is now in his eighties. Another traveled to KCI with his son but they both took separate planes in order to, as the father put it, make sure that the son enjoyed his inheritance. Because of an ice storm, their separate flights to Manhattan were canceled. They proceeded to rent a taxi for $130 and rode in the same car over icy roads to Manhattan.

I remember explaining to one lecturer that attendance was difficult to predict. I was preparing him for an embarassingly small crowd. As we walked down the hill to McCain he remarked, "Never fear, the students know _________ _________ is here." So much for arrogance. Another lecturer refused interviews with the media but agreed to meet a Northview Elementary School class that was doing stories about the lecturer. This same individual told of hitting Eleanor Roosevelt in the buttocks with a slingshot during a barbecue.

A senior Senator told of his recollections at a pre-lecture dinner party of every President he served with. His favorite was Harry Truman, but he refused to discuss Lyndon Johnson. Finally, as I returned him to the hotel, I remarked, "Every time I brought up Johnson, you changed the subject." He looked at me and grinned, "He is where he belongs!" This, of course, was several years after Johnson's death.

Another lecturer, in discussing the Kennedys, remarked about Teddy, "It is obvious that Rose didn't have triplets." The thoughts of the mighty, the intellectuals, and the history-makers behind the scenes both renew our faith in mankind and remind us of the narrowmindedness that is in us all.

The chairman of the series is in a unique position to judge but only, of course, subjectly. After re-reading all the lectures, here are my judgments for what they are worth:

The most personable—	Shirley Temple Black
The perfect gentleman—	Gerald Ford
The most knowledgeable of current events—	Howard Baker
The most intellectual—	Hugh Sidey/James Schlesinger
The most articulate—	John Connally
The least cooperative—	Charles Percy
The most blunt—	Barry Goldwater
The most reserved—	Mike Mansfield
The most sure of himself—	Milton Friedman
The most nervous—	Thomas Eagleton/Charles Collingwood
Alf's favorite—	Charles Mathias
The most delightful personality—	Carl Rowan
The most humble—	Norman Borlaug
The most knowledgeable about his particular field—	Bob Bergland
The most serious-minded—	David Broder
The most comical—	Malcolm Forbes
The best prepared—	Walter Mondale
The most scientific—	George Gallup
The most likeable—	Edmund Muskie

In total, 21 great Americans. What a privilege to share in just a few fleeting moments of their lives.

Postscript: I would be remiss and less than true to my values if I didn't mention the Ian Smith affair. The former Rhodesian Prime Minister delivered his speech to a somewhat unruly crowd in McCain Auditorium, but not under the auspices of the Landon platform. Removing him from the Landon Series was, in my judgment, a mistake. A university, of all places, should stand for freedom of speech regardless of how much one disagrees with an individual's particular views and actions. The Landon Series has attracted this nation's top history-makers and a few individuals that have changed the course of world history. Smith was a significant player in that field. As a Zimbabwe student said that day, as some in the crowd attempted to shout down Smith, "To refuse his request to speak is totalitarianism which on Smith's part, we condemn." I was especially grateful in the backing of the *Manhattan Mercury* in the Smith affair. As the editorial stated, "Why not Idi Amin?"

William L. Richter, Chairman from March, 1981 to May, 1984

In December, 1980, I was asked by KSU President Duane Acker if I could attend lunch with Governor Landon in Topeka. No explanation was given for the invitation, but I was delighted to accept, since I had not seen Governor Landon for several years, possibly since the late sixties, when he had visited one of my introductory political science courses as a guest lecturer. On December 19, we had a lengthy and enjoyable lunch at the Topeka Club, with the focus of conversation primarily on politics. A few weeks later President Acker asked if I would chair the Landon Lecture Series. I accepted with little hesitation. From its beginning in 1966, I had regarded the Landon Lecture Series as a tremendous asset to our students, faculty, and fellow Kansans and as an outstanding forum for public dialogue on major issues. I would discover during the next three years many other sources of satisfaction in managing the series: the pleasure of working with President Acker, the excellent secretarial assistance of Lavon Wells and Shelley Bunker, the fine performance of campus security personnel under Chief Art Stone, the outstanding support of the Landon Lecture patrons, and the often exciting tasks of hosting major public figures on their visits to campus.

Some major changes occurred during the three plus years I chaired the series. In reaction to the "Ian Smith affair" the previous year—in which the Rhodesian Prime Minister's visit had engendered widespread campus protest and ultimately the withdrawal of the Landon auspices from his public lecture—President Acker and I agreed on a more formal system of consultation concerning prospective Landon Lecturers. I would touch base on every proposed speaker with at least half a dozen people, including the student body and faculty senate presidents, the chairperson of the university

343

convocation committee, and the chair of the Landon Patrons. Usually President Acker or I would also consult Governor Landon or his daughter, Senator Nancy Kassebaum, although we retained the ultimate decision on whom to invite. I regret that I did not visit with Governor Landon in Topeka in the manner of earlier series chairmen, but I did enjoy greatly my frequent discussions with Senator Kassebaum. Always willing to take time from her busy schedule to assist the series, she played a central role in securing several of our top speakers, including President Ronald Reagan and Senator Edward Kennedy.

A second important change was the expansion of membership in the Landon Patrons. As Bill Boyer's reminiscences note, the patrons' organization was formed in 1968, under the able leadership of Manhattan businessman J. Robert Wilson, to provide financial support to the series. Its numbers grew gradually during the 1970s, from approximately two dozen couples to more than two hundred individuals, but membership remained largely limited to local civic and business leaders and a handful of campus people. In consultation with President Acker and Bob Wilson, I decided to broaden the base of membership by advertising to faculty and students that all who were interested in supporting the series were welcome to join. The response was very strong. President Reagan's visit in September 1982 gave a further boost to this effort, with a resultant increase of more than 30% in patron membership.

The Landon Lecture Series, Kansas State University, and the Manhattan community lost a valued friend when Bob Wilson died unexpectedly in March 1983. He and his wife, Barbara, had provided fifteen years of dedicated service to the Landon Lectures. In May, Edward Seaton, publisher of the *Manhattan Mercury,* was chosen as Bob's successor. The choice was a most fortunate one, for Edward has played a very active role not only with the patrons but frequently in helping to get speakers and facilitate arrangements.

A third change was the decision to avoid speakers' bureaus as an occasional source of speakers. Governor Landon, Senator Kassebaum, and I opposed the use of agencies both because of their higher cost and because they detracted from the distinctive quality of the Landon series.

We did provide honoraria to some of the speakers, and we usually provided transportation and local hospitality, but arrangements varied tremendously. Federal Reserve Chairman Paul Volcker drove out for the day from Kansas City where he had scheduled official business. Sheikh Yamani not only provided his own transportation, but did so in grand style. He flew to Kansas City in his own Boeing 707. The day before his lecture he flew to Manhattan in a smaller private jet, then returned to spend the night in his hotel in Kansas City. The next day he arrived in the 707, which remained parked at the Manhattan airport until later that day when he departed directly to Boston and Europe. At the other end of the transportation spectrum, Charles Kuralt arrived in Manhattan by a commercial flight, carrying his own bag, and apologizing for the fact that anyone should have gone to the trouble to meet him at the airport.

A final change worth mentioning has been the internationalization of the Landon Lecture Series during the 1980s. By bringing former British Prime Minister Sir Harold Wilson and Saudi Oil Minister Sheikh Ahmed Zaki Yamani to the Landon series, we set a precedent for the inclusion of later foreign speakers, including Salvadorean President Jose Napoleon Duarte. This change was not without some risk. The Yamani lecture was disrupted by a group of approximately one dozen anti-Saudi protesters. Unable to locate and remove all of the protesters safely and easily, we emptied McCain Auditorium, then readmitted the audience to hear Yamani's belated, but excellent, presentation. Despite some subsequent discussion whether foreign speakers ought to be avoided for security reasons, we decided—and President Acker reaffirmed—that the potential benefits of such Landon lecturers would greatly outweigh the risks.

Anyone associated closely with the Landon Lecture Series over a number of years has a treasure of anecdotal memories: Paul Volcker's imposing physical presence and equally imposing intellectual presence; Sir Harold Wilson's charming repartee at dinner at the Manhattan Country Club the evening before his lecture, followed the next day by a presentation so rambling that several months of subsequent editing efforts could not transform it into coherent printable copy; jogging three miles at dawn with Agriculture Secretary John Block and KSU Vice President Chet Peters; reminiscing with Oregon Senator and long-time friend Mark Hatfield, and watching Charles Kuralt engage in similar reminiscing with Manhattanite and former CBS cameraman Wendell Hoffman; leading Congresswoman Pat Schroeder by the hand up the treacherously icy outside steps to her suite on the top floor of the University Ramada Inn because an ice storm had knocked out the electricity and the elevators.

President Ronald Reagan's visit was especially memorable. Besides all of the normal arrangements for a Landon Lecture, we had numerous special concerns for the visit of an incumbent President. Governor Landon attended, the only time he has been able to do so in recent years, and seemed thoroughly to enjoy the occasion, his ninety-fifth birthday. The federal government provided the transportation, ferrying Reagan and Landon in by helicopter from Topeka and landing on the playing field of the Memorial Stadium south of Ahearn Fieldhouse. Getting the·President safely to the platform in the fieldhouse, however, required special safety measures. After discussing several alternatives with the presidential advance team, we finally had constructed a temporary wall which stretched from the fieldhouse across 17th street to the K-State Union, to provide a protective route for the president's limo. Protesters were another issue. Despite the feelings of some University staff that any protest would be "undignified" and should be strictly controlled, I contacted groups whom I knew to be planning some form of protest and worked out with them a set of ground rules which allowed them to express their sentiments in a public area outside the building and permitted the President's speech to proceed without interruption inside.

Press relations, a factor in any Landon Lecture, were considerably more extensive for the Reagan visit. My favorite press memory of the event, however, concerned the editor of the Kansas State *Collegian,* who telephoned a week or so before the scheduled visit to ask where President Reagan would be spending the night in Manhattan. In an unguarded moment, I said, "You know, Charlene, it is like the story of the 800-lb. gorilla—the President sleeps where he pleases." There was a long silence at the other end of the line and I realized that she was contemplating making use of the comment, possibly in conjunction with some "Bedtime for Bonzo" headline. I was grateful she agreed, however reluctantly, not to print the statement prior to the President's visit.

Of the various matters which the presidential advance team and our local arrangements team had to handle during the two weeks prior to the Reagan visit, the one of least substantive importance was probably the most time-consuming: the issue of what to give President Reagan as a gift. KSU staff member Mitsugi Ohno's magnificent glass sculpture of the White House, would be most appropriate, but that was much too large and fragile for presentation in the fieldhouse. I suggested the donation of one of Ohno's Klein bottles. These graceful and artistic bottles, illustrating the mathematical principles of a one-sided geometric figure, were first created by Ohno, and only a few glass-blowers in the world can duplicate his feat. The President's advance team ignored all these considerations and vetoed the suggestion because the bottle wouldn't be sufficiently photogenic! The student government president suggested purple and white horse blankets, one each for Reagan and Landon, both avid horsemen. President Acker's assistant, Mike Johnson, was deputed to contact horse blanket manufacturers, but found that none had blankets in purple. Meanwhile, some faculty raised objections that such a gift would convey nationwide too narrow and traditional an image of Kansas State University. Finally, only hours before Reagan's arrival, President Acker solved the problem. Two purple K-State football jerseys were presented by the student president, President Reagan's with no. 1 and Governor Landon's with no. 95 in honor of his birthday. The jerseys proved eminently photogenic, showing up in *Time* and on the evening news.

During spring 1984 I was awarded sabbatical leave to continue my research work in India and Pakistan. I did not believe it would be fair to ask anyone to serve as acting chair for a year, so I tendered my resignation to President Acker. I was pleased when Professor Charles Reagan agreed to assume the Landon Lecture responsibilities. The continuing excellence of the series has been ample testimony to the wisdom of that appointment.

I thoroughly enjoyed my experience with the Landon Lecture

Series. Although the lectures were not always brilliant and Murphey's Law often controlled logistical arrangements, it was time and effort well spent. The Landon Lecture Series has brought well-deserved honor to Governor Alf Landon, distinction to Kansas State University, and enhanced public awareness to a generation of students. Besides that, it has been great fun.

Charles E. Reagan, Chairman since May, 1984

Bill Richter, in his reflection above, has explained how I came to be chairman of the Landon Lectures in May of 1984. This honor came as a complete surprise. In fact, President Acker called me in Cincinnati where I was attending a meeting of the American Philosophical Association. Bill gave me a briefing, introduced me to the Landon Lecture secretary, Shelley Bunker, and turned me loose. Since he was remaining on campus, he offered his continued assistance. I called on him frequently for advice and counsel.

I continued with the precedents set by Bill Richter in consulting with President Acker, Senator Nancy Kassebaum, and faculty and student leaders about our selections. I prepared a list of everyone in the news or in positions of influence who I thought were potential speakers. I would then recommend to President Acker which persons we should invite in which order, and we would try to plan about a semester ahead. Senator Kassebaum has always been very helpful to me both in discussing potential speakers and in helping us get acceptances once we have sent invitations. She has made it clear to me that she is happy to be an advisor, but the choice of speakers remains with the chairman and the University.

My first lecturer was Secretary of Defense Caspar Weinberger. His lecture was relatively easy to arrange, once we had a confirmed date. He advocated acceptance of the Strategic Defense Initiative which had recently been announced by President Reagan.

The second lecturer for whom I was responsible was President Duarte of El Salvador. At about the same time I became Landon Lecture Chairman, he was elected President under the new constitution of El Salvador. In late September, I got some vague hints that he might accept our invitation, but nothing definite. We timed our invitation to coincide with his appearance at the Interamerican

Press Association meeting in Los Angeles. Ed Seaton had tipped me off in early June that President Duarte was probably going to speak there.

I was notified only about two weeks in advance by the Salvadorean Embassy in Washington that President Duarte would accept. Then we began a whirlwind of preparations. For most of our Landon lecturers, the preparations are fairly easy and we have done it so many times that everyone involved knows just what to do. But for heads of state or vice presidents, the arrangements are complicated by security requirements. I must say the Secret Service and the various protective agencies are accommodating and easy to work with.

The usual procedure is for the Secret Service to send a lead agent several days in advance. This agent walks through the entire schedule, and carefully checks each of the principal sites, such as the airport, the auditorium or field-house, and the Student Union. Then he/she calls in separate agents to be in charge of each site. This person must develop the security plan for his/her site and determine how many agents will be required on the day of the event. Finally, the night before the event, all of the agents arrive in Manhattan and are briefed by the lead agent and the site agents. In the meantime, the technical agents have arrived and established a communications post and headquarters, usually in one of the local hotels. The final group to arrive are the agents who, with the help of trained dogs, will perform a security sweep of the fieldhouse or auditorium a few hours before the event. They look for bombs, persons hidden in the building, and weapons. Once they have finished with the building, all entrances are closed except where there are magnetometers or agents watching all those who enter.

I have learned that they prefer that we make all of our preparations and complete our schedule of events before they arrive. Then, they will work around our plans, changing only things like doors used, or paths taken from one site to the other. They are always in close contact with local police agencies. The chief of the campus police, now Charlie Beckom and formerly Art Stone, is our liaison with local and state police, and works closely with the secret service. All of these security arrangements, while not difficult, are time-consuming and require careful coordination among everyone working on the lecture, including Mike Looney, our television and radio technician, Tim Lindemuth, who is in charge of press relations and news coverage, and many other people who have specific duties during a lecture.

In making preparations on short notice for the visit of President Duarte, I was faced with two principal difficulties. First, I had to arrange transportation for President Duarte and his party from Los Angeles to Manhattan. He was originally scheduled to come by commercial airline. I discovered that in order to do this, he would have to leave Los Angeles, where he was to give a banquet speech to the Interamerican Press Association the night before his lecture here, at 11:00 p.m. and travel all night in order to get to Manhattan by 10:00 a.m. the next morning. I was afraid that once he discovered his arduous all-night journey, he would lose interest in coming, so I offered to arrrange more direct transportation. I tried for several days to get a government plane, but since he was on a private visit to the United States, the U.S. government was reluctant to provide one. I believe that another reason was that the U.S. election would be held the following Tuesday. There may have been some worry that it would look like President Duarte's widely covered speech at Kansas State was only a pre-election publicity stunt. Indeed, Senator Kassebaum was running for re-election, and her democratic opponent made precisely that charge. Since he was not a credible candidate in the first place, his charge received little notice. At one point, I was frustrated that the government was willing to fly in an armoured limosine, but not the man who was to ride in it. I finally chartered a Lear jet to bring the President and his party to Manhattan. Ed and Karen Seaton, who were at the Interamerican Press Association meeting, accompanied President Duarte to Manhattan.

Humorous note on how even the best laid plans can go awry: The Secret Service also chartered a jet to bring the agents who were accompanying President Duarte on this trip. Their jet left half an hour before his. So, when the first jet landed at the Manhattan airport, we expected it to be the Secret Service plane. No one was ready for an official greeting. And, of course, out came President Duarte and not the Secret Service agents we expected. We hastily assembled for the greeting, and then waited another twenty minutes for the other plane to get here. It was a different model jet and was a bit slower.

The other problem I had was of a political nature. Some of our colleagues at Kansas State invited Arnoldo Ramos, a spokesman for the Salvadorean guerrilla groups, to speak on campus at the same time as President Duarte. I got a call from Captain David Manguia of the Salvadorean Presidential staff saying that they had heard that Ramos was coming. Captain Manguia asked if we had invited him and was there to be a debate. I responded that the Landon Lectures had invited only the President and that there would be no debate. Then, I had to give my word that there would be no meeting nor face-to-face confrontation between the two. I assured him that while it was the case that anyone could invite just about anyone to speak at an American university, we had not arranged this and could do nothing about it, but that there would be no debate or confrontation. Captain Manguia said that under those conditions, the President would come.

It took me several days of serious discussion with my colleagues to get their assurance that I could keep my word. At first they argued that Ramos had a right to be in the auditorium and, if he wanted to, to ask a question. I answered that it was not an issue of rights, but of conditions for the acceptance of an invitation. I felt obliged to call President Duarte and tell him if I could not keep my word about a confrontation. They finally realized the practical reality: If Duarte cancels, few students—and certainly no news cameras—would notice if Ramos came to campus. It turned out to be a splendid day of speeches and counter-speeches, news conferences and counter-news conferences which greatly benefitted those students who wanted to become informed about the opposed viewpoints on El Salvador.

One of the great pleasures of being a Landon Lecture chairman, as my predecessors have mentioned, is the opportunity to spend time with some of the major figures in our political and public life. In the case of President Duarte, I spent two hours with him, most of it alone, at the airport in Kansas City where he was awaiting a commercial flight to Miami, on his way back to San Salvador. He gave me a fascinating first-person account of the difficult days in El Salvador at the end of 1979 and the beginning of 1980. His perspectives on both President Carter and President Reagan were interesting.

I haven't the space to tell about each of the speakers whose lectures I have arranged, but two other experiences are worth reporting. All of the speakers I have worked with have been pleasant and kind. Tip O'Neill stands at the head of the list. When I met him in Kansas City, we went first to Topeka where he was doing a fundraiser for Rep. Jim Slattery (who also has been helpful to the Landon Lectures). After that, we flew to Manhattan. He kept everyone—including President Acker, Jim and Linda Slattery, and two of Slattery's aides—in stitches with his funny stories and jokes. At the Manhattan airport, where I had arranged for an interview with the student newspaper, a woman came up to him and said, "I recognize you; you're on the pro golf tour!" He hugged her and said that that was the nicest thing anyone had said about him. Later, in the hotel, he told me, "Chuck, tell me what you want me to do and who you want me to meet and talk to. I'll do whatever you like while I'm here." He reminds me of the way Gerald Ford made Barry Flinchbaugh's job easier a few years before. Seasoned politicians must appreciate the difficulties organizers face.

The last anecdote is about Secretary of State George Shultz. Making the arrangements for his visit were fairly easy and made easier by the skill and professionalism of his advance team of Janice Settle and Nancy Stone. We all had a nice time preparing for the visit. On the Sunday before the Monday lecture, I was getting nervous that Secretary Shultz would cancel because of the tense international situation with Libya and because the vote on aid to the Contras in Nicaragua was to be on Wednesday of that week. Janice Settle called me to say that they were sending a secure satellite telephone and could I arrange to have a station wagon and driver at the airport for the technicians and their equipment. I said yes and asked her what she thought about the situation. She said the secure telephone was a good sign and she was doubtful he would cancel.

He came and gave an interesting lecture (reprinted in this volume). Afterwards, the questions from the audience were all about the Contras and U.S. policy in Central America. Backstage after the speech, he asked me if anyone here was interested in Libya. I responded that attention was focused primarily on Central America. At the Patrons' Luncheon, again no questions were on Libya, and again he asked me about it when I accompanied him to his car. I thought nothing of his question until I turned on my evening news and discovered that we had bombed Libya that day and that the mission was underway while he was speaking at Kansas State University. That evening, after President Reagan's press conference announcing the attack, Tom Brokaw interviewed Caspar Weinberger, George Bush, and George Shultz. Everyone of them had been a recent Landon Lecturer. That explains why the Series has the reputation it has. I am pleased that as of this writing I have the privilege to serve as its chairman.

Dr. William W. Boyer, Jr. is the Charles Polk Messick Professor of Public Administration in the Department of Political Science at the University of Delaware. He was formerly the Head of the Department of Political Science at Kansas State University

Dr. Joseph Hajda is Professor of Political Science at Kansas State University. He was formerly Director of International Programs at Kansas State.

Dr. B. L. Flinchbaugh is Professor of Agricultural Economics. He was formerly Assistant to the President at Kansas State.

Dr. William L. Richter is Professor and Head of the Department of Political Science. He was formerly Director of the South Asia Center at Kansas State.

Dr. Charles E. Reagan is Assistant to the President and former Head of the Department of Philosophy at Kansas State.

THE LANDON LECTURES
1966–1986

Governor Alfred M. Landon *New Challenges in International Relations* December 13, 1966

Ralph McGill *The Emerging South: Politics and Issues* May 17, 1967

Governor Ronald Reagan *Higher Education: Its Role in Contemporary America* October 26, 1967

Governor George Romney *The Challenge of International Development* December 6, 1967

Senator Robert F. Kennedy *Conflict in Vietnam and at Home* March 18, 1968

Governor Nelson A. Rockefeller *Our Country's Problems, Solutions* May 9, 1968

Arthur Schlesinger, Jr. *The 1968 Election: An Historical Perspective* November 14, 1968

Senator Mike Mansfield *A Pacific Perspective* March 10, 1969

General W. C. Westmoreland *The Role of the U.S. Army in Today's World* April 9, 1969

Senator Edward W. Brooke *National Security: Dollars, Demands and Dilemmas* October 6, 1969

Hubert H. Humphrey *How We Can Make Our Government Work* January 9, 1970

Archbishop Fulton J. Sheen *Three Forms of Love* March 17, 1970

Secretary Walter J. Hickel   *Be Part of the Solution, Not Part of the Problem*   April 6, 1970

President Richard M. Nixon   *It's Time to Stand Up and Be Counted*   September 16, 1970

Chief Justice Earl Warren   *The Alternative is Chaos*   October 21, 1970

Senator Hugh Scott   *Implications of Foreign Policy*   April 26, 1971

John Kenneth Galbraith   *Foreign Policy: The Next Reform*   May 7, 1971

Leonard Woodcock   *The Economic Game Plan*   October 19, 1971

Secretary Elliot Richardson   *Human Needs and Government—A Realistic Assessment*   January 24, 1972

Secretary William D. Ruckelshaus   *The Crisis of Trust and the Environmental Movement*   April 12, 1972

Secretary Earl L. Butz   *The Future Belongs to Those Who Prepare for It*   May 4, 1972

Dan Rather   *Reporter's Notes*   November 16, 1972

Rear Admiral Alan Shepard   *How Do We Stand in Space?*   April 3, 1973

General Alexander Haig   *A Strategic Overview*   April 24, 1973

William F. Buckley, Jr.   *The Assault on the Free Market*   November 2, 1973

Ambassador Anne Armstrong   *Crisis and Challenge*   February 12, 1974

Reverend Billy Graham   *The Divine Answer to the National Dilemma*   March 4, 1974

Walter W. Heller   *The Energy Crisis and the Economy*   March 19, 1974

Senator J. William Fulbright   *Energy and the Middle East Interests and Illusions*   February 13, 1975

Secretary William E. Simon   *Restoring Our Prosperity*   March 18, 1975

Ambassador Daniel Patrick Moynihan   *The World in the Year Ahead*   May 7, 1975

Senator Henry M. Jackson   *America and Freedom's Future*   January 21, 1976

Senator Charles McC. Mathias, Jr.   *The Alternatives to Detente*   April 27, 1976

Carl T. Rowan   *What Jimmy Carter's Election Will Mean*   November 18, 1976

Senator Thomas F. Eagleton   *1977: Year of Opportunity in the Middle East?*   December 8, 1976

Senator Charles H.. Percy   *Does the United States Have a Responsibility to Feed the World?*   March 4, 1977

Senator Mike Mansfield   *Best of Times—Worst of Times*   April 12, 1977

Secretary Bob Bergland   *Toward a National Food Policy*   September 9, 1977

David S. Broder   *American Politics in the Carter Era*   December 9, 1977

Malcolm S. Forbes   *Where We're At and Where We're Headed*   January 24, 1978

President Gerald R. Ford   *The War Powers Resolution*   February 20, 1978

Milton Friedman   *Free Trade: Producer Versus Consumer*   April 27, 1978

Charles Collingwood   *Reflections on Power (and Influence)*   November 3, 1978

Senator Howard Baker   *Toward a New Republic*   March 8, 1979

Dr. Norman Borlaug   *Civilization Will Depend More Upon Flourishing Crops Than on Flowery Rhetoric*   March 20, 1979

Ambassador Shirley Temple Black   *It's All Perceptions Now*   April 10, 1979

Vice President Walter F. Mondale   *SALT II: An American Decision*   July 17, 1979

Senator Barry Goldwater   *The World Today*   February 25, 1980

Governor John Connally   *America in the '80s*   March 20, 1980

Hugh Sidey   *Power and the Media*   March 27, 1980

Secretary James R. Schlesinger   *American Security and Energy Policy*   April 28, 1980

Secretary Edmund S. Muskie   *Long-Term Issues*   December 4, 1980

George Gallup, Jr.   *The Mood of America*   February 11, 1981

Paul A. Volcker   *Dealing with Inflation: Obstacles and Opportunities*   April 15, 1981

Sir Harold Wilson   *Western World: Economic Crisis*   September 30, 1981

Secretary John R. Block   *Clearing the Road for Tomorrow*   October 30, 1981

Senator Mark Hatfield   *Foreign Policy in a Transition Era*   April 26, 1981

President Ronald Reagan   *Rebuilding America*   September 9, 1982

Charles Kuralt   *America: The Long View*   November 22, 1982

Ahmed Zaki Yamani   *Control and Decontrol in the Oil Market*   March 28, 1983

Senator Edward M. Kennedy   *The Changing Relationship Between Politics and Public Policy*   January 30, 1984

Representative Patricia Schroeder   *Great Expectations: From Abigail Adams to the White House*   March 19, 1984

Hodding Carter III   *Whose News Is It?*   April 6, 1984

Mayor Tom Bradley   *There Are No Impossible Dreams for Possibility Thinkers*   April 16, 1984

Secretary Caspar Weinberger   *Arms Reduction and the SDI*   September 27, 1984

President Jose Napoleon Duarte   *The Democratic Process in El Salvador: The Meeting at La Palma*   November 2, 1984

Lesley Stahl   *The Press and the President*   November 29, 1984

Senator Bob Dole   *The Dream of America*   March 25, 1985

Speaker of the House Thomas P. 'Tip' O'Neill   *Half a Century of American Achievement*   April 22, 1985

Vice President George Bush   *Looking Forward to the Summit Conference*   September 9, 1985

Tom Brokaw   *The Role of Television in Our Lives*   March 24, 1986

Secretary George P. Shultz   *Moral Principles and Strategic Interests: The Worldwide Movement Toward Democracy*   April 14, 1986

Secretary William Bennett   *Once More, A Plea for History*   September 9, 1986